Gilbert E Sabre

Nineteen Months a Prisoner of War

Gilbert E Sabre

Nineteen Months a Prisoner of War

ISBN/EAN: 9783744754187

Printed in Europe, USA, Canada, Australia, Japan

Cover: Foto ©ninafisch / pixelio.de

More available books at **www.hansebooks.com**

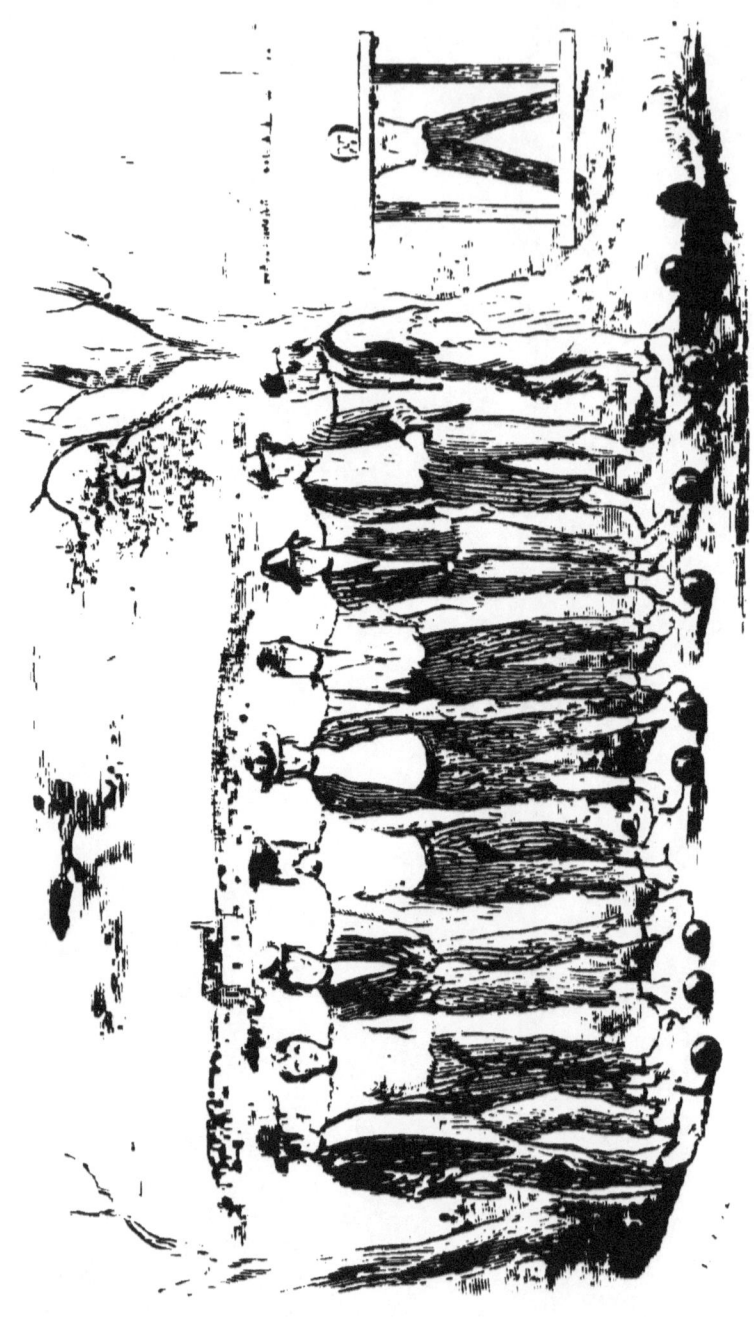

THE CHAIN GANG

NINETEEN MONTHS
A PRISONER OF WAR.

NARRATIVE

OF

LIEUTENANT G. E. SABRE,

SECOND RHODE ISLAND CAVALRY,

OF

His Experience

IN THE WAR PRISONS AND STOCKADES OF MORTON, MOBILE, ATLANTA, LIBBY, BELLE ISLAND, ANDERSONVILLE, MACON, CHARLESTON, AND COLUMBIA,

AND

HIS ESCAPE TO THE UNION LINES.

TO WHICH IS APPENDED,

A LIST OF OFFICERS CONFINED AT COLUMBIA,

DURING THE WINTER OF 1864 AND 1865.

NEW YORK.
THE AMERICAN NEWS COMPANY,
119 & 121 NASSAU STREET.
1865.

Entered according to Act of Congress, in the year 1865,
By THE AMERICAN NEWS COMPANY,
In the Clerk's Office of the District Court of the United States for the Southern District of New York.

RENNIE, SHEA & LINDSAY,
STEREOTYPERS AND ELECTROTYPERS,
81, 83, and 85 Centre-street,
NEW YORK.

R. CRAIGHEAD, PRINTER,
Caxton Building, 83 Centre street.

CONTENTS.

CHAPTER I.

A Prisoner—Morton, Miss.—Mobile, Ala.—Atlanta, Ga.—A Foretaste of Southern Inhumanity—Off for Richmond............... 9

CHAPTER II.

At Richmond—Libby—Terrible Forebodings—Belle Island—Its Appearance—How the Prisoners lived—The daily Bill of Fare—Deliberate Torture......................,...................... 19

CHAPTER III.

Reduction of Diet—Conflict between Life and Death—Revolting Extremities—Surgeon's Call—Richmond Hospitals—Mortality—Soldiers buried alive... 29

CHAPTER IV.

Sharp Practices of Rebel Surgeons—A New Way of Making Money—Convalescent Hospital in Richmond—Efforts to Escape—Discovery—Back to Belle Island............................. 88

CHAPTER V.

The Winter of 1863 and '64—Miseries multiplied—Arrival of Prisoners from Burnside's Army—Their terrible Sufferings—A

CONTENTS.

Night of Horror—Fearful Extremities of Cold—Pitiable Expedients to keep Warm—The Number of Deaths during the Winter—Burial of the Dead.. 42

CHAPTER VI.

Punishments—Bucking and Gagging—Riding the Horse—Great Sufferings and Torture under the rigors of a fiendish Vindictiveness.. 50

CHAPTER VII.

Theft—Police Regulations of the Island—Regulators and Raiders—Summary Punishments—Treachery of the Camp-guard.... 53

CHAPTER VIII.

National Airs—Hatred of them by the Southern Soldiers—Greenbacks and Contraband Trade—Speculations in Food—In Money—Quotations—The Richmond Brokers—How the Yankees outwitted the Guards.. 58

CHAPTER IX.

Desertions to the Enemy—Twenty-eight Renegade Cobblers—The Devotion of Southern Union Soldiers—Contribution of the Sanitary Commission—The Treatment received from the Rebel Government.. 63

CHAPTER X.

A special Exchange—Sad Disappointment—A Revolt organized—Details of the Plan—Its discovery—Precautions of the Rebel Authorities.. 68

CHAPTER XI.

Clearing Belle Island—Expectations of Home—The over-buoyant Spirits of the Men—Fatal Consequences—Sad Realizations...... 72

CONTENTS.

CHAPTER XII.

PAGE.

From Belle Island to Andersonville—A Terrible Journey—What we Experienced on the Way—Universal Sympathy of the Negroes.. 74

CHAPTER XIII.

Arrival at Anderson—The Condition of the Men—Brutality of a Rebel Officer—The March to Camp Sumter—Description of the Camp...... 81

CHAPTER XIV.

Going Back to the Old Treatment—The Expedients for Shelter—Rations—Withholding Rations as a Punishment—Cooking in Prison...... 86

CHAPTER XV.

The Arrival of the Summer Season—The Crowded Condition of the Camp—Appearance of Summer Diseases—Poisonous Odors—Immense Swarms of Flies...... 90

CHAPTER XVI.

Sickness and Mortality—The Nature of the Diseases—Their improper Treatment—Hospitals—The Immense Mortality—Vaccination and its melancholy Effects...... 93

CHAPTER XVII.

The Consummation of Suffering—Despair and Insanity—The Conversation of One of the Victims—Moon-blind—Its Effects........ 97

CHAPTER XVIII.

Plans of Escape—"Chickamauga"—He serves the Rebels as a Spy—The Death of Chickamauga—"Mugging the Guard"—A grand Conspiracy—Eight Thousand Prisoners to Revolt—Discovery of the Plot—Punishment of the "Traitor"—Efforts to Escape by feigning Death.................................... 100

CHAPTER XIX.

Traitors in Camp—Their Punishment—Tempting Prisoners from their Allegiance—Discovery of a guilty Shoemaker—Meting out Justice... 106

CHAPTER XX.

Amusements within the Stockade—Establishment of the Markets—Scene on Market-street—Competition in Business—The Effects of the Markets upon those who could enjoy them..... 109

CHAPTER XXI.

Raiding at Camp Sumter—Detection of a Number of "Raiders"—Their Trial—Sentenced to be hanged—Their Execution—The Effect of extreme Measures.................................... 112

CHAPTER XXII.

Removal to Macon—An agreeable Journey—Prison Life at Macon—An extraordinary Privilege—Description of Macon—More Prisoners Arriving—Preparations for another Transfer.... 118

CHAPTER XXIII.

Off for Charleston—Enthusiasm of the Prisoners—The Displeasure of the People—Under Fire—Nobody Hurt—Relieved—An Exchange—Presents from Home................................ 123

CHAPTER XXIV.

Transferred to Columbia, S. C.—The Expressions of the People on the Way—General Grant's Combinations beginning to Pinch.... 128

CHAPTER XXV.

Extract from the Diary of Lieutenant J. N. Whitney, 2d Rhode Island Cavalry.. 131

CHAPTER XXVI.

The Escape of Lieutenant Whitney and Captain Van Buren—Their Experiences on the Way—Attacked by Hounds—Arrival at a Mill—Obliged to Turn Back—A Sorghum Boiling.............. 143

CHAPTER XXVII.

Off the road—Discover a Pea-stack—Rest—Morning—Where the Travellers found themselves—Making themselves known to the Negroes—The Hospitality of the Negroes..................... 150

CHAPTER XXVIII.

The Travellers again on the Way—Their Guide—Peleg's Home—A final Parting—Dense Forests—Again off the Road—Strike the Savannah River—Efforts to find a Negro—Run into a Rebel Picket—Again in the Hands of the Enemy..................... 156

CHAPTER XXIX.

Taken to Augusta—Back to Columbia—Meeting old Friends—Another Exchange—Prisoners transferred to the Yard of the Lunatic Asylum—Building Quarters—Suffering...................... 163

CHAPTER XXX.

Sherman again in motion—Speculations as to his Destination—Removal of Prisoners to Charlotte—Our concealment—We leave our Hiding-place at Night—Fired upon—Meet two Rebels—Succored by a true Union Lady................................ 168

CHAPTER XXXI.

The Occupation of Columbia—We are within the Union Lines—The Burning of the House of our Benefactress—Our Efforts on her Behalf—Home.. 172

LIST OF UNITED STATES OFFICERS, Prisoners of War, Confined at Columbia, South Carolina........................ 175

NINETEEN MONTHS

A PRISONER OF WAR.

CHAPTER I.

A Prisoner—Morton, Miss.—Mobile, Ala.—Atlanta, Ga.—A foretaste of Southern inhumanity—Off for Richmond.

As I seat myself to indite the following narrative of my experience in Southern prisons, I am impelled by no motives of courted martyrdom, nor a desire to appear before the world as a hero: I rather sicken at a repetition of what were once inexorable realities. Indeed, when I become deeply absorbed in a recollection of the scenes still fresh and vividly before my mind, I sometimes forget that I am again surrounded by friends and humanity, and become despondent and oppressed. A person hardened to all sorts of wretchedness for nineteen long months is often apt, for some time after, to overlook his freedom. The mind, accustomed to long subjection and restraint, is slow to realize its acquired liberty, and lurks mournfully in the dark sepulchres of the past, brooding over miseries gone, yet present, mental agonies, whose lacerations time may heal, but the scars remain forever the indelible marks of a terrible ordeal.

In telling my story, I will confine myself exclusively to the narrative style, not striving for literary effect, but to state plainly what I witnessed and endured. In doing this, I must be understood as not awarding to myself an undue claim upon the sympathies of the Christian and enlightened people of the North, but using my own trials as an example, as the mouth-piece of thousands of others, many of whom have endured wretchedness compared with which mine has been nothing. With this understanding I will begin.

On the 2d of July, 1863, the expedition, Colonel J. N. Hannan commanding, of which my command formed a part, left camp, near Port Hudson, with orders to occupy Jackson, Louisiana. At this time, General Banks was closely investing Frank Gardner, in Port Hudson, and it was confidently believed there that he must soon surrender. The object of our movement was to reconnoitre the country adjacent and in the rear of our lines, to watch the operations of small parties flying about the country, and give timely notice of the approach of a considerable hostile force to succor the beleaguered garrison, and oblige General Banks to raise the siege. After pursuing our route for some distance, on July 3d I was detached with twenty-five men, of the Third Massachusetts cavalry, to move and make observations on another road. Upon nearing Concord Church, four miles from Jackson, I suddenly encountered the whole of Colonel Logan's brigade of rebel cavalry. Almost simultaneously my command was attacked on all sides, and after a desperate conflict against overwhelming numbers, I gave what are termed in military parlance "stampeding orders," in hopes that by taking to the woods some of us might escape; but so completely were we invested, that nearly every man before night was picked up. I was taken with a squad with which I was endeavoring to cut my way back to our lines.

Scarcely had the firing ceased, than a drove of rebel soldiers fell upon me like a pack of rapacious and ravenous wolves. After unceremoniously depriving me of my hat, boots, and blankets, they made me disgorge the contents of my pockets, and finally "swapped" clothes. A sneaking fellow, who secured my jack-knife, seemed particularly fortunate, and rejoiced. After each one of our party was subjected to an involuntary distribution of his property, I was sent to the rear, in a squad of fellow-prisoners. Two days after, the whole party, under guard of twenty-five rebel cavalry, was marched off to Morton, Mississippi, a small town on the Jackson and Meridian railroad, about twenty-five miles east of the former place. The distance we were obliged to travel was about one hundred and fifty miles. The weather was simply torturing. The sun poured down upon our hatless heads a perfect stream of fire. The intense heat falling upon our ill-clad persons raised painful and feverish blisters, and the abrasion of what remnant of clothing we had upon us rendered our sufferings still greater. Our feet, swollen and torn, were made doubly painful by the heated roads. The country through which we passed was poorly supplied with water, and when at hand, it was not the limpid, refreshing, fatigue-dispelling element of the mountain, but the dead, slimy, green, vegetable, and animal decomposition of the bayous, the haunt of the alligator and foul reptiles. Thus day after day we trudged, rather were driven on our way. Some of our party often fell to the ground, overpowered by the combined effects of heat and exhaustion. For a few moments we would be halted for the unfortunate one to revive. These were treasured moments. They were often for hours our only chance of escape from the intolerable heat. Singular that the torments of a comrade should give so much satisfaction! In time of misery, men care only for themselves. Self seems to be naturally a predominant impulse. When we resumed our march, we set out wondering who would be the next to suffer, that the rest might have another moment's respite.

After a lapse of about three weeks we reached our destination, and though the inhospitable chambers of the prison awaited us, this prospect, in view of our painful march, was rather a source of joy than of despair.

Our place of confinement at Morton was an old negro prison, in which, at the time, in an adjoining room, were thirty of this unfortunate race. Some were shackled and manacled with great cruelty, and the most fiendish punishments, from their piteous cries, must have been applied to them. The greatest crime of the larger number was a desire for freedom.

While at Morton, I first heard of the surrender of Vicksburg and Port Hudson, and that General Sherman had routed and driven Johnston eastward of the Pearl river. I now observed, also, that General Johnston was sending large numbers of his troops eastward, by rail,— as I since have learned, with a view to reinforcing and assisting Bragg in the operations which culminated in the sternly contested battle of Chickamauga.

I remained at Morton about seven days, and embarked by rail for Mobile. On the way to that city I was prostrated by a severe spell of illness, and left at Lodlan Springs. By the efficacy of a strong constitution and little drugging, I speedily recovered sufficiently to be able to resume my journey. I was again placed upon the train, and arrived at Mobile in the latter part of August.

Upon reaching the city, I was placed with my comrades in a building which in former times was used for mercantile purposes, but since the war had been converted into a prison, miscellaneously for Yankees and all sorts of villains. On the first floor were nine or ten men of the Second Tennessee cavalry; these poor fellows, on account of their devotion to the old flag, were treated with additional severity, and subjected to every humiliation. On the second floor, General Neal Dow was confined, awaiting trial at the hands of the civil authorities, in whose power he had been placed, after his capture by the military. The crime charged against him was "permitting his men to pillage the inhabitants of certain districts, while conducting a raid of national troops through Mississippi."

After undergoing a close confinement of two weeks at Mobile, our squad again resumed its travels, this time bringing up at Atlanta, Georgia.

At Atlanta we got our first glimpse at, and began to realize the wretchedness and misery of Southern captivity. We were rudely turned into a small pen or stockade, a short distance south of the city. In this inclosure were promiscuously confined four hundred national prisoners of war, and about five hundred rebel soldiers. The latter were awaiting trial for desertion and other capital military misdemeanors. The bloody code of Southern tyranny upon these unfortunates was executed without even a show of clemency or regret, and with an exacting fiendishness. Without a moment's warning, some were dragged from their hovels and conveyed to an adjacent field, where they were brutally shot; others were hanged, or rather suspended upon trees and choked to death, without the mitigating appliances of a regular scaffold. Another set were sent under guard to the front, as the condition of military operations at different points was uncertain. I cannot express my horror, when I sat brooding over the unhappy lot of these men, and questioned myself whether I and my comrades, though prisoners of war, had any thing to expect from wretches who had so little heart.

To speak in detail of life in the Atlanta stockade would be to give, on a smaller scale, the horrors endured on Belle Island and at Andersonville. As my object is to be as brief as possible, I will leave those two haunts of pestilence and woe as the representative types of what it is to conduct war on chivalric principles.

A short time after my arrival at Atlanta, a small batch of prisoners were brought in from Rosecrans' army, operating south of Chattanooga. The advent of this new lot of "Yanks" was a matter of the highest satisfaction to the prison guards, who immediately suggested an exchange of rebel notes for greenbacks. These financial transactions were always numerically in favor of the prisoner, though the guards always reaped largely the benefits of a knowledge of the money market, and never failed to falsify the price of greenbacks. There was but one resort, and that was to make the exchange as quickly and secretly as possible, or the possessor of greenbacks stood a fine chance of being deprived of them without any return whatever. At the time of my capture I had a small amount of money concealed; fortunately, I was not deprived of my jacket, though I had on my body, when I arrived at Morton, scarcely a single other article with which I left camp at Port Hudson. The secretion in the lining of my jacket of funds for a campaign, was a precautionary measure I always adopted before starting. Realizing that Confederate notes, under the circumstances, were a vastly more secure investment than greenbacks, I prudently exchanged at the best terms I could get—namely, six dollars rebel notes for one of greenbacks.

The Atlanta prisoners, at the time of my arrival, were receiving rations in quality enough to sicken the most hardened; and in quantity, a close calculation upon the amount of sustenance required to prolong or eke out life, without supporting it.

The daily rations at this time were:

One half-pound of corn-meal, and one ounce of raw beef.

The corn-meal we were obliged to use without salt, and the beef we boiled into a kind of weak soup.

I was at Atlanta until the 6th of September, 1863, when a large detachment, in which I was included, was ordered to prepare to be transferred to Richmond. Prisoners, particularly in Southern prisons, carry little luggage, so we were ready in about an hour, and were at once marched for the depot. On the way we passed a number of persons, principally women, children, and mechanics, on the streets. It was difficult to determine from their expressionless faces whether they felt any commiseration of our condition. It seemed not. They all wore a look of apathy. This may have been the result of habitual humiliation, and the tyranny of the Southern aristocrats. Occasionally we would hear a word of indignity cast at us; on our part, we moved with sealed lips, and gave no cause for remarks; whenever any thing was said by the inhabitants, it was from pure vindictiveness.

I may here say a few words about Atlanta; my opportunities, of course, were not the best to judge of the town, in the mere aspect of a city, for, from the time I entered the stockade gate until ordered for transportation to Richmond, I never crossed the prescribed limits of the camp and its adjacent privileged space. Atlanta, as Sherman, our country's great explorer, has already informed us, was, before he visited it, a city of about twelve thousand resident, and probably no less than forty thousand transient population, made up of officers, soldiers, and men employed in the itinerary workshops of the rebellion. As a railroad centre, it was one of the most important in the South, having communication with all parts. At all hours of the day and night trains could be heard arriving and departing. Often when my mind, despondent and wearied by the *ennui* of captivity, seemed ready to give way, I listened to the laboring puff and shrill whistle of the locomotive, and followed the rumbling cars off in the distance,—thinking often, that leads to liberty; and then catching up the sound of the remote approach of an incoming train, would follow it back, noting the increased volume of noise until brought to a stop at the depot. From the incessant activity of trains, I could well judge of the importance of the place, and the hum of machinery, the smoke of various industrial establishments, convinced me that much of the material of war consumed by the rebellion was manufactured there. The success of our arms along the borders of the rebellion had driven a great deal of the machinery used elsewhere to that point for safety. In consequence of this, private dwellings were converted into workshops, or temporary sheds were erected, in which the machinery was set up, and applied to useful purposes, until Atlanta became rather a city of manufactories than residences. I am satisfied that the capture of Atlanta was one of the severest blows to the material interests of the rebellion that up to that time it had sustained.

Of the country surrounding, I only speak from outside information, though I observed in approaching the city and in my departure, that we passed through a region of fine agricultural merits. We were continually impressed by the guards with the fact that Georgia was one of the most fertile States in the South; but we never experienced any tangible evidences of this fact in our prison diet. I believe, though the remark of the guards was true, that the lack of abundance was owing to the interruptions of labor by the great pressure of the war interests of the country. I cannot admit, however, that food was so scarce as to necessitate the meagre allowance issued to us; for money could always command any quantity. It was, without question, one phase of the studied inhumanity which the degraded character of the Southern leaders had adopted to exercise their intense animosity.

We left Atlanta towards evening, and crowded as we were in close cars, we all felt a glimmer of liberty. The fresh air of the country filled our lungs with vigor. We drew deep inhilations, and felt revived. For a moment we forgot our destiny, and looked out upon a fine and ever-changing prospect of plantations and indications of former wealth, forests and swamps, bayous and rivers, valleys and hills. The people seemed to be advised beforehand of our coming, for the road at many points presented groups of women and children, white and black, and at every station there was a large turn-out of those not gone to the wars to see what they considered the fruits of the prowess of their chivalry.

During our journey, particularly across Georgia and South Carolina, I noticed the movement of large numbers of troops. I inquired their destination, and was informed they belonged to Longstreet's corps, moving to reinforce Bragg, in Tennessee.

While stopping at a station, on what was termed Stone Mountain, there occurred a little incident which displayed the devotion of even the children of the South to the cause of treason. The moment our train came to a stand, about fifty youngsters congregated about the cars. Our appearance was so forlorn that the little fellows took us for rebel soldiers. Sympathizing with our situation, a number of them disappeared for a short time, and soon after returned heavily laden with cornbread, ham, and yams. These acceptable donations were readily received by the occupants of the cars. After all had been distributed, one of the youngsters discovered the persons they were thus gratuitously feeding were not "Confederate" soldiers but "Yanks;" whereupon the congregation set up a terrible lamentation, and denounced us as mean and contemptible, and they hoped we would get sick. As these infantile invectives were perfectly harmless, and many of them incomprehensible, we relished our unexpected meal, and considered the freely expressed opinions of the children an exceedingly cheap rate. As the train moved from the station, some of the youngsters threw stones after us, but not materially lessening our gratitude for their kindness.

CHAPTER II.

At Richmond—Libby—Terrible forebodings—Belle Island—Its appearance—How the prisoners lived—The daily bill of fare—Deliberate torture.

EIGHT days after leaving Atlanta, we arrived in the rebel capital. We were met there by a large crowd of hangers-on, loafers, and hard cases generally, who were idling around the depots. I saw very few of what I took to be the better class of people. At Richmond, as well as everywhere along our route, there were those who delighted in ridiculing our situation; and one more callous to magnanimity than the rest would make remarks, which were received with the highest approbation and merriment by the surrounding crowd. As we had already learned to endure this species of torment, we kept down our galled spirits, not, indeed, without a frequent wish for a single pounce upon some superlatively provoking wretch near by.

It was night, and from the depot, in the darkness, we were marched without delay to Libby prison. I could not enter the portals of this abode of suffering without a shudder. So much had been said about its horrors that I even borrowed misery from wretchedness itself. Detachments of our party were unceremoniously turned into the respective quarters we were to occupy, as if so many animals. Each made a dash at some choice spot which first met his eye, and immediately took possession. All fellow-feeling was lost, and the strife was for the greatest comfort of self. It fell to my lot to triumph over several disputants, and secure sufficient room to lie down at least. After all became quiet, I tried to sleep, but it was impossible. Tired and sore from continuous travel, burning with thrist and craving with hunger, my brain in a perfect whirl of confusion, I tossed about, turned from one side to the other, thought of every thing, performed all sorts of dry mathematical calculations to induce sleep, but sleep was impossible, the deep and gloomy future yawned before me, full of the most terrible forebodings. It is not so trying to suffer when we see before us at least a prospect of good, but to endure anguish of body and mind, and have not even one ray of cheer, is a test against which human weakness stays the tide, only when moved by that invincible impulse, despair. Towards morning I forgot my condition, and fell into a broken sleep, from which I was very soon aroused by the morning call. As the clothes on our backs answered the manifold purposes of wearing apparel by day, and night-shirt, bed-linen, and counterpane by night, we were not long in dressing and making beds. The whole party was then marched out for ablution, which was performed in the most primitive manner, several tubs answering the necessities of the whole party, and evaporation, aided by a fragment of a shirt or coat, or probably shirt or coat itself, took the place of a towel. This being finished, we were marched off to breakfast, which was slow in coming, and painfully limited in quantity.

During the morning after my arrival at Libby, I had the pleasure of exchanging a note and a few words with Lieut. J. H. Whitney, of the 2d Rhode Island cavalry. He was also a prisoner, having been captured about two months before. We had little to communicate that was not familiar to both, as we were captured about the same time. However, the satisfaction of meeting a friend was in itself a joy, and we compared notes upon our experience as far as it went, and exchanged words mutually encouragiug.

During the same morning officers of the prison came in and searched all those who arrived the night before for greenbacks. We were informed that if we would give them up they would be returned to us.

We had so often in other places, during our captivity, been deceived by the mean, low-bred proclivities of our high-born and chivalric keepers, that our wits were immediately set to work to devise some method of escaping the force of this extraordinary financial transaction. I felt so strongly convinced of my own ability to take all necessary care of my money, that I proposed to an intimate comrade to be searched among the first, and upon being sent above, which was the routine, to lower a string through a hole which I spied in the floor, to which I was to affix my valuables. As he had no money he was soon disposed of. The string soon made its appearance. The room being poorly lighted, and the investigating committee very deeply occupied in their systematic robberies, I rolled my money, which amounted to some hundreds of dollars, and my watch, in a small bundle and fastened it to the string, and in a few moments I had the satisfaction of seeing the string and package disappear through the lucky hole. When my turn came, I was accordingly found an unprofitable subject and speedily passed up stairs. Here I rejoined my comrade and received from him the package. I now took care to secrete it so as to avoid eliciting the attention of the prison-keepers. The money of the party had scarcely been stolen when we were ordered below to prepare to be marched to Belle Island, a beautiful name for a spot whose record is so big with one phase of the infamy and the everlasting damnation of every man who has ever supported the treason of the South. After considerable delay, late in the evening we were in motion. It was ten o'clock at night when we left the gloomy precincts of Libby, and marched through one of the principal streets of the rebel capital. On our route every thing was perfectly quiet. There were but few people on the streets. They took but little notice of us. Occasionally we would pass a night patrol; he would perhaps halt for a moment out of curiosity and then pass on without remark, or even an evidence of feeling for the horrors which awaited us at our destination. Having marched about a half an hour we crossed the main bridge over the James River, to Manchester. Thence following along the river a short distance on the south side, we crossed another bridge, which spanned the southern channel and terminated on Belle Island.

When we arrived at the main entrance of the prison limits we were unceremoniously turned in like a drove of cattle, and left to shift for ourselves. The least we expected was some accommodations, even the rudest. But no, the camp was already crowded to its full capacity, and the only resting-place we could find was on the bare ground, without shelter or covering save the broad canopy of heaven.

My first night in Libby was one of indescribable sensations. Though the terrible place was palled in darkness, my imagination conjured up pictures of emaciated forms, starvation and disease struggling for their victims, and all sorts of human woe in its most hideous forms. The very air was full of the foul exhalations of a miserable existence. Dark forms could be seen tottering about, and often through the dreadful night issued moans from the agonies of a dying victim. I took no sleep my first night on Belle Island. Every thing was too strange, too awful to be real. I often pondered over my situation, and wondered to myself whether it was not all a dream.

At the earliest gray of morning I arose from the ground, shivering from the chill and dews of the night. But I soon forgot my own miseries in the scene of desolation and suffering which unfolded itself before the great luminary of day.

Having taken but a general glance at what was passing before me, my first inclination was to find out something of the location and appearance of the island, before penetrating the sickening details of its wretched occupants.

Belle Island, an oblong tract of land—the whole dimension but one mile in length, and less than one-fourth of a mile in breadth—is situated in the James River, between Richmond and Manchester; the channel passing on the Richmond side being nearly one-third wider than between the island and the south bank. The island was reached alone from the Manchester side of the river, and by a rickety bridge, upon which was laid a branch of the Danville Railroad for the convenience of the Old Dominion Iron Works, which were located on the upper end of the island. The prison camp was situated on the extreme lower end of the island. The site seemed to have been chosen for its capability of adding to the wretchedness to which our brave men were compelled to submit. The ground was low, wet, and flat, and calculated to breed every character of fatal diseases. The area occupied by the prisoners was not over the size of an ordinary regimental camp—say about four acres. Around the whole was an embankment about three feet in height, somewhat resembling in appearance a hasty field defence. The ditch lay inside, and was about two feet in depth. The ditch and bank formed the boundary, beyond which it was death for a prisoner to wander. Here was the fatal "dead-line," outside of which, encircling the whole camp, were a chain of sentinels, ready to carry out their instructions to kill at every opportunity. The death of a Union prisoner always secured a furlough. Still further from this were the guard and officers' quarters, cook-house, hospital, and graveyard. A ridge of low hills surrounded and overlooked the camp. Here were posted, at different points, four pieces of artillery, charged with shell and canister, and pointed to rake all parts of the camp. Cannoneers were always at the pieces, ready at an instant to open upon any indications of a revolt. North of the camp was the graveyard, in plain view, and thickly marked with evidences of its dense population of bodies wantonly deprived of life. West of the graveyard was the hospital, the stepping-stone from the camp to the grave.

While I was quietly sauntering in the vicinity of the guard-line, towards the north channel of the river, I was accosted by a grim specimen of Southern chivalry.

"Hello thar, Yank, how d'ye make it?" said he.

"Nothing to complain of yet," I replied.

"How long you've been in thar?" he inquired, with an eminently tantalizing accent.

"Just as long again as half," I replied, not wishing to gratify his curiosity.

"You're a mighty bright un," answered the inquisitive gentleman, somewhat nonplused by being cut off so short.

After a few moments' pause, as if collecting his ideas, if he ever had any, he again broke out—

"Hello, smart Yank, in thar, do you want something to eat?"

"No. Do you want some greenbacks?" asked I.

"Yes," said he, with a greediness which Uncle Sam's currency always calls forth among Southern soldiers.

"Well, you can get plenty of them up North," I answered.

"That's so. Again taken down. You're a d——d sharp un, you are."

Not wishing to continue this conversation, for fear of trespassing too far upon the temper of the guard, I walked off to another part of the prison inclosure; seeing which, the fellow exclaimed after me—

"Oh, Yank, call again if you want something to eat, or a nice new blanket,—here's the place to get it."

As this was said merely to bring before my mind these comforts, most painfully deficient, I treated the remark with silent contempt.

My first visit through the camp was a theme of the greatest horror. I lost all consciousness of self. I felt a perfect agony of exasperation at what was suffered there. I could not even withhold a bitter censure of the government. I thought of the humanity which has characterized all its acts towards men who have lost all rights. I thought of rebel prisoners in the North, living upon the best of food, and abundant in quantity, with every medical care, and then asked myself the question whether it was humanity to nurse an enemy and condemn a friend. I thought not of my own gloomy future, but the horrible past of this abode of misery and suffering.

It would be utterly impossible to convey more than a general idea of the picture presented by the sufferers on Belle Island; and my own lot cast with them was indeed often a subject of painful contemplation. Around me were seven thousand men, human beings, massed, literally massed, within a space which was not sufficiently large to conveniently accommodate one-half that number. The quarters were constructed of any thing and every thing, and of all styles of architecture, from the rudest and most dilapidated species of cabins, which were considered palaces, down to a burrow or a piece of blanket, the centre raised upon two sticks, eighteen inches in height, and the four corners pinned to the ground, thus allowing one or two men to slide under horizontally. The materials used in the construction of these hovels were principally pieces of board, strips, mud, earth, strips of tenting, coats, pantaloons, and shirts, rudely lashed together,—in fact every conceivable thing not eatable, and not absolutely necessary for cooking. Rude and squalid as was their exterior, infinitely worse were they within. For economy of material many of the hovels were sunk several feet in the ground, and the loose earth was banked up to give height on the surface. The interior dimensions varied from six feet square and upwards to about two or three times that size, and sheltered from three to twelve men, and sometimes even more. The accommodations inside were of the rudest character, consisting merely of a board, or a piece of a blanket, to raise the body from the damp ground; and in some cases men did not possess even this luxury.

The majority of the hovels were without light and ventilation, the means of ingress and egress bearing no pretensions above what would be called a hole. How men managed to survive the damp and confinement of such places I could not divine, and doubted the strength of my own constitution to successfully struggle against the test.

The camp was deficient in even an attempt at drainage, and consequently every rain added greatly to our discomfort. As the result of this defect, there was no regular plan observed in the laying out of the camp. Each hovel was erected upon the most eligible site standing out of the way of the frequent floods.

The James River, which washed the island on all sides, answered a variety of purposes. About one hundred and fifty feet of river front was set apart for the sink. A space of ten feet adjoining the upper limit afforded all the conveniences allowed for washing, and ten feet above this was marked off for drinking. According to the regulations of the camp, no one was permitted to visit the sink during the night. It is therefore unnecessary to describe the scene presented every morning after eight to ten weary hours of darkness and suffering : it can be better imagined.

About thirty-six hours after my arrival on the island, I began to realize the effects of the reduced state of the commissariat, for the supply of prisoners. The daily allowance per man, at this time, was as follows :

One half pound of corn-bread, about half baked.
One pint of bean soup.
One to two ounces of meat.

This liberal supply was served in two instalments, morning and afternoon.

The soup could hardly be classed among the nourishing fluids generally recognized under that head, and would have been a curiosity to any one but an inhabitant of Belle Island. He was indeed himself the more curious to satisfy the hungry curiosity of his stomach. The fact of its being bean soup was sometimes patent in the appearance of a stray bean on the surface. Any one who discovered a dozen beans was considered in luck. The recipe used in the manufacture of bean soup for prisoners was, in general terms, a few wormy hog-beans, the more worms the better, a superabundance of James River water, and occasionally an imperceptible quantity of salt or saltpetre.

We had in name at least one luxury, and that was coffee. It was not the valuable product of the tropical plant known by that name, but a manufactured article of which the sum and substance was burnt bread-crust. The merit of this species of coffee was guaged by bringing it in contact with the greatest amount of heat without being consumed. The maxim accepted in regard to this article of diet was, the blacker the breadcrust, the better the coffee.

CHAPTER III.

Reduction of Diet—Conflict between Life and Death—Revolting Extremities — Surgeon's Call — Richmond Hospitals — Mortality—Soldiers buried alive.

PATIENTLY, day after day, the victims of rebel barbarism on Belle Island endured their sufferings without a murmur. Day after day as the winter grew they felt the harsh hand of hunger and cold, disease and death, seizing them with a tighter grasp, and yet they kept their peace. What was working in those minds full of anguish and despair no one knows, but with the fortitude of martyrs they asked nothing of their enemies, trusting in God.

About the middle of the month of November our greatest sufferings commenced. This new *régime* of torture was inaugurated by a perceptible reduction in our diet. At that time the issues of meat suddenly disappeared, and by the expiration of the month the soup also ran out. In the place of soup about twice a week two spoonfuls of beans unboiled were graciously issued to each man. But here another obstacle arose. Our daily allowance of wood was so limited that it scarcely lasted more than half an hour. This was sufficient time only to soften the beans, or set the water to boiling. Hence our alternative, under these circumstances, was to give the beans and the water the full benefit of the fire, and when that gave out, to eat the parboiled mixture despite the consequences.

The growing scarcity of food soon brought numbers to the most revolting extremities. Frequently I remember seeing men of noble frames, but emaciated to mere skeletons, crawling about the camp, voraciously snatching the veriest crumbs dropped or thrown away by some new arrival. It was a daily sight to see men supporting themselves with one hand, and plunging the other into a barrel of refuse matter in search of a bone or a bean. An old bone which had been repeatedly examined and gnawed at, was often a subject of bitter strife between several starving contestants, and frequently the victor triumphed to his disappointment, in finding the bone familiar to him as the object of former struggles.

One day while resting against the chimney of a cabin near my quarters, I witnessed a similar though more agonizing contest. Two men so reduced that they could scarcely keep on their feet, were fighting with all the energy they had left, for the possession of a bone which some new-comer had thrown away. They held the cause of the conflict between them, and turned and twisted, repeatedly both falling to the ground, and rising again together to renew their efforts. After about twenty minutes thus occupied, they undertook to compromise the matter by more peaceable means. At this juncture a third party stepped up, suddenly seized the bone, and ran off. The two men immediately shuffled and staggered in pursuit. In a few moments the three had disappeared among the huts.

The most disgusting scene of all, I saw a few days after while walking through the camp for exercise. I mention it as but a single instance of the extent to which the men were hardened by their sufferings. Two soldiers lying on the ground were apparently in conversation, one of them being sick suddenly ejected the contents of his stomach. His companion, incredible and revolting as it may appear, perceiving a fragment of undigested meat, drew it from the vomit and without hesitation placed it in his mouth, masticated and swallowed it with apparent relish. This was too much for me. I turned my back and hastened to my quarters: while on the way I passed a poor fellow in the very embrace of death, alternately coughing and singing. I halted, and after contemplating him a few moments said to him, "My man, you seem to be in a happy mood," not at first perceiving the impulse of his song.

He looked at me a moment, grinned and again began, "Hard up, hard up! I never shall forget the day when I was hard up; but I'll be well off yet, I'll be well off yet!"

The manner of the man's expression soon told the whole story. His mental faculties were gone. The intensity of his suffering was more than he could endure. He was a maniac in the camp, strolling about chanting his mournful refrains, "Hard up, hard up! I never shall forget the day when I was hard up; but I'll be well off yet." Yes, I thought, when death puts an end to your misery.

Probably the principal cause of suffering, and one I think to which the insufficiency of food and clothing was secondary, was the want of proper shelter.

The crowded state of the camp, and the scarcity of building material, often obliged men to lie in the open air without the covering even of a blanket, for weeks at a time, awaiting their turn to step into the quarters of some comrade who had succumbed in death to the mis-cries of the place. While undergoing this test many of the unfortunates themselves died. In the matter of clothing, the first stroll I took through the camp I discovered hundreds of shoeless feet and bodies almost naked. About one-half of the men were without overcoats or blankets. The result of this deplorable neglect was an immense mortality. The prevailing disease of the camp was diarrhœa, which coupled with exposure and starvation, reduced the men to a most frightful condition. Many looked more like hideous spectres than human beings—their eyes were wild with the delirium of suffering, and their faces sunken, wan, and sad, and were fit subjects to affright the stoutest heart.

One day standing at the gate leading to the hospital I observed a mournful procession. It was made up of between two and three hundred suffering men, attending "surgeon's call." This was the daily average. As the line moved slowly by it wavered and staggered with the weight of wretchedness. Some of the men, with almost superhuman effort, succeeded in carrying themselves erect, others tottered along, often grasping for support a comrade, who, unsteadied by this unexpected shock, seized another; thus the struggle spread until nearly the whole line was affected. Numbers of men were unable to walk alone and were assisted by some stronger companion. Those who were not able to keep their feet at all, were either left behind to die or conveyed by their comrades in a blanket.

Surgeon's call was more a form than a blessing. The medical department of the Island was attended by an insufficient and inefficient corps of men. Judging from their manner many of them had never seen a work on medicine, and most probably were graduates of the school of horse medicine, or that sphere of medical experience which relates to the treatment of the white trash of the South. The surgeon-in-chief of the rebel armies evidently made it a merit to send the poorest of his craft to practise upon the Yankees.

One day while watching the passing of the victims of surgeon's call, perceiving one man tottering along with decrepitude, brought about by the weight of woe, I stopped him a moment—

"Comrade," said I, "you are very ill, why don't you get a permit for the hospital?"

He looked up surprised at my question, and merely asked,

"Have you ever been there?"

"No," I replied.

"Well, then don't ask such a question."

"But pray is the hospital any more than what you suffer here?" I inquired.

"Ten or a hundred times: just as much more as it takes to quickly put an end to a man," he said, gloomily.

He seemed for a moment in deep meditation, and then continued:

"I had two brothers, both older and stronger than myself; we belonged to the same company and the same regiment, and were captured in the same battle."

"Three brothers captured in the same battle!" I repeated, with some commiseration.

"Yes, three brothers taken in the same battle. After fighting hard all day, late in the afternoon, while on picket, we were run down and taken prisoners, and carried to the rear. After stealing all we had, and making us exchange clothing, we were sent off by the rebels to this terrible place."

The man again became quiet, and seemed to be revolving in his mind awful scenes.

"What has become of your brothers?" I asked.

"We were not," he replied, "on the island two weeks before one of them was taken down sick. He was sent out there (pointing to the hospital) for treatment. Four mornings after, I was counting from the guard-line the number of dead laid out for burial. Among the number I recognized the face of my brother. I felt reckless, and would have crossed the dead-line, and let the guard shoot, so that I might have another look at my brother. As I started forward a companion with whom I had been conversing seized me, held me back, and persuaded me not to commit a folly which would inevitably result in my own death. I obeyed, but all the morning watched from within the limits of the camp the dead body of my brother without. At noon I saw him rudely tossed into the dead-cart, and hauled off to the silent grave."

Here the man shed tears, and supporting himself on my shoulder, remained thus giving vent to a grief that had hitherto been unable to escape. Drying his eyes on his coat sleeve, or rather on the rags which represented it, he again spoke:

"My second brother," said he, "gave way about a week after the first died. After the experience of the first he refused to go to hospital. He went to surgeon's call, but that did him no good. One night we laid down in our hut. About midnight he said he was cold. I gave him all the blanket I could. The next morning I looked at him, and found he was stark dead."

Here the soldier thought for a moment, and then looked me full in the face, and with a wild grin said, in a voice as hollow as the sepulchre itself: "And I expect they'll have the trouble of carrying me out in a blanket one of these fine mornings." With this remark the sick man continued on his way to surgeon's call.

I watched as the victim parted from me; death's stamp seemed fixed upon him. Two weeks after, I uncovered a dead body which was about to be carried to the graveyard. It was the last of the three brothers. I could not stay a tear, and thought of the anxious mother awaiting their return or some tidings from her three sons.

By a rule of the camp, the most severe types of disease were, at the expiration of each week, sent to hospital in Richmond, where they received but little better treatment than on the island. On the subject of the Richmond hospitals I conversed one day with Corporal Bowie and others, who had facilities of ascertaining. I learned that the accommodations of the hospitals were limited, and always more than filled. The patients were closely ranged along the floors, with scarcely sufficient room to pass between them. The rooms were without ventilation, and were so filthy that the greatest surprise was the non-appearance in the city of some terrible plague originating in the hospitals. Medical supplies were scarce, and sometimes absolutely exhausted. But the worst feature of the place was the inattention and brutality of the rebel nurses. Men in the last struggles of death were permitted to lie unheeded in the most violent paroxysms. Others, from their inability to move, made their evacuations in their beds, and lay for whole days in the filth, and surrounded by the foul effluvia. Others, in the delirium of fever, fell savagely upon some patient near by, and after striking and tearing him with a perfect frenzy of passion, fell exhausted and powerless, or perhaps a corpse ; while the sufferings of the victim of his insanity were increased or terminated.

But if life in the Richmond hospitals was terrible, death itself was no alleviation. The average daily mortality was twenty. The bodies were often permitted to remain in the beds until putrefaction had set in, or sometimes in haste were hurried off to the dead-house before life was fully extinct, to make room for some new patient. The dead-house is said to have presented a horrible sight; the bodies were piled upon the floor, sometimes several deep, awaiting sepulture. In the mean time innumerable rats, attracted by the ovation laid out for them, feasted themselves without interruption, and morning revealed a horrid sight of ghastly and mutilated faces, some devoured entirely, and others without eyes and noses.

On the island I found, of my own observation, the disregard of human life, and the neglect to which human bodies were condemned, most mournfully verified. I shall never forget one evidence of this. On January 12, 1864, I was passing where I could see five bodies of soldiers, lying side by side, in the rear of the hospital, preparatory to burial. I stood a moment in deep contemplation watching them. I soon discovered what I supposed to be a convulsive action in one of the bodies. I looked more closely and found the man, though laid out to be buried, was not dead, and was then endeavoring to turn over. The doctor, in making his round, considered the poor fellow dead, or so nearly so that he might as well be taken out to make room, in expectation that he would die before the remaining four would be buried.

Another instance of the carelessness, we can hardly

suppose it ignorance or design, of persons in charge of the sick I witnessed one day, while watching the process of disposing of the dead. There were a number of coffins lying in the vicinity. In one I noticed two men unceremoniously cast a corpse, and were nailing down the lid: suddenly I was startled to find the lid lifted, and a man, partially naked, by a miraculous return of strength, seat himself upright in the coffin. The man was not dead. What a fortunate return of consciousness! I thought how many, in the extreme exhaustion and lethargy of disease, thus revived when too late. My blood chilled as I thought of perhaps scores, maybe hundreds, after enduring all the horrors of Southern barbarism, awake to find its consummation in being buried alive.

CHAPTER IV.

Sharp Practices of Rebel Surgeons—A New Way of Making Money—Convalescent Hospital in Richmond—Efforts to Escape—Discovery—Back to Belle Island.

A SHORT time after my arrival on the island I entered into an arrangement with one of the doctors, whereby I expected to better my condition, by being transferred to a Richmond hospital as an invalid. As I discovered afterwards, I was merely the victim of a sharp practice in vogue among the surgeons of the island and a number of accomplices at Richmond. It appeared these men had organized a well-understood arrangement between themselves, in order to secure money from prisoners of war. The plan, as I learned by experience, was this. When a prisoner was considered "flush," a doctor immediately set upon his track, and, after a brief familiarity, introduced a conversation which invariably terminated in a suggestion that for fifteen dollars in greenbacks he would be sent across the river to the city convalescent hospital as an invalid, and there be paroled with the sick. The accommodations at these establishments, in view of the small sums occasionally realized, were a vast improvement on any thing experienced in other places devoted to the uses of prisoners of war. If the prisoner had money sufficient to meet the expense of this privilege he handed it to the doctor, and in a day or two the first part of the bargain was consummated—he was passed into a boat, and conveyed across the river.

This agreeable change lasted usually, at the utmost,

from two to four weeks, at the expiration of which time a new set of doctors were sent around, purporting to overhaul the city hospitals. The individuals invariably knew the subjects of the arrangement, and at once ordered them back to the island, unless they could purchase extension of their privilege by paying for it. Men, however, once thus gulled kept their money for better uses, and accordingly refused. The result of this was a document certifying or rather announcing the recovery of the patient, who was immediately restored to the island and permitted to reflect upon his bargain.

Having money, I was induced to victimize myself by putting confidence in persons who had frequently before given evidence, either personal or towards my comrades, of their bad faith. Two months I passed in hospital in comparative comfort, but after the lapse of this time I was informed that I must either return to the island or to some city prison. When we were alone my companions and myself held a council of war, during which we determined not to go. We resolved for the time being to ransom ourselves from the island. The surgeon accepting the proposition three besides myself gave him twenty-five dollars each to be invalided for two months longer; in the mean time we planned measures of escape.

For some days after this arrangement we were engaged in observing all parts of the hospital premises affording the most practicable chances of escape. Having selected the wash-house as the scene of our attempts we commenced taking up the boards. It was our purpose to dig out by tunnelling the foundation. Our labors in the beginning went on magnificently, and the third night found us under the sentinel's beat. We could hear his cry "All's well," and so we thought were we, and looked hopefully upon the issue of our undertaking. The fourth night, however, found our operations summarily checked. During that day the rebel sergeant of the guard looked suspiciously upon us. Whether he had been informed or merely suspected us, or whether our fears and imagination had a great deal to do with our alarm, we were unable to determine, but concluded that this should not be an obstacle to a prosecution of our labors that night. Expedition was now every thing.

Shortly after dark, one of our party being on guard, three of us crept to the wash-house and resumed operations. We were working vigorously, when the suspecting sergeant visited our beds and found them vacant. Immediately but quietly instituting a search, he came upon us by surprise. We were digging away, and whispering our instructions to each other in the quietest manner, when lights appeared and the sergeant and several men approached. Our hearts sank within us. No opportunity presented itself where we could secrete ourselves. Our only alternative was to face our misfortune manfully. For a time my mind was filled with an inclination to settle my accounts with life, make my peace with God, and stand up and meet death on the spot. The manner of the sergeant soon, however, calmed my fears and though all of us were roughly buffeted, we suffered no other punishment than a few bruises, and numerous epithets less beautiful than expressive and potential in the dialect of profanity.

We were at once placed under guard and hastened to Libby. After passing the remainder of the night in calm reflection and frequent self-congratulation that we were alive, we early the following morning experienced the sensation of a march back to the horrors of Belle Island. Thus terminated my first effort for liberty, but I was determined it should not be the last. I was convinced of one thing by my experience—that if the traitor government desired, the condition of prisoners could be immensely ameliorated without much additional outlay. The hospital in which I was an inmate because I paid the surgeon's fee, though rude in accommodations and management, still was infinitely better than the abodes of filth and misery which prevailed in the buildings used for the general sick. It appeared the whole system of treatment of prisoners of war was a conflict of vindictive and mercenary motives. When the patient had money which had escaped the cupidity of his captors, and the insatiate pack of deliberate thieves he met at his introduction to prison life at Richmond, he was allowed privileges; but when that money was all consumed, he was treated, if possible, more severely than those who never had means. Those who had no money at all from the beginning, felt the full rigors of the despotism and inhumanity of the chivalry of the South.

CHAPTER V.

The Winter of 1863 and '64—Miseries multiplied—Arrival of Prisoners from Burnside's Army—Their terrible Sufferings—A Night of Horror—Fearful Extremities of Cold—Pitiable Expedients to keep Warm—The Number of Deaths during the Winter—Burial of the Dead.

My absence from the island now proved worse for me than if I had remained and endured all its privations. Winter was not yet passed, and the quarters which I had occupied before leaving were now in possession of another. By a fortunate circumstance, one of my companions and myself succeeded in securing a shelter—which, by a stretch of imagination, was called a tent by the islanders sufficient, by care and close contact, to accommodate two. This at least had the effect of lessening our exposure, though we were obliged to lay on the ground and had only such covering as we could secure by the polite manner in which we approached the guard and a prompt levy upon the late possession of a dead comrade.

The winter of 1863 and '64 was a terrible one for the miserable inhabitants of Belle Island. The season was colder than had been known for some years. The cold winds, rains, and snows swept the island mercilessly. It seemed to blow fiercer than ever, to increase our wretchedness. Those who had tents or huts were comparatively comfortable, and still they suffered; but the misery and suffering of those unfortunates who were without any protection whatever, cannot be told. All night long the emaciated forms of the outcasts could be seen staggering through the camp in order to keep from freezing. The scarcity of fuel drove them to it. In the darkness, or perhaps in the calm cold light of the moon, they could be seen moving about, feebly striking their shoulders with their hands like spectres preparing for some terrible exhibition of demonology. The only rest which these men found was during the day, to get in a sunny place and take the repose nature demanded.

Two days after my reappearance on the island my attention was attracted by four men carrying out of the camp the remains of a soldier. I inquired the boy's history, for he was a boy not more than sixteen. The soldiers informed me that he was brought in about a month before. When he came he was without any thing, his captors had robbed him of his overcoat and blanket. He could find no shelter. There was no mercy among the miserable beings on the island, and the boy was obliged to shift for himself. The night was extremely cold. He ran about the camp trying to keep his blood warm, but despite his exertions, the merciless wind pierced him to the very heart. At last, overpowered by his exertions, he fell to the ground exhausted: the cold throwing him into a stupor, he soon fell asleep. It was his last sleep. The next morning he was picked up by some companions stark cold, and lifeless, as a piece of marble.

In the latter part of December some new prisoners arrived on the island. The men were greatly fatigued by their trials. They were all without blankets and overcoats, having shared the fortunes of all their predecessors who had fallen into the hands of the enemy. I noticed two, who seemed to be particularly devoted to each other. The one was yet strong and healthy, the other weak and in poor health. He was completely overcome, and the whole of the first night his companion belabored him with his fists to keep him awake. The night was cold: the weak man could not overcome his desire to sleep, and would rouse himself at the urgent wish of his companion, but almost immediately again fall asleep. At length the night was passed, and as the sun rose the strong man conducted his companion to a small fire where he laid him on the ground. Between the slight heat of the fire and the scarcely perceptible warmth of the sun the weak man fell asleep, and did not awake until aroused by his companion late in the afternoon.

On the last day of the year 1863, during a terrific storm of wind, snow, and sleet, several hundred of Burnside's men who were captured in the defence of Knoxville, East Tennessee, were brought in. I never gazed on a more forlorn, dilapidated, miserable set of men in my life. They were fit subjects to be the companions of the tortured beings of Belle Island. Their captors had stripped them of every thing, even the clothes on their bodies, giving them in exchange their own ragged and filthy garments. Nearly two-thirds of them were without shoes, and not more than a score out of the whole number were permitted to keep a blanket or overcoat. Very few of the new-comers could find shelter, and the remainder were left out in the open air to swell the record of misery nightly experienced. The men reported the most terrible suffering on their way to Richmond. Part of the way they were obliged to march over mountains, through swamps and streams. The wind, and rain, and cold beat upon them fearfully. Their clothes were a sheet of ice, and their feet were blue, swollen, and frostbitten. In this condition they were driven daily on long marches, while their keepers were riding by their side mounted. At night the miserable procession would halt. There were no axes with the party; they were therefore obliged to gather sticks and dead-wood for fire. Invariably before midnight the fires were out, and the tedious hours until morning were spent in shivering and watching. The rations of the men were limited to what could be gathered by parties of the guard detailed as foragers. They always had an eye to themselves, but their indolence or inhumanity generally found the prisoners short. When this batch of prisoners arrived on the island a large number commenced dying within three days, and many others before the expiration of a week were obliged to submit to amputation of frozen limbs.

One night in January, 1864, was the worst I remember on Belle Island. The day had been clear, but very cold. Men who usually sought rest at this time were obliged to keep up and bestir themselves to keep warm. Many sought and found a few moments rest during the day in the quarters of a comrade, but those who were deprived of this privilege dreaded a night which would probably prove their last. Night came. A piercing fierce northeast wind was sweeping ruthlessly across the Island. The men who had blankets and quarters were frequently driven to the necessity of running through the camp to keep warm. What then must have been the sensations of those outside! About midnight I could no longer stand my shivering, and jumped into the open air for exercise. I never shall forget the scene I witnessed there. The whole camp was crowded with men, dashing about, jumping, stamping their feet, and swinging their arms according to their strength and the degree of heat still left or awakened in them. I joined the throng, clasping my hands rapidly around my shoulders and jumping occasionally to start the circulation in my feet. While undergoing this process of warming, occasionally dashing across an open space in the camp, I saw numbers of men move from tent to tent begging and crying piteously, their jaws rattling with cold, to be admitted. As far as there was any possibility of accommodating another they were admitted, and the huts and tents were crammed to double their capacity. Frequently the too incautious entrance of a stranger would demolish the frail shelter of the occupants, and the whole were driven out to pass the rest of the night a victim of their sympathy. Refusal where the quarters were absolutely full, only multiplied the desperation of the men disappointed, when in the consummation of their sufferings they fell frantically upon their knees and attempted to burrow with their nails into the frozen surface with a perfect frenzy. When disappointed in this, the wretched men would throw themselves in a heap, one on the other, in order to aggregate the warmth of their bodies, so as to make a sensible effect through the whole mass. In these efforts the recklessness of the men was really painful. They would fall upon one another and struggle to be beneath. Here a desperate fight ensued, having at least the good effect of exciting the men and firing their blood. In these struggles the strongest invariably found the warmest part of the mass, and the weakest, lying on the outside shivering with the wind, would keep his place for a moment and jump up and strike for himself. This would bring the cold on the next. He too would jump up, and so on until the whole mass would be broken up and the men seeking other means of comfort. Thus the weary night wore away, rendered doubly long and cruel by the anxious wretches who were praying for morning. I could not return to my quarters. Several attempts found little comfort there, and the next morning I found myself well-nigh overcome.

The scene presented by the return of day was horrible. All through the camp bodies of men frozen to death were found. Many made insensible by the cold had fallen asleep, and been frozen. Others would fall asleep, but arouse at a timely moment to save themselves from the fatal stupor. I now observed a large number seat themselves, hugging their knees close to their bodies. Others would fall over and sleep a few minutes, and then start to their feet, as if in doubt whether they were frozen or alive. Nature seemed to sympathize with the wretchedness, and as the morning grew, the sun rose bright; it was never so comfortable and full of warmth. The sufferers of the night now assured of a chance of awakening, gave way to exhausted nature. They lay everywhere through the camps, on the sunny side of hovels, and seemed to enjoy their slumbers as though they reposed on beds of down.

About noon a burial-party searched the camp for the dead who had fallen during the night. I watched the sad office. The detail was from the island guard, and the manner in which they performed their duty was brutal in the extreme. Many a poor fellow who was comparatively comfortable was well shaken and disturbed in his slumbers, by the heartless inquiry: "Hello, there, are you dead yet?" The frozen, or rather those who made no reply to the questions of the burial-party (and no one knows how many of these, by proper treatment, were capable of resuscitation), were placed in rude pine boxes, and conveyed to the graveyard, where they remained several days, and were finally buried.

At the time, during the winter, when the suffering of the men was at its height, there were from exposure alone as many as twenty-seven, and sometimes fifty deaths in a single night; and so completely insensible had the men become to these scenes of wretchedness, that scarcely a word passed on the death of a most intimate comrade, and frequently frozen bodies would lie a whole day in camp, exposed to the view of everybody who chose to look at them. What else could be expected than this awful mortality? Nine long weeks, during the months of December, January, and February passed, without the issue of a single load of wood to the prisoners on the island. Who was to blame for this heartless oversight, neglect, or indolence, is of course not known. Daily, hundreds of men would call upon the officers of the guard, and beg that some fuel be sent; even if necessary to cut down the rations. But no, no wood came, and many a long night and weary day, under every description of weather, the prisoners endured their dreadful lot. I often thought how many lives, by a single stick of wood, might have been saved. But to save life was evidently not the wish of the traitors; they seemed to care nothing for that. There was to them an evident satisfaction, next to his suffering, in the death of a Union soldier.

I shall never forget the month of January, 1864. This was the worst of the winter. Every day, after witnessing some new phase of horror and human suffering, I could not but breathe a prayer that God, in his inexorable justice, would deal with our enemies according to their deserts. I tried to suppress a desire for revenge with my own hands. I looked on all sides of me. There were stalwart frames, wrecks of men who left their homes at the patriotic impulse of love of country and constitutional liberty, men who had stormed the breach and marched upon the cannon's mouth, now helpless victims of the outrageous crime of Southern treason.

CHAPTER VI.

Punishments—Bucking and Gagging—Riding the Horse—Great Sufferings and Torture under the rigors of a fiendish Vindictiveness.

Not satisfied with the sufferings of the men from the want of food and shelter, there were numerous punishments inflicted upon them from the slightest causes. There was a red-whiskered sergeant of a portion of the rebel guard on the island, who particularly revelled in inflicting the grossest torture. His chief delight was to buck and gag the men, and he executed his diabolical work upon the slightest pretences. Bucking and gagging was carried out by obliging the victim to seat himself on the ground. Next his hands were tied, and his arms forced around his knees. The next situation was a stout stick shoved horizontally between the arms and the knees, passing over the former and under the latter, securing the man completely in a most painful position. A block of wood was then fastened in the mouth by means of a string. Men in this situation were often permitted to remain, weak and half clad as they were, without food, seated for a whole day, and in extraordinary cases a day and a night, on the cold ground, exposed to the cold and pelting rain, without the power of extricating or moving a limb. Kept in this constrained and painful attitude, the suffering of the unfortunate victim may be imagined. The author of the cruelty, or at least the medium of its execution, looked upon it with peculiar relish.

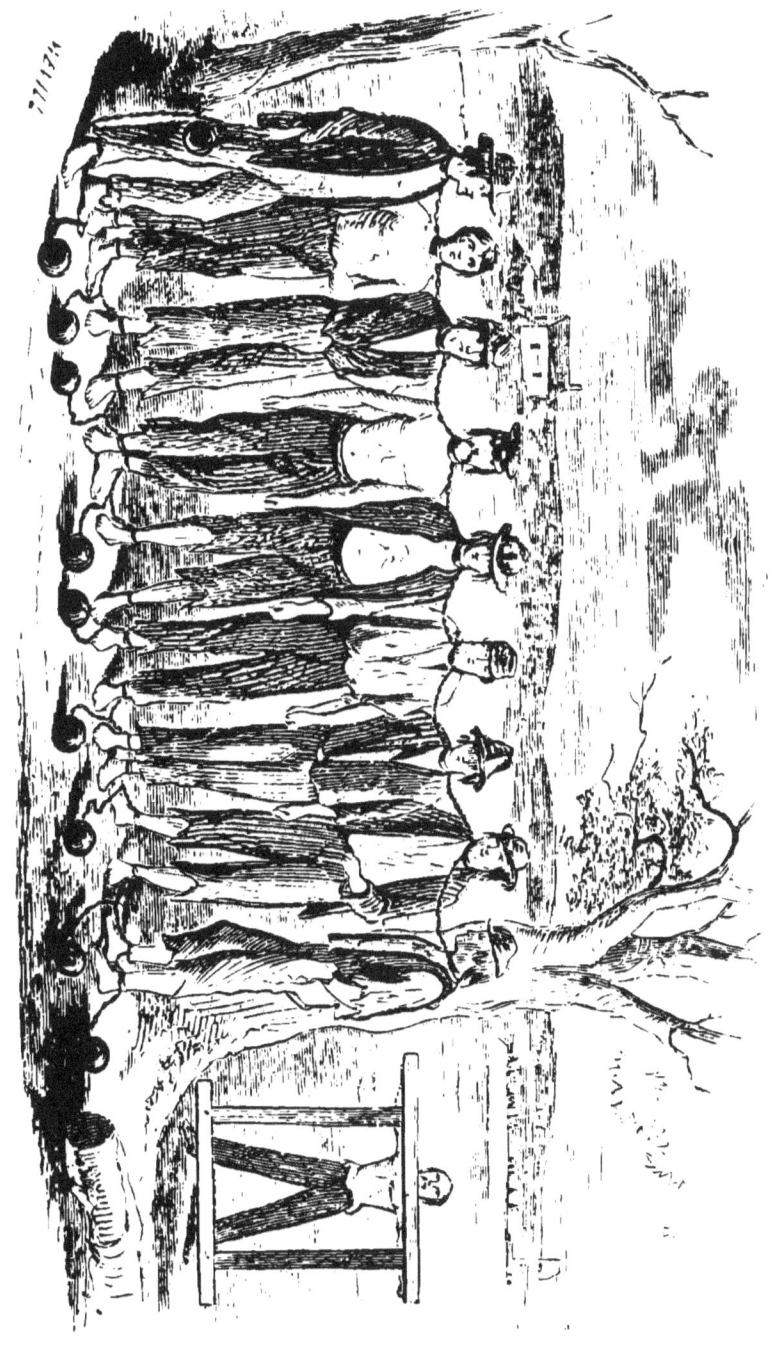

THE CHAIN GANG.

During one of the raids or sudden movements in February, 1864, against Richmond (I could not learn the exact nature of the affair), the rebel capital was evidently thrown into great anxiety, judging from the manner of the guards on the island. Their fear of speedy retribution instead of effecting a relaxation of their severe measures, rather heightened them. A few days after the first excitement was over, a small number of captured raiders were brought on the island. The red-whiskered sergeant was particularly delighted at his new subjects. His mind seemed immediately to plan some original torture for the new-comers. The first day—and it was rainy and terrible—he compelled three of these men to place themselves astride a wooden horse. He then fastened a rope to each foot, and drawing the limbs apart, fastened the other extremities of the rope to stakes previously driven in the ground, about six feet on either side of the horse. The men then had their hands secured behind them, by means of a rope attached to stakes in the rear; their heads were then drawn back, and another rope run through their mouths, between the teeth, and both ends fastened to a thirty-two-pound shot. Two of the men fainted in the beginning of this brutality, but no heed was given them, and the three were kept in this condition of torture for fully an hour and a half.

Harmless as we were, it was impossible to retaliate or interfere. With burning rage, day after day, we were obliged to witness our miseries, manifold in number, increased by the brutal arts of a fiend, who was encouraged in this inhumanity by the applause of all true-hearted Southerners who visited the island. Often have I studied the brute's features, his form, his manner, his voice, and then looked again to be sure to fix him in my mind. How many have done this! For what reason, let the first meeting say.

It would be impossible and a profitless task to undertake to mention all the different modes of punishment. The full round is familiar to every man who ever was a victim of Belle Island. This was but another means of manifesting the mean and vindictive spirit, impotent insomuch as the National Government was concerned, and a lasting disgrace to the perpetrators of the fiendish work upon those who, through the casualties of war, were thrown into their hands.

CHAPTER VII.

Theft—Police Regulations of the Island—Regulators and Raiders—Summary Punishments—Treachery of the Camp-guard.

Surrounded by so much misery, prison life has a general tendency to encourage all the evil of men, and very little of the good. I allude to those acts called forth by the instinct of self-preservation, for the struggle upon Belle Island was one of life and death, and the men were often driven, by the necessities of their situation, to acts of which they disapproved, and which, under any other circumstances, would have called forth a cry for summary dealings. The practice most troublesome on the island was theft. Any person possessing a coat, or blanket, or haversack, was obliged to carry them about his person, or leave them in charge of a reliable comrade. Any thing wearable, eatable, or usable in any shape to add to the comfort of the possessor, could not be left unguarded for a moment without mysteriously or openly disappearing.

Theft was not confined to any particular class of persons, in a moral point of view, but was carried on as a matter of the most desperate necessity, by those who were without the necessary article. The prisoners were much ridiculed by the Southern press for their stealing and cheating propensities, but forgot to lay the cause where it justly belongs. If each man had been reasonably well supplied, these things would not have occurred. But when a man was freezing to death, whether it is right to steal a coat or a blanket, or when another was starving to death, neither person will hesitate long to speculate upon the moral right of an opportunity to alleviate his sufferings and save life. Not one man out of ten, when he arrived on the island, had a single thing calculated to make him comfortable. Even their clothes were nothing but the homespun and tattered cast-off garments of a rebel soldier or citizen. The men were obliged to meet their wants somehow, and were compelled in a majority of instances to do it by stealing or purchasing the clothing of the dead.

If the necessities of many drove them to theft to supply their deficiencies of clothing, shelter, and food, there were another set who, being supplied, for their own protection, established a self-constituted police, known on the island as "Regulators." This force was highly efficient, prompt, and severe in its way, and was particularly the terror of evil-doers. The party against whom they were banded were known as "Raiders." The "Regulators" patroled the camp with watchful eyes, and the "Raiders," equally on the alert, were continually on the lookout for a chance. If a "Raider" was discovered carrying off any thing, a party of "Regulators" immediately gave chase. The pursuit was generally a matter of strength on the part of the pursued and the pursuers. If the former had more strength than any one of the latter, he escaped. If not, he was overtaken and brought to trial. The "Regulators" were armed with sticks, and if the "Raider" was found guilty, they made him first disgorge and then belabored him most unmercifully. From the effects of such a beating several deaths occurred during my confinement on the island.

During the month of February, 1864, shortly before my transfer to Andersonville, there was an instance of "raiding" which proved more disastrous than was usually the case. One of the guard had thrown his blanket across the bank to dry. While his back was turned an expert "Raider" seized it and made off. The guard immediately after, on looking for his blanket, found it gone. In his exasperation he levelled his piece and fired into the crowd of prisoners near his beat, instantly killing one, severing an artery in another who bled to death in a few moments, and severely wounded a third. This so enraged the remainder of the crowd, that in co-operation with a squad of "Regulators" they started on a hunt for the "raider." In their rage, there was not the least doubt that if he had been discovered at the time he would have been hung without ceremony—not for the crime of "raiding," but for committing an act which he knew would endanger the lives of innocent men. The lieutenant of the guard, about an hour after, ferreted out the culprit and had him conveyed outside the camp limits, and ordered him to be stripped and receive twenty lashes on the back. The man handling the lash being a rebel soldier, laid it on the victim with his whole force. The lieutenant remarked that the punishment "was not for being the cause of the death of a couple of Yankee prisoners, but for stealing the blanket."

About shooting prisoners the guard was perfectly reckless, and at one time the number of deaths from this cause became so great, that it was a common remark in camp that if "twenty-five or thirty Yankees did not die daily in the Richmond hospitals, the guard shot enough on the island to make up the deficiency."

The treachery of the island guards often proved fatal to the lives of venturesome prisoners. One instance of this I will mention. In February, 1864, the Sergeant-Major of the 77th Pennsylvania volunteers, who had for a long time been a prisoner on the island, sighed for freedom. For some time he had been intimate with one of the guard. While in conversation with him on one occasion the guard informed the Sergeant-Major that for a certain sum he would pass him and two comrades outside the chain of sentries and row them across the river. The Sergeant-Major relying on the sincerity of the offer, found two prisoners who had the money and were willing to pay and hazard the attempt to make their escape. The guard received the money, and the same night the three men were passed out the gate according to agreement. They were quickly stealing towards the river; arriving near the bank, they felt as if they could almost see and feel freedom in their grasp. They were staggered with surprise when suddenly a volley of musketry was fired at them. Immediately four guards sprang from an ambuscade. Two of the guard had been severely wounded by their own fire; the remaining four clubbed with the butts of their muskets the three bewildered prisoners, exclaiming wildly, "Your time has come, you G—d d—m Yankees! Your time has come, you can put on your overcoats in the morning." The three men would have been beaten to death on the spot if a lieutenant, aroused by the noise, had not arrived at this juncture and interfered on their behalf, placing a guard over them. The next day the three men were searched and robbed, after which they were stripped and turned into camp. This act of brutality so aroused the sympathies of the rest of the prisoners, that a contribution of clothing not in use, or fragments of clothing was taken up, out of which the unfortunate men were clad.

The guard who practised this diabolical scheme, boasted and laughed over his smartness, calling it a "Yankee trick."

CHAPTER VIII

National Airs—Hatred of them by the Southern Soldiers—Greenbacks and Contraband Trade—Speculations in Food—In Money—Quotations—The Richmond Brokers—How the Yankees outwitted the Guards.

The vindictive spirit of the Southern hatred of the United States was frequently exhibited, particularly in the dislike manifested at the old and familiar national airs. All tunes like the "Star Spangled Banner," "Columbia, Gem of the Ocean," and all airs calculated to revive a recollection of the days when we were one, were absolutely proscribed. There was not so much hostility felt against the tune "Red, White, and Blue," as these colors were disgraced by application to the flag of treason. The guards often could be heard singing this air, though in a different language and a less exalted spirit than characterized the old song. As for "Yankee Doodle," this was still more odious than the worst. The tune originally applied in derision to the patriots of 1776 had become too closely interwoven by too many glorious recollections in the minds of the lovers of the institutions for which our forefathers fought, to sound harmonious in treason's ear. There were too many memories of justice and principle associated around it, to sound well in the ear of the outlaws of civilization.

On one occasion, while a party of prisoners were singing national airs, a guard who lost his peace of mind in listening to the familiar sounds, discharged his musket into the tent in which the prisoners were sitting. The music ceased suddenly. Fortunately the deadly missive passed through without harming any one. The offence was too sacred.

There was one article of Yankee ingenuity to which the rebel soldiers, officers and every other species of rebel, took a great fancy. That article was a "Greenback," and any prisoner who saved any of them during the thieving processes through which he was put in the beginning of his experience as a prisoner, had a sort of omnipotence and received a courtesy quite bending in view of the lofty-pated character of the rebels. By means of greenbacks, whilst they lasted, a prisoner was enabled to live comparatively quite comfortable, orders to the contrary notwithstanding.

Trading, by the rules of the camp, was strictly prohibited. This gave rise to a brisk contraband traffic on the part of the guard and a few "speculators," prisoners. These transactions are worthy of some detail. The guard by some means contrived to bring a few trifling articles on the island. Upon exposing these for sale an arrangement was immediately made with a speculator, who purchased at an enormous price. These speculators in course of time commenced their operations more openly, until they established themselves on the main street running through the camp. For the reason of these mercantile pursuits, the street was known by the name of "Market-street." This avenue soon became the scene of busy agitation, and in the bustle at least, if not the business, would rate favorably with places of considerable population. The speculators took their stands at prominent points, and managed their sales with great dexterity and noise. Considering that nine men out of ten were entirely out of money, and nine out of that ten had very little and held it as a reserve for some greater necessity than they had yet experienced, the "speculators" were an indefatigable set, and kept up a terrible hullabaloo without eliciting much money.

One could be heard yelling at the top of his voice—

"Walk up, gentlemen, walk up! Here's where you get every thing you want!"

Another would sing out in the interrogative form—

"Who's the lucky man to buy this last slice of bread for ten cents greenback or one dollar Confed?"

Another could be heard—

"Step up, gentlemen, and buy a spoonful of salt—ten cents greenback or one dollar Confed."

These and various other invitations usually attracted a large crowd, but very seldom a purchaser. The speculators were a despised set, but as their performances during the long weary hours of prison-life drove away the *ennui* of idleness and gave much amusement to those whose sufferings had not completely overwhelmed them with despair, they were tolerated.

It frequently, however, happened where the men were obliged to carry on a species of trading urged by necessity. If one had an article of food which he could dispose of for something less valuable and more bulky in the stomach, he would take this means of meeting his wants. A common practice was to trade with a sick man coffee for corn-bread.

Fresh meat was a luxury. As an article of trade it commanded from twenty-five to fifty cents per ounce, and few there were able to buy it. Several times during my imprisonment on the island dogs strayed within the dangerous precincts of the "dead-line." So it emphatically proved to the dog. In a few moments he was the subject of contention among as many as could lay hold on him. The animal always set up a piteous howl, only so forcible as could be drawn from the treatment he might expect from men made desperate by hunger. In the midst of the *melée* the dog was literally torn to pieces,—men bearing off the legs and ears, and a half dozen still struggling over the possession of the carcass, dragging out the entrails and making a most offensive scene. The guards generally laughed at these exhibitions of the desperate straits to which the prisoners were reduced.

Money was a legitimate article of speculation with everybody. There were three parties interested. The prisoners, the guards, and the Richmond brokers,—the latter remotely. The money market had its quotations, its fluctuations, and dealers made fortunes and experienced failures: that is, in a run of good luck they became "flush;" and the reverse, "broke."

The current rates, generally running on the ascending scale, were:

BELLE ISLAND: Confederate bills, $10 to $15 for $1 greenbacks.

RICHMOND: Confederate bills, $16 to $20 for $1 greenbacks.

The guards were led on by the Richmond brokers, to whom they sold the proceeds of their speculations, when permitted to visit the city.

In their money dealings Yankee ingenuity generally triumphed. In numerous cases it was a triumph of artistic skill over blind cupidity. The prisoners, by means of a lead-pencil, rendered small bills easily convertible into those of a higher denomination. For instance, a one they altered into a ten, and received from some unsuspecting guard from $100 to $150 in Confederate currency. The fraud was palpable at a glance and would have been detected by a child at the North, but combined avarice and fear of detection by their officers, allowed the guard only sufficient time to see that the bill was *green*, had on it a picture of " old Abe" or some other dignitary of the United States, and represented a certain amount, when they quickly deposited it in the barrel of their rifles and resumed walking their posts.

The guards usually realized the full force of the deception upon settling up with their banker, as was evident from the character of their countenances when again seen at their beats.

CHAPTER IX.

Desertions to the Enemy—Twenty-eight Renegade Cobblers—The Devotion of Southern Union Soldiers—Contribution of the Sanitary Commission—The Treatment received from the Rebel Government.

DURING my confinement on Belle Island there were a small number of men who renounced their loyalty to the national Government, and gave in their adherence to the rebels, by taking the oath of allegiance to support their cause. These acts might receive some palliation, if they had occurred in the cases of those who found it the only alternative to save life. But it happened that the traitors were those who had always been the best treated, and were the worst, most degraded and vile-looking set of human beings I had ever seen, even in the dens of iniquity and crime in the large cities. The men who "deserted," as it was termed, were always applied to some purpose in the employ of the rebel government, and were never sent to the front. They seldom had trades, and therefore were of but little use at the best. There was one purpose to which they were applied, that multiplied their baseness and degradation. I mean in the service of the prison guards. We had a squad of this class on the island, and a more despotic and cruel set could not be imagined. And even while doing their greatest to please their masters, they were the object of distrust. Some of the men had conscience enough left to repent of their guilt, but having taken the fatal step, it was too late to retract.

Another case I will mention occurred on the 15th of

December, 1863. Notice was given in camp that a certain number of shoemakers were wanted, and would receive three dollars per day for working at their trade in Richmond. There was considerable talk about the offer, and it was supposed there were none who were so totally forgetful of their flag as to consent. The hour for those accepting the proposition to make their assent known arrived. All the prisoners able to stand were congregated near the main gate, to witness the issue of the call. A rebel officer soon stepped forward, and called upon all those who accepted the offer to step forward. Every thing was quiet. Directly twenty-eight renegade cobblers, hanging their heads in shame, and moving reluctantly as if their legs refused to carry them, went over to the enemy. The men hissed them loudly, and turned away in disgust. The cobblers were placed under guard, and marched off the island.

I cannot pass a matter unnoticed which has elicited the admiration and respect of all true Union prisoners. I allude to the men of Southern birth who adhered to the national Government, and took up arms in its defence. Every one is aware that there are in the service a number of these men, and a number of organizations bearing the names of their native States. I am not much an admirer of Southern Unionism, in the general sense of the term, particularly among that class of men so largely in the majority, who cry loyalty to the United States, but remained at home giving aid and comfort to either side who happened to be in the neighborhood. Policy, so far as my experience goes, is nine-tenths of Southern fealty to the Government.

But to the point: the inhabitants from the liberty-inspiring mountains of East Tennessee are loyal, and have shown their loyalty by sending to the war for the Government a large number of brave soldiers. It has been particularly noticeable that these men, falling in battle, wounded or prisoners of war, were subjected by their capture to the grossest insults and cruelty. In prison they were held as hostages, and during exchange of prisoners were the last exchanged. Their prison treatment, if possible, was more severe than that sustained by men of Northern regiments; and upon the most trivial charges they were bucked, gagged, murdered, starved, and every thing else that increased the horrors of prison life. But with all the deep-seated and special vindictiveness and animosity shown them, they bore their trials manfully, never complaining, but always ready for the worst. I take much pleasure in placing this testimony on record, of the lofty and self-sacrificing patriotism which has characterized the loyal representatives of the South.

In the month of January, 1864, the prisoners of Belle Island were the recipients of a large quantity of clothing, as an evidence of the thoughtfulness and charity of the United States Sanitary Commission. This was the second lot received since the commencement of the winter.

With the clothing came an officer, who was released from Libby prison, to act as agent for its distribution. The newly delegated powers evidently greatly puffed the officer. He came on the island, and during his whole stay acted with an overbearing manner greatly beneath the dignity of a gentleman. On his first appearance he "bucked" and "gagged" several men, on a most trivial cause. During the existence of his brief authority he exacted the greatest deference to his rank, and took his own time. He was perfectly wound up in red tape, which looked very much like "putting on style," or, as the men termed it, "showing off." I mention this fact, as it was the common remark of prisoner and guard.

It was painful in the extreme to see scores of sick and emaciated men, who could scarcely keep on their legs, obliged to stand and wait several hours shivering in the cold, until his tardy efforts brought their turns. But above all, to see him deliberately sit down at a fine dinner in the presence of his suffering countrymen, and eat with rebel officers provisions sent from the North and for prisoners, was exasperating to the highest degree. I feared several times the men would overstep the hard necessities of their situation, and rise in desperation and despair at such consummate selfishness. At length, after the clothing was distributed, there was a momentary joy overspread the camp. A smile or a shout of rejoicing was not an unusual thing. "Hurrah for Jersey City!" "Three cheers for Maine!" "How are you, Pennsylvania!" "Bully for little Rhody!" "Good for Minnesota!" and so on, each man expressing the source whence came his share in the donation. But two days had not passed before this glimmer of sunshine was dispelled by a darker cloud than had previously overshadowed the island. The same day of receiving the clothing, the prisoners' rations were cut down almost one-third. This reduced it considerably below the minimum amount previously received. There was but one alternative to save life, that was to dispose of their clothing. One by one the prisoners got rid of one article and another. It was, too, a curious and noticeable fact, that the guards were unusually well supplied.

In less than one week after the clothing was distributed almost every article had passed over to the guards. The prisoners were again reduced to their primitive condition, and their rations were accordingly raised to the original standard. It was palpable to every one that the scarcity was a cover for the securement of the clothing sent on the island, giving the transaction, as the enemy supposed, a shadow of legitimacy.

CHAPTER X.

A special Exchange—Sad Disappointment—A Revolt organized—Details of the Plan—Its discovery—Precautions of the Rebel Authorities.

The latter part of the month of January, 1864, brought great rejoicing in camp, over a report spread among the prisoners that five hundred were counted off for exchange, and that the island was to be cleared in less than a week. No sooner had the men heard this than all seemed to rise in strength and spirits. Again cheers, though from feeble lungs, were heard, and all were talking of home, and a speedy escape from past misery. Indeed, all that we had suffered was forgotten in the word liberty, and many thought, as they were soon to leave the scene of their trials, that they had at least learned one lesson, how to appreciate the blessings vouchsafed them by the Government in whose service they had suffered all. The good news had a sensible effect upon the money market, and prisoners having Confederate bills to sell were the losers. Large inducements were offered, but the guards preferred the greenbacks. One prisoner passing through the gate offered sixty-eight dollars in Confederate bills for one dollar in greenbacks, and found no one to take him up.

The first batch of prisoners had left, and patiently we of the remainder were awaiting our turn. A whole day passed, and no more news was received from the Richmond authorities. The second day came, and still no orders to prepare. In the afternoon a rebel officer was seen riding towards the camp: all supposed it was a call for another batch, and many were already preparing for their departure. In half an hour after, we were informed that the first lot were merely to meet a special exchange. The revulsion was terrible, some cried, others beat themselves, and others withdrew to their huts to mourn over their frustrated hopes.

Disappointment, heaped upon misery, drove us to the very brink of despair. Where all betokened speedy relief from our trials, were now clouds doubly black with gloom. For several days we forgot our wretchedness in the melancholy contemplation of shattered expectations. But that dash of light which hope developed only whetted the desire to be free. Escape, desperate resolutions, though always in the mind, now assumed form, and the men determined to make an effort.

For some weeks the plan of a general uprising was discussed by the most prudent and sagacious of the prisoners. Several methods were presented and analyzed, but without result. None were feasible under the most favorable circumstances. A month passed, and still nothing was determined; at length, in the beginning of February, a scheme was proposed, which, with prompt action, might terminate at least in the escape of a portion of our number, if not all, in a condition to bring to the task sufficient strength.

It was generally believed that the greater portion of Lee's army was menacing Meade's cantonments on the Rappahannock, and that Richmond was merely held by garrisons confined to the defences several miles from the city. Accordingly, five hundred prisoners were advised of the details of the plan of escape; having approved of which, they received their instructions. At each post on the guard-line there were to be three men, and a sufficient number were to rendezvous at a point as near the reserve guard as possible. At a preconcerted signal, each post and the reserves were to be overpowered and disarmed, and, under penalty of death, required to follow quickly, and hold their peace. Simultaneously, the remainder of the camp was to be informed of the revolt, and, under the excitement thus occasioned, were to be called to strike for liberty. The piece of artillery on the island, not more than one hundred yards distant, was to be carried by assault by a quick movement of a detail made for that purpose. The remaining three pieces, being in position across the river, could not be reached, and, therefore, their fire we expected to sustain. According to the arrangements, those taking part in the revolt were to cross from the island by the bridge on the south side, and thence get on the north bank by the main bridge crossing to Richmond. It was intended that the movement should be so quick that immediately after the weapons of the guard were secured, about one hundred men thus armed should clear the way, followed by those yet without arms; and, by the time they were well under way, the parties holding the rebel guards, destroying the artillery and boats, were to cover the rear, and destroy the bridge, if possible, after them. After gaining a foothold in the city, two detachments, previously designated, were to strike out on an independent errand; one to liberate all Union prisoners in the city, and arm them with captured weapons; the other to seize all necessary arms and ammunition in store there. In order to heighten the confusion, the city was to be fired by independent parties. It was supposed that one hour would suffice to accomplish matters thus far. It was then intended to make a rapid march by way of the peninsula to our lines at Yorktown. This route was selected, because it was at the time one most poorly defended in point of numbers, and the country afforded the best protection in case of pursuit.

February 7th found all our plans come to naught. For some reasons the enemy suspected something brewing. Whether it was treachery on the part of any one connected with the secret of the uprising, or whether it was merely a suspicion that our actions were not all right, we never learned. Nothing was ever, to my knowledge, whispered on the subject. But the fear and suspicions of the guards were evident; for several battalions of home organizations arrived on the island that day, and morning and evening, subsequently, went through company and battalion drill in front of the camp. The old guards were relieved by troops from the front, a new set of sentinels were posted at different points, and the provost-guard in Richmond was strongly reinforced. The same day, while going to the river's bank for water, I discovered on the camp gate this notice:

Hereafter any person coming within six feet of the bank, after tattoo, runs the risk of being shot.
By command of
V. BASSIEUX,
Lieutenant-commanding

This convinced me and every one else that we were suspected, and the subject of escape was indefinitely postponed.

CHAPTER XI.

Clearing Belle Island—Expectations of Home—The over-buoyant Spirits of the Men—Fatal Consequences—Sad Realizations.

About the middle of February, the rebel government directed Belle Island to be cleared. Accordingly, detachments of several hundred prisoners, every few days, were taken off, and it was supposed, by those remaining, the exchange was resumed. On account of this supposition, excitement again prevailed. Men, haggard and weak, leaped with joy. The sick, even, crawled from their filthy and vermin-covered resting-places to share in the universal shout. The eagerness of the men knew no bounds. Many, too impatient to await their turns, rushed past the guards with the first squad, and were clubbed, unmercifully, back by rebel soldiers. During the second detachment, I observed about twenty men make an effort to force themselves by. This act so exasperated the lieutenant commanding the rebel detail that he seized a musket from one of his soldiers, and made a lunge, impaling a prisoner upon his bayonet, killing him instantly. Not satisfied, he seized the piece by the barrel, and reversed it, striking a prisoner on the head with the butt, producing a fearful and mortal contusion of the skull; a third was knocked down by a blow on the shoulder; while a fourth, in warding off a blow, was severely wounded in the arm. This piece of brutality accomplished its purpose, and the men, thenceforth, patiently awaited their names to be called.

At the expiration of four days my turn came. The prospect of again being under the protection of the stars and stripes was a subject of more comfort in imagination than I looked for really in fact. Nothing was said on the island about the destination of the men which were sent off. I judged from this that they were merely being transferred to some point further in the interior. When we were placed on board the cars, I inquired of one of the guard where they were taking us. His reply was, to Camp Sumter, in Georgia. I was not at all surprised at this piece of intelligence, and made up my mind for the worst.

CHAPTER XII.

From Belle Island to Andersonville—A Terrible Journey—What we Experienced on the Way—Universal Sympathy of the Negroes.

THE day upon which we took our departure from the rebel capital was February 17, 1864. It was a day long to be remembered for its discomforts and food for gloomy thought. The day was raw, wet, and cold; one of that peculiar atmospheric compound only known in Virginia. None of us were in a condition for travel. The long and weary months of the winter, with their scenes and experiences of deliberate barbarism towards the prisoners of Belle Island, had reduced us all to a degree of exhaustion and debilitation which verged upon death. A distant journey was now in store for us. It was evident that numbers would never see their destination.

The train upon which we were embarked was made up of a series of old rickety box and platform cars. From a slight examination of them, as we were awaiting orders to get aboard, it struck me that they had been in the service of that and other roads for at least ten years, and for five more laid up as condemned and unfit for use. In these we were to be conveyed, as we were told, to Georgia. I made up my mind, in which, luckily, I was disappointed, that if some did not lose their lives, or were not in some way horribly mutilated by a number of railroad accidents, it was no fault of the cars or the rebel authorities.

As in every other instance of rebel treatment towards prisoners of war, the train was about half large enough for those who were to be accommodated. We were, accordingly, huddled miscellaneously, the sick and the well, into the same cars. Some were weak, and rendered almost powerless from starvation; others were perfectly helpless from the combined effects of starvation and disease. To add to our misery, not even sufficient room was allowed for us to lie down : the only alternative, therefore, was to fall down in our places and trust to the chances of escape from being trod or smothered to death by the compact and struggling mass.

After several hours' delay the train got under motion. The fact was very apparent that the engineer seemed determined to add to our tortures, by giving two or three heavy jerks, which jammed the inmates of the cars one upon the other, throwing some upon the floor. These wretched men, when the return motion of the mass took place, were unavoidably trodden upon and bruised in a terrible manner. They lay there crying for mercy and help, until lifted to their feet by the humanity of some kind-hearted companion.

As we moved away from the island, the scene of five months' experience, which probably has never been endured by human beings other than those who have had the misfortune to fall into the hands of the rebel government, I could not help looking back and casting a farewell glance upon a spot so awful in its scenes of misery.

The camp presented a fit picture of its history. Desolation and ruin reigned everywhere. The very air about the place hung like a shadow over the spot; a pall hiding one crime of the greatest of all crimes recorded in history. Thousands of graves, many still fresh from the burial of death's victims during the night, could be seen; the sad mementoes of our trials, and the lasting evidences of the inhumanity of those responsible for the all-absorbing offence of treason. As we parted from these mournful associations, I could not repress a tear and an ardent prayer that the distance which would probably intervene between our place of future incarceration and the seat of the rebel government would at least lighten our yoke, and bring our wretchedness within the scope of human endurance.

Our route southward lay immediately to Burkesville Junction. At this point the train stopped for about an hour to await several upward bound. Thence we proceeded to Danville. Thus far we saw few troops, in fact very few persons, except old men, women, children, and negroes. At all the stations, as we passed, the whole population was assembled to "see the Yankees." We found many who seemed to feel a compassion for our misfortunes, and though, as a general rule, nothing was said favorable or disfavorable of us, certainly not the former, we were at least grateful for the silence. Occasionally a woman, always showing signs of high birth, or an old man more intensely vindictive than the rest, would give vent to a round of epithets, which, however, were received in silent contempt by us, and seldom applauded by those hearing them. There was something eminently pleasing in this fact. It showed, at least, that the people, as a mass, had no blame in our sufferings, and where curiosity tempted them to view us as we passed, there were, unquestionably, in the assembled crowd, many sympathizing hearts.

It happened several times on the way to Danville that

some miserable wretches threw stones into the trains, and in several instances men were severely injured from that cause.

After a tedious as well as tardy run, we reached Danville the day after our departure from Richmond. Here it was necessary to lay over several hours to get rations. As another example of rebel inhumanity, we were put on board the train without food, and kept there in our exhausted condition, jostled and tossed about in the most barbarous manner, by the wilful act, no doubt, of the engineer. The rations which we received at Danville were short of the standard at Belle Island. The motion of the train had excited our appetites, so that what we received, instead of appeasing our cravings, only excited them. Before taking our departure the corpses of several soldiers, who died on the way, were taken from the train for interment.

From Danville our next run was to Greensboro, thence to Salisbury, North Carolina; thence to Charlotte, Columbia, Kingsville, and Branchville, South Carolina. Our journey was slow, the roads were in bad condition, and the weather every thing calculated to add to our wretchedness. In South Carolina the people displayed a more bitter hostility than yet experienced. All their words, however, fell as harmlessly upon our ears as though they were not heard. Some would remark: "You infernal Yanks should all be hung for coming down here, and meddling with our rights." I thought, in answer to this fellow, that the United States was just giving the rights they deserved, and of which they would reap still more bitter fruits before they got through. Another would exclaim: "You d—d Yankee mudsills, I hope every one of you will die in that prison where they are taking you." I thought, in reply to this, that many of us stood an admirable chance of being disposed of in that way, but that we would at least prove that we were mudsills in a very strong superstructure. I felt that there would be a reckoning some day, when all would be made right.

The greatest satisfaction which we enjoyed in travelling through the Carolinas, was the universal good-will and sympathy of the negro. They heard of our coming, and along the route, and despite the terrible stories of their owners, they would congregate apart from the whites, oftentimes where the woods were most dense, and as we passed, wave their turbans, their eyes glistening and running over with honest tears. Not unfrequently they would cast a corn pone, a piece of bacon, or something eatable into the cars; and when witnessing the conflict between the starving men within, they would wring their hands, weeping bitterly, and exclaim: "De Lor hab mercy on you! May de hand ob the Lor protec his people, de Yankees!" and the like. These simple words, contrasted with the haughty spirit of the higher class of whites, were to us like soothing balm. One word of consolation and hope from the poor negro, that innocent child of nature, did more to alleviate, at all events our mental anguish, than did a whole volume of the vile and opprobrious epithets of the rich whites tend to increase it.

We were, in the second stage of our journey, furnished with the usual short supply of rations, at Salisbury, Columbia, and Branchville. The effects of our transfer and weak condition now commenced to show a more alarming increase of mortality from exhaustion. It was useless to undertake to reason with the officers in charge, at their downright murder of prisoners; they invariably would reply: "Well, if you would have stayed at home, instead of trying to subjugate the South, you would not be here."

At Branchville I had quite a conversation with an old female, who, judging from a basket on her arm, and sundry undefinable-looking objects therein, was guilty of the genuine Yankee act of peddling for a living. I beckoned her to me. She came, rather hesitatingly, however.

"Well, old woman," I asked, leaning out of the car, "what have you in your basket?"

"Them's pies and cakes," she answered, in a very summary way, looking around to see whether any one was watching her.

"How d'ye sell them?" I asked.

"I don't sell 'em," she said, again looking around for spies; "I mean I don't sell 'em to you'ens.

"Well, to whom do you sell them?" I inquired, feigning ignorance. "Did you ever see any greenbacks?" I added.

"I once hear'n tell on 'em. They is what you Yanks use like our Confederate money?" she said, with an inquisitive turn of the head.

"Yes; only they are as good as gold up where the Yankees come from," I replied.

The old lady twisted up her mouth, and gave utterance to a peculiar utterance, "Whip, whoo, I'd like to have some on 'em; I haven't seen any gold these long time. They tells us down here they keeps all the gold in Richmond, to use for the army; and my old man has fit three years without getting any of it."

Just at this juncture, while the old lady was disposing

herself to receive some Yankee money for her pies, a rebel officer appeared moving towards her. The old lady spied him, and, without further delay, took to her heels.

The officer came up, and said he would " put a stop to this talking out of the cars, by giving orders to the guard to shoot somebody." This being the case, nothing more was said.

From Branchville our train proceeded to Augusta, Georgia. At this place the enemy seemed to have established a large manufacturing centre for the supply of war material for the Southern armies. At Augusta we struck almost due south to Millen, and thence west to Macon. At the latter place we were again delayed. After a great deal of controversy on the part of some rebel officers, we again got under way, and after a ride of sixty miles reached Anderson, which we soon discovered was the end of our journey.

CHAPTER XIII.

Arrival at Anderson—The Condition of the Men—Brutality of a Rebel Officer—The March to Camp Sumter—Description of the Camp.

Upon our arrival at Anderson we were compelled to remain on the cars for some hours, while preparations were being made to transfer us to camp. Since our departure from Belle Island we had not been permitted to leave the cars, very seldom even to answer the most urgent necessities. Some idea may therefore be formed of our condition. Those who were not entirely overcome by the journey were cramped and stiff, and covered with filth and vermin from long and close confinement. The sick and exhausted were little better than merely alive. These wretched men lay in the cars surrounded by the most intolerable filth and foul smell, but were unable to move to any opening through which to draw a breath of fresh air. In the car in which I rode there were several dead or dying. The former having died the day before, gave unmistakable evidences of rapid putrefaction. To add to our condition of misery, we had received nothing to eat for twenty-four hours, and were consequently, even those who were not sick, well-nigh overpowered by weakness.

After every thing seemed to be ready, an officer came around and ordered the men to get off the cars. The men, to the extent of their ability, obeyed. When all that could stand were out, there were still half of the number that started on the journey unable to rise to their feet. A number who had succeeded in getting to the door of the cars were unable to go further, and many who reached the ground sank down, their strength completely given out.

Having waited a few moments, the rebel officer, exasperated at the tardiness of our movements, went through the cars, kicking and cuffing helpless men who were lying on the floors unable to move, exclaiming: "Get up there, you G—d d—n Yankee, none of your playing possum around here!"

One man, who managed by a desperate effort to partially rise in his place, but fell back again, he took hold of and handled most unmercifully. The man was too weak to say any thing, but with the most heartrending signs, imploring compassion, he asked the heartless wretch to deal more humanely with him, or kill him outright.

Another man, who stared at the officer as he passed, with a pair of expressionless, glassy fearful eyes, was kicked in the face because he made, in his delirium, no recognition of the officer's command.

It was, indeed, a terrible scene. Men were even thrown from the car, and injured or broken limbs added to their sufferings. The feeling of the men who were witness to all this was deep, but not a word could be said, nor a warding hand be raised without bringing down upon all some new form of brutality.

The rebel officer being thoroughly convinced that he had exercised his cruelty upon each man unable to leave the cars, directed the guards to march us off to camp. As we moved, or rather tottered away, I gave a last glance at the unfortunates left behind. I wondered what new device of inhumanity would forever relieve both fiend and victim of their pains.

As we filed along to the stockade, we passed a number of women, children, and negroes, but very few men. Nothing was said to us by these lookers on, but I could plainly discern that they were terrified at the treatment to which we were consigned by their leaders. As we drew in sight of the place of our future incarceration, I felt sick at heart. There was the rude stockade, the sentinels and sentry-boxes, and though the camp was then but recently established, that place of horrors, the hospital and the graveyard, were not missing, in the exterior view of the camp.

When we reached the main entrance, and on the way, many of us were again subjected to the thieving process. However, as we came direct from Belle Island, it was generally admitted as a consequence that we were not rich either in money or effects. It was considered that what the Belle Island officials and guards left was not worth stealing. We were hence not very closely examined.

As usual, we were turned into Camp Sumter like so many beasts, to take care of ourselves, and without any thing with which to do it. What we wanted particularly was food, but our most urgent wants seemed to be a good argument on the part of the authorities for delay. Accordingly, we had several long hours of hunger left us for reflection and rest. When our first rations were issued, we found them not perceptibly differing in material and quantity from what we had experienced at Belle Island.

Camp Sumter is situated near the village of Anderson, Sumter County, Georgia. Anderson is a station on the Southwestern railroad, about midway between its two branches, each running abruptly to the west, to the Chattahoochee River, at Columbus, Georgetown, and Fort Gaines, Georgia. The camp derives its name from the county in which it is located. It was finished in the beginning of February, 1864, and by the middle of the same month received its first instalment of occupants. The remoteness of the locality convinced me that the frequency of successful escape from Richmond and Belle Island was the main reason for its construction; for, as I found, of nine prisoners who managed to elude the camp-guards, not one ever succeeded in reaching our lines.

The camp, for the more secure confinement of the prisoners, in addition to the usual chain of sentinels, was completely surrounded by a stockade sixteen feet in height, and originally inclosed an area of about sixteen acres; but the large increase of prisoners by June, 1864, required an enlargement, which was made to the extent of four acres, making twenty acres in all. About ten feet from the stockade was a rude railing, investing the entire camp, called the "dead-line." In the centre was a swamp, covering about one-third the original space, and through the middle of which ran a small stream. This furnished the water for washing, drinking, and cooking, while the swamp was used as a sink. An attempt was made by the prisoners to drain this, by running transverse ditches, communicating with the stream. But this was found to be worse than to allow the swamp to remain undisturbed, as the filth emptied into the creek made the water absolutely unfit for any purpose whatever. An attempt was subsequently made to remedy this evil by sinking wells. These undertakings met with but partial success. Few implements were allowed the men, for fear they might be applied to other purposes, such as "digging out." However, about six or eight wells were sunk, though the result was little for the general good, as they furnished but a scant supply of water, and were owned and guarded by the squads that dug them.

With the exception of the first three thousand prisoners sent in—and unfortunately we were not of that number—no shelter was provided for the occupants of the stockade. When we first arrived, some leniency was granted, giving us opportunities, though accompanied by a strong guard, to leave the inclosure, to gather wood, brush, and leaves, in an adjacent wood. Out of the material thus accumulated, a few of us were enabled to construct huts and hovels, which, in a measure, sheltered us from the sun, and heavy night-dews, for which the climate is remarkable. Against the rain, however, our accommodations were less comforting.

There was some show of a plan in the laying out of the camp, but nothing further. Every thing else was of the meanest and most primitive character.

CHAPTER XIV.

Going Back to the Old Treatment—The Expedients for Shelter—Rations—Withholding Rations as a Punishment—Cooking in Prison.

It was evident, when our party first arrived at Camp Sumter, that some effort was to be made to practise a little more leniency. The new order of things, however, worked but a very short time.

As the number of prisoners increased, the conduct of the camp officers and guards reverted to the old rule of things. They made a trifling exception in the cases of a few higher commissioned officers of white regiments, but all others, officers and privates, white, black, and mulatto, were thrust into the inclosure to shift for themselves. Two months after my arrival at the camp the crowd of prisoners became so great, and the tyranny of the guard so uncompromising, that the gates of the stockade were even closed against any one leaving under guard even for wood to build a shelter. The substitutes which were now made to take the place of wooden huts gave the camp the poverty-stricken and squalid appearance of Belle Island. The new men, too, when brought in, as in every other instance, under my observation, were deprived of blankets and almost every thing, except the clothes which they had upon their backs, and which were rebel uniforms, ragged and dirty, exchanged for their own. These the men were frequently obliged to tear up to protect themselves from the weather, sunshine or rain, while others burrowed into the earth.

Indeed the expedients of the men on the subject of shelter were rather novel and various. At one place might be seen one of the United States shelter tents, setting at naught the raging of the elements; next a brush shanty, hot, dirty, and damp, partially tempering the sun's rays, but not by any means water-proof during a rain. At another place, while walking off the main avenues and alleys of the camp, a person frequently stepped upon something which instantly moved, and from beneath a voice would be heard, in emphatic terms, "Get to hell off my Shebang." Upon examination, it would be found that the speaker was none other than a soldier lying at full length in a cave, into which he entered horizontally, and feet foremost, his head resting in the entrance. At another place, a prisoner, changing his positior continually, would be found reclining beneath the shadow of a pair of pants, or an old coat spread out after the fashion of an awning.

The ordinary ration, I mean in quantity, at Sumter I found a few days after my arrival was materially larger than was issued at Belle Island, though still insufficient to keep a man in health. It consisted, in general terms, of one-eighth of a pound of meat, and corn-bread enough to sustain life. In the place of corn-bread uncooked meal or mush was frequently issued. But both, as well as the corn-bread, was not fit for the stomach of a human being. In the North I had seen a better quality cast aside as unfit for a hog. The meal was unbolted, about one-third being made up of hulls and cobs.

The supply of rations, however, was irregular, and often withheld entirely for twelve to twenty-four hours, upon the slightest pretexts. If there was a prisoner unaccounted for, the whole camp was obliged to suffer.

One day a prisoner could not be found. As usual, the commandant of the camp refused to issue any rations that day unless the prisoner was found or accounted for. A search and inquiry were instantly made, and the man was soon found laid out with a row of dead bodies awaiting burial. He had died but a few hours before.

There was not the least apology for either the character or the quantity of the rations issued to the prisoners at Camp Sumter. The contiguous country was fertile, and, judging from appearances, a fine crop was planted and harvested during the season of 1864; besides, for a circuit of several hundred miles no hostile or contending columns had ever penetrated. The camp-guards were well fed, fat, and hearty. It was not want or scarcity, but deliberate, vindictive, and uncompromising enmity. Whatever may have been the instructions to the officers in charge of the camp, whether they were to be rigid or lenient, one thing is certain, the first few weeks of our imprisonment at Sumter were tolerable, but in less than two months after, we were again subjected to all the cruelty endured at Belle Island. The conduct of the men was certainly not the cause, for during the few weeks of better treatment there never was known the same class of men better behaved and under better subordination. But when inhumanity again commenced its terrible work, the men were driven to many acts called mutiny, out of sheer despair.

Our cooking conveniences were generally in keeping with the other arrangements of our prison life. There were a few, but very few, who possessed kettles, either of tin or iron, but the utensil mainly used was a flat board. On this the corn-meal, when not already made into bread, was prepared and baked. The meat always came cooked. Considering their situation, the men speedily brought the art of cooking, in their primitive way, to great perfection; and invariably, when wood was abundant, their own cooking, in point of health, was infinitely preferable to the prepared food issued by the commissary.

CHAPTER XV.

The Arrival of the Summer Season—The Crowded Condition of the Camp—Appearance of Summer Diseases—Poisonous Odors—Immense Swarms of Flies.

During the first few months at Camp Sumter existence was endurable, but the approach of the hot season, coupled with the increase of numbers and decrease of diet, gradually brought about a degree of suffering to which it would be difficult, at least in my experience, to find any thing superior or even equal. At Belle Island we underwent all the bodily discomforts and miseries which could spring out of exposure to cold: now we were obliged to battle against the oppressive heat.

Summer in Southwestern Georgia is every thing that can possibly be involved under that name. The mornings are heavy, sultry, and full of miasmatic poisons; at meridian the sun pours down with a temperature ready to scorch man or beast to the crisp; the evenings are close, and the nights cold and damp. If this, under the most favorable of unfavorable circumstances, was not sufficient to produce the most complicated set of diseases, the case of Camp Sumter, during the summer of 1864, certainly did not prove the contrary.

Towards the middle of July our numbers swelled, it seemed, to about twenty thousand men, who were brought in from all parts of the theatre of war. If we had to believe the extravagant stories of the rebel guards, we would long have given up the cause of the Union as hopeless.

Every time a batch of prisoners were added to the camp, the guards fabricated a wonderful narrative suited to the occasion. But whatever they said, for very excellent reasons, we disbelieved, and particularly after the new prisoners themselves confirmed our views, greatly to the discredit of rebel veracity.

Any one who can imagine twenty thousand men confined to a space of twenty acres, in the midst of summer, without shelter, and with rations barely sufficient to allay the pains of hunger, can form some idea of our situation. Midsummer in Southern Georgia, under any circumstances, is simply terrible; but now, infinitely worse, the men were crowded together so as to admit of scarcely room for circulation. No accommodations for cleanliness were allowed. The result was vermin and disease. To successfully combat the former, in camp language, it was necessary "to skirmish" two or three times a day, in order to gain some respite from persecution. In regard to the latter, the men were at the mercy of their own constitutions. Not even soap was allowed, with which to wash; and we were obliged to use sand, the abrasion of which partially supplied its place.

A crowded camp, excessive heat, and scarcity of food, were in themselves sufficient, it seemed, to consummate our trials. But no; the camp atmosphere was alone more fatal than all the rest put together. It will be remembered, as already mentioned, in the midst of the camp was a swamp, which was used for every purpose of washing and a sink. The hot sun had developed all its pestiferous poisons, and the foul effluvia which arose hence was terrible. It would be absolutely impossible to convey a better idea of the stench, than merely to state that even we, who had been trained to all sorts of noxious odors could not endure it, and were obliged often to crowd to the windward, or find some distant part of the camp and lie down, nose to the ground. Myriads of flies, and every kind of insect, attracted by the numerous impurities of the camp, visited us in clouds. It seemed like a plague. The aggregations of these little insects was so great, that the hum of their innumerable wings could be heard resembling the sound of an approaching wind. Though troublesome, these very flies so often bitterly condemned, were unquestionably the great sanitary agencies at work, to lessen, in a measure, the dreadful havoc of death amongst us.

CHAPTER XVI.

Sickness and Mortality—The Nature of the Diseases—Their improper Treatment—Hospitals—The Immense Mortality—Vaccination and its melancholy Effects.

The very natural result of the camp atmosphere, and our exposure at Sumter, was a wide-spread and alarming sickness and mortality. The most fatal of the diseases to which we were subject were scurvy and diarrhea, though every other possible form of bodily complaints were perfectly familiar to us, and the victims were at the mercy of capricious chance, as proper medical treatment was entirely out of the question.

The hospitals of the camp were rude, without ventilation and supplies, and presided over by a more ignorant and vain class than were found at Richmond. Infinitely the best class were the hospital stewards, who were detailed prisoners. They did all in their power to lessen the sufferings of the sick committed to their charge, but they could do nothing without means, and to complain would result in an order to return to camp. They were thus obliged to look on, and see their comrades carried away, without being able to lift a finger to save them.

The prisoners' hospitals were composed of a limited number of very small "wedge" tents, battered and torn, and during a rain no protection whatever to the inmates. In each of these tents from four to six sick, depending on the nature of the disease, were confined. In our own service, five healthy men to an ordinary "wedge" tent for privates is considered a large number; what then, can it be imagined, must have been the condition of the sick prisoner, breathing day and night the impure and poisonous exhalations not only of himself, but of four or five others? Few ever entered the hospital to return; and when a sick man was seen being borne thence on a stretcher, every one thought to himself his next step will be the grave.

The mortality consequent upon our treatment, well or sick, was more than alarming. Even as early as the latter part of May, while our treatment was the best we had ever received in a rebel prison, and before there were four thousand congregated, I often saw within the stockade, awaiting transportation to the dead-house, as many as forty corpses placed in a row, showing the proceeds of death's work the day before. What made the scene still more appalling was the fact that no epidemic or contagion raged in camp. A few cases of small-pox broke out during the spring, but were carried to a distant point outside the stockade, and treated separately.

The men soon became so hardened to these constant and multiplying scenes of death, that the removal of a corpse from the camp was made the subject of no more feeling consideration than the remark: "Well, whose turn will be next?"

As the number of prisoners increased, so did the number of sick; and for want of room the hospitals were removed without the stockade. We were now able only to judge of the deaths in camp. These were numerous. What they numbered in hospital must now have greatly exceeded the highest number ever attained. Out of thirty of my personal acquaintances sent to the hospital but one returned, and the rest I have never heard of. In April, 1864, our squad numbered ninety persons; in July, the whole number alive was twenty.

From a very trustworthy source I learned, that by the expiration of two months, after Camp Sumter was established, one thousand Union soldiers had died, and this out of less than four thousand, the aggregate number then in the camp. In July following the mortality was at its height, ranging from one hundred to one hundred and fifty deaths daily. I had witnessed death and suffering in all shapes on the battle-field, but this was nothing to the sickening sensation of death from the terrible agency of disease.

On a scorching day in July, while standing on a knoll within the camp, and looking over and beyond the stockade, the dead could be seen carried away in wagons, and piled fifteen and twenty, one upon the other. Judging from this, it is not difficult to form some idea of the rudeness of their interment.

The hospital soon became a word which involved all that was horrible, until the men feared to be sent there. The result was, hundreds suffering from the severest types of disease determined rather to run the chances of recovery without medical treatment. It was no uncommon thing in the morning to find, scattered through the camp, the dead bodies of men who had thus died, the victims of brutality on the one hand, and fear on the other.

In spring, as already mentioned, the small-pox made its appearance in camp, and orders were given to have all the prisoners vaccinated. Very few fortunately submitted to the precaution, preferring to run the risks of escaping rather than be contaminated with all sorts of constitutional impurities. Many of the men who acceded to the orders, in a few weeks after found their arms swollen and sore. Instead of healthy indications of the taking of the scab, they found malignant chancres, which devoured their flesh to the very bone; and running sores broke out all over their bodies, and in a few months the patients were loathsome victims of scrofula, syphilis, and other taints. The sufferings presented by these unfortunate men were pitiable in the extreme. They prowled about the camp, shunned by everybody. They were seen for a few months, daily giving evidences of the literal eating away of their very lives, until death, which must have long been a wished-for termination to their misery, overtook them. The treatment of such diseases at the best is no easy task, but to watch them day by day, taking full course, without the least effort or ability to check them, was a phase of suffering a fit climax to the horror and wretchedness every day witnessed in Camp Sumter.

CHAPTER XVII.

The Consummation of Suffering—Despair and Insanity—The Conversation of One of the Victims—Moon-blind—Its Effects.

THE height to which the suffering of the prisoners attained, before I was transferred from Sumter, resulted in the most heart-rending derangement of the mental faculties of large numbers. The men of this unfortunate class were the objects of the most unparalleled misery. Their disturbed minds wandered in the midst of scenes connected with the wretched past, and those who had strength were running madly through the camp, asking every one to shoot them, and then standing back, laughing madly, and exclaiming, "It is too good." Others, in a state of complete nudity, strolled about, their bodies nothing but skin and bone, and covered with immense sun-blisters and vermin. Others could be seen crawling about in the filth, and asking the guard to shoot.

The spectacle presented by these men has probably seldom had its counterpart anywhere in the history of persecutions. But nothing in the shape of human suffering was remarkable or extraordinary to us, but all was considered a natural part in the gross outrages against nature and humanity perpetrated by the execrable leaders of the rebellion against the helpless victims at their mercy.

One day while washing a coat in the camp-ditch, a prisoner came up to me and opened a conversation. His eyes glared with delirium or insanity. His voice had much of death in it. He was a sad example of which there were too many at Sumter. I asked no questions, but rather chose to hear than speak. The whole drift of his words was that of the deepest despair. He spoke quickly and mechanically; his reason at intervals would indeed seem to flash a little light, but in an instant all was again madness. His words, which I could but occasionally understand, were to the effect that his life had long been a burden; that he saw no end of his misery; that he had borne up as long as possible, and that the only obstacle to his taking his own life was the thought, whenever he had made up his mind, of a widowed mother and sisters. A recollection of them seemed to intervene and check the last act of desperation. I gave him what encouragement I could, but encouragement in such a place was poor consolation—a set of empty words, idle fancies. He walked off. Less than fifteen minutes after, I saw him crawl under the guard-line, and dare the guard to shoot him. Several of his companions laid hold of him, overstepping the fatal bounds at the peril of their own lives, begging the sentinel "not to shoot a crazy man," and dragged him by force back within the limits of the camp.

I mention this as but a single instance of this terrible affliction; there were hundreds who suffered in different degrees. Their roaming thoughts were continually running upon scenes of woe, which their tongues were mechanically and constantly narrating. They threatened suicide, or begged the guards to shoot them. During a sane moment they would talk of home, from which they would soon wander, and talk about some horrible deed or tale of woe which their invention would suggest. In time these cases became worse; and unless checked by some treatment or rather care, however rude, the sufferers were a source of danger and disturbance by their wild behavior. When their condition reached this extremity, these unfortunate men usually mysteriously disappeared from camp, and nothing more was heard of them.

There was another calamity which afflicted many, and when subject to the disease, were called by the prisoners "moon-blind." This was from the fact that the men affected lost the power of sight, and were unable to distinguish objects except by fires. No medical treatment was known by the camp physicians for this malady. The sufferers were permitted to move about at night, stumbling and bruised by coming violently in contact with some unseen object.

It would be impossible to give an adequate idea of the depth and variety of suffering which was endured at Camp Sumter during the nearly five months that I was confined there. There were deaths in fearful numbers; disease in every conceivable form, and derangement which was a kind of half-way step between life and death. If the history of Camp Sumter contained only acts of deliberate inhumanity recorded against the rebel government, an eternity of repentance would never wipe out the infamy, but to remember that it was but a single example, will make the rebellion of the South, if for no other reason, the execration of all time.

CHAPTER XVIII.

Plans of Escape—"Chickamauga"—He serves the Rebels as a Spy—The Death of Chickamauga—"Mugging the Guard"—A grand Conspiracy—Eight Thousand Prisoners to Revolt—Discovery of the Plot—Punishment of the "Traitor"—Efforts to Escape by feigning Death.

As the only relief from their wretchedness, the minds of the most desperate turned to schemes of escape. Tunnelling, strategem in passing the gate, organizations to assault the stockade, to overpower the guard and capture the artillery, were all planned but never carried out. As at Belle Island, the camp was full of rebel spies, who reported to the guards all understandings among the men looking to revolt, and all our movements were closely watched and guarded. One of these fellows, a Union soldier nicknamed "Chickamauga," having lost a leg in that battle, was detected giving the guards information concerning the designs of the prisoners. This ingrate was always treated with the greatest kindness and care by the men, and when discovered felt his humiliation and disgrace so deeply that he tempted the guard several times to shoot him. The prisoners upbraided him for his treachery, and tormented him so continually that one day he again crept under the "dead-line." The guard, pitying his miserable condition, held his fire, calling to a prisoner to draw him back. "Chickamauga" resisted, falling upon the ground, and using all sorts of language to the guard,

CARRYING OUT THE DEAD.

calling him a coward, and afraid to shoot. Several prisoners, who sympathized with the man for his wellknown bravery in a number of battles, endeavored to induce him to desist from his desperate intention, to return to his comrades, and strive to do better, promising forgiveness. But he would not listen. His recklessness and insults went too far. The guard near by brought up his piece and fired. A bullet through the head instantly finished the miserable man's career. The prisoners who witnessed the act turned away from another scene of wanton bloodshed without saying a word. No one wished the unfortunate man to be shot, though his crime was not too good for such an end. The guard, however, laughed, after the act was done, saying, "Well, there's another d——d Yankee done for."

In the beginning, efforts to escape were frequently made by small parties. I remember an instance which occurred in April, 1864. A guard was sent with three prisoners for wood. The party left early in the afternoon. Several hours on such an errand was generally considered over the time. Night came, but no prisoners and no guard returned. The next day, however, the guard made his appearance, but came alone. When questioned, he told the story of his adventures rather excitedly. It seems the "Yanks" induced him to escort them more than the usual distance from camp, by the promise of a few brass buttons. As soon as the prisoners got him pretty well out of hearing, and in a remote, secluded spot, they disarmed him, and marched him about fifteen miles. Here one of the party obliged him to swap clothes, and then bound him securely to a tree. The three prisoners, leaving the guard to be extricated from his predicament by some passers·

by, started for the Union lines. The guard stated that he remained tied until morning, when, in the midst of his yelling, somebody rode up to inquire his trouble. When he told his story he was released, and hastened back to camp. This operation was known in camp as "mugging the guard." It was frequently practised, but seldom the prisoners succeeded in getting off. Two days after the guard had returned, the three prisoners were brought in, having been arrested and secured by citizens.

Soon after this occurrence, myself and several others attempted to escape by the tunnelling process, and succeeded in burrowing thirty feet; but the sandy nature of the soil defeated our undertaking, when on the eve of completion, by caving in and attracting the attention of the guard.

One object in removing the prison-camp to such a remote region was, undoubtedly, to put an end to the fair chances of reaching our lines, as when prisoners were kept further north. I found, even when one or more succeeded in getting a good start on their way to freedom, they were overtaken by means of bloodhounds, which were able to scent a man two days after he left the camp, and followed until the fugitive was overtaken, and held at bay until their masters rode up and secured him. The killing of the dogs seldom bettered the escaped man's fortunes, as the attention drawn towards his escape, by the pursuit, by means of hounds, set the inhabitants on the alert, and at the first place he stopped for food he was invariably picked up, and sent back to camp. What little service came from the negroes was always for the benefit of the fugitive; they satisfied all his wants, and gave him directions about the woods. But fear of their masters made them reserved and cautious, their timidity and caution being frequently the cause of the exposure of the fugitive.

All recaptured prisoners, on being brought back to camp, were immediately chained and balled,—some by means of balls attached to their ankles, and others by the same fastened to the neck. A more scientific mode of this kind of punishment was adopted, by fastening by the necks of three or four prisoners, sometimes a dozen, standing in a row, with a twenty-four-pounder shot attached to the ankle of each, and sixty-four-pounder fastened to the chains around the neck, so as to oblige each victim to bear an equal share of its weight. In the early part of July, 1864, with twelve others I effected my escape from the stockade, through the cook-house. We were out several days, but one by one were retaken and brought back. As each came in, he was fastened by the chain to the one who was brought in immediately before him, until we were all ironed together, neck and hands, with a twenty-four pounder shot attached to the right leg of each. The latter we were forced to wear for several months. From the effect of the cruelties practised upon prisoners after recapture many died, and numbers with the irons on them. There were almost continually about one hundred prisoners ironed, for the single offence of an attempt to escape.

A gigantic conspiracy, in which no less than ten thousand men were engaged, was arranged in June, shortly before my departure for Charleston, numbering in its accomplishment the active participation of eight thousand men. This force was organized into companies and battalions, and the appropriate officers assigned to each. Six tunnels were dug, and a day appointed.

Every thing was ready to be carried out, when reinforcements arrived, and other measures taken to defeat our purpose, and let it be known that we were discovered. The plan failed as usual, through information given the authorities by spies among our own number.

The first decided intimation we had that we were discovered was the appearance of the post-quartermaster within the stockade, accompanied by a guard and a body of negroes, equipped with spades and shovels. The official's knowledge of the tunnels which he had come to destroy was so accurate, that he went directly to them, and set the negroes to work upon their demolition.

Measures were at once set on foot to bring the informant to justice. Several weeks had passed, and the task was about to be given up, when the villain was detected. He was accused, and, after a close examination, admitted that he did it for a plug of tobacco. He also accused other persons, who, upon subsequent examination, were found innocent.

It was now resolved to make a good example of the guilty man. One side of his head was shaven to the skull. He was then forced to lie upon his back, and held down, while an old man-of-war's man pricked upon his forehead the letter T, to mark through life his infamy as a traitor. The culprit was then obliged to run the gauntlet from one end of the stockade to the other, between two lines of about eight thousand prisoners, who groaned and hissed him as he passed. The culprit, having passed through his humiliation, hid himself in an obscure corner, and was so disheartened, that he probably would have died there, if the officer of the day, with a guard, had not removed him several days after from the stockade.

A novel method of escape was successfully practised for some time, by feigning to be dead, and being borne out by men at the hospitals who were favorable to the interests of the prisoners. The bodies were placed with the dead in the dead-house, whence they took their departure after dark. At least fifty men were unaccounted for at the expiration of several weeks. This large deficit in his rolls, and the number of men on hand, started the captain of the guard to a diligent search by means of his spies. After several days, the method of escape was discovered. A guard was immediately placed around the "dead-house." The same night two of the dead suddenly resuscitated, and were making their way out when they were picked up, much to their own astonishment, and sent to camp, where they were safely secured by the ball and irons.

4

CHAPTER XIX.

Traitors in Camp—Their Punishment—Tempting Prisoners from their Allegiance—Discovery of a guilty Shoemaker—Meting out Justice.

NOTWITHSTANDING their sufferings and humiliation, the men, as a general rule, were true to the loyalty which had moved them to fight. In my own experience, up to my departure from Sumter, I had known but about one hundred, who so far forgot their duty to the national Government as to swear allegiance to the rebellion. Twenty-eight of this number were the renegade cobblers of Belle Island. How many men were secretly inimical, from various causes, it would be impossible to tell. That there were spies in our midst was, in several instances, shown by the detection of the despicable scoundrels giving information. Our plans of liberation set at naught by timely precaution, just as they were to be carried into effect, was very sure evidence that the rebel authorities were kept advised by somebody. Whether these persons were of their own number, aping the holy martyrdom of the prisoners, or whether a prisoner alleviating his own sufferings at the expense of his comrades, was always an unsolved question, except in the several instances where the criminal was discovered.

The manner of treating those detected in their infamous treachery was summary and deserving. It several times occurred, as already mentioned, that the guilty parties, out of a sense of shame, hid themselves, or tempted the guard to shoot them, in which latter extremity they were too often readily gratified, and released alike from their degradation and their misery. There were others whose depravity and lack of conscience thought lightly of their crime. These were, therefore, brought to justice by the unrelenting hand of those who suffered by their evil doings.

The mildest form of punishment, as far as bodily comfort was concerned, was the scorn and reproach of their comrades. This, however, applied only to those sensible of such treatment. Another, and more violent and offensive method, was to pitch the culprit into the filthiest quarter of the camp sink, and keep him there until well saturated with the foul matter and powerful odors, when he was permitted to come out; after which the crowd at once proceeded to kick and cuff him out of the stockade. Tonsorial operations were much in vogue, as a mild punishment of traitors and scoundrels generally, one half of the head being shaved from the front to the back of the neck, after which the delinquent was escorted through the camp by a noisy crowd, and laughed at by everybody.

A fellow named William Carrin, of a Massachusetts regiment, was discovered one day making the rounds of the camp, inducing men who were shoemakers to desert and join the Confederacy. They were to follow their trade, for which they were to be well paid. Among the arguments used to convince the men were such as had a powerful influence upon the weak-minded. For instance, he told them there would be no more exchanges or paroles during the war; that the black flag had been raised, and the two armies were slaughtering each other promiscuously. He would also urge the point of personal comfort, stating that they would have excellent quarters, their food and clothing would be of the best, and their wages enormous. The renegade had himself taken the oath to the rebel government, and had been working for them for a long time. Fortunately the cobblers of Camp Sumter were not to be so easily deceived. One of those tempted exposed the errant shoemaker, who was at once brought before a committee called on the spot. After a clear analysis of his crime, he was forced to acknowledge his guilt. His person was searched, and papers found placing his offence beyond all question. He was sentenced to have his head shaved. The sentence was summarily carried out. He also took an oath not to aid the enemy any more, and that he would remain within the stockade. The same day he broke his oath, and informed the commandant of his treatment. The rations were at once withheld until the principals in the affair were discovered. The three persons most active in the affair at once stepped forward. Of this party, I was one, Peter Donnelly, of the Excelsior brigade, another, and the name of the third I have forgotten. The camp commandant gave vent to his rage in a few oaths, and then dismissed the matter, much to our surprise, as we expected, at least, some more effective and durable manifestation of his ire.

CHAPTER XX.

Amusements within the Stockade—Establishment of the Markets—Scene on Market-street—Competition in Business—The Effects of the Markets upon those who could enjoy them.

As at Belle Island, those of the prisoners who had strength enough to partake in amusements to wile away the dull and monotonous hours of prison life, devised various means for their sport. These amusements always formed a sad counterpart of the experience of those unfortunate men, prostrate by sickness and disease. But men bound only by the common impulse of a common cause, suddenly thrown together by some misfortune, soon lose the warm feelings at first engendered between them under happier circumstances. The more they suffer, the wider the breach that divides them, until misery makes each man nothing more than a mere animal, struggling for self-existence, regardless of the wishes and efforts of every one around him.

The source of a great deal of interest and excitement at Sumter, to those who could enjoy them, were the markets. They were originated by a few of the prisoners inclined to speculations, who had a little surplus meal, and baked it into slap-jacks and biscuits. These they would offer for sale. Those who had money, and having as well a taste for this agreeable transformation of ground corn, purchased liberally. Soon after the markets were established, trade received a powerful impetus by the arrival of a large number of prisoners captured at Plymouth, North Carolina. By a remarkable exhibition of generosity on the part of the enemy, the prisoners were permitted to retain their money and clothing. After these persons arrived, the money they brought with them was soon put into circulation through the camp. The enterprising speculators reaped largely the benefits, and at once extended the scale of their operations. They purchased at wholesale, from the guard, a number of articles not recognized in a prisoner's rations. The rebel authorities seeing their opportunity, established a sutler at the post, and allowed him such privileges as enabled him to do a lucrative business. He was also even permitted to bring his produce and goods within the stockade. Capitalists purchased of him in quantities, and then retailed in suitable amounts to the men. Frequently a number of prisoners, allowed to go outside with working parties, bought from the farmers in the neighborhood. This resulted in a competition of prices, as the latter were able to sell at a much lower rate than the sutler.

By the time I was transferred from Camp Sumter, Market-street had grown into a business mart of considerable respectability. Booths and tables were erected, and a display of eatables spread out quite flattering to the fertility of Southwestern Georgia. The only obstacle in the way of unlimited operations was the exceedingly limited supply of "legal tenders." Even to those however who had no funds, the markets were a source of benefit, in the amusement they afforded, and the relief of the mind from the wearying sameness of our every-day life.

There were several other methods of occupying time among the well, when the camp was first organized, but these gradually wore out, until there was nothing left but *ennui*, and a restless craving for freedom. The opening, or rather toleration of the markets, by the rebel officials, I found one of the most fortunate events in the history of the camp. Though there was no apparent diminution in the fearful mortality which carried off scores every day, those whose constitutions and physical strength were superior to the horrors and wretchedness of our situation, were occupied by the new source of entertainment allowed. I have not the least doubt, that among those iron men who successfully bore up under all their sufferings, that is, kept their feet, the sickness was very materially lessened by the excitement and occupation of the thoughts upon matters enlivening and calculated to dispel despair.

CHAPTER XXI.

Raiding at Camp Sumter—Detection of a Number of "Raiders"—Their Trial—Sentenced to be hanged—Their Execution—The Effect of extreme Measures.

The system of "raiding," which was carried on with so much annoyance at Belle Island, was practised, with even greater industry, at Camp Sumter. The class of vagabonds who thus indulged their thieving propensities, spent their nights in prowling through the camps, carrying off every thing they could lay their hands upon.

The sick and helpless were particularly annoyed by their depredations, but every one suffered more or less. It was impossible to possess any thing, unless it was closely watched. While one man was absent, it became necessary for a comrade to remain as a sort of guard to the property. At length the evil became so great that it was determined to set a terrible example.

Quietly, one afternoon, a small number of the prisoners held a secret meeting to consider the nuisance and adopt measures to stop it. After exchanging views upon the subject, it was determined to organize a small and reliable detective force, to keep watch and draw out any suspected parties, in hopes of discovering the ringleaders.

The same night the detectives commenced their duty. A close surveillance was kept upon different parts of the camp, but morning came without making any discoveries. The following day was passed in mixing with several suspected parties, but without avail. The second night met with the same results. It was now supposed that the raiders had got wind of the efforts to find them out, and they had taken the wise precaution of desisting, at least temporarily, from their labors. During the same day, however, a blanket was missing from a poor fellow who was dying from the effects of chronic diarrhœa. The "detectives" immediately started in quest of the "raider." After an hour's diligent search he was discovered, and drawn from his hiding-place, not only with the article last stolen, but numerous other evidences of his guilt, and which were at once claimed by their owners.

A preliminary examination drew from the arrested man an acknowledgment of his crime; and at the same time the names of a number of others implicated in the same acts were elicited. The entire party was arrested, and a trial called.

On the next morning the sergeants of the different messes were assembled, and, out of this number, twelve were chosen to act as a jury. Several officers were brought down from Macon to witness the trial. Those of the sufferers by the depredations of the "raiders," who were able to attend, were summoned to appear as witnesses, and the accused were permitted to choose their own counsel and witnesses. During the excitement of the arrests a number of men were held for trial, but who, upon proving their innocence, were at once discharged.

The trial of the "raiders" was conducted with the strictest impartiality. After hearing all the evidence, the respective cases were argued with considerable ability. The verdict given, was for the leading "raiders" to be hanged by the neck until dead, and the remainder to suffer such other punishments as the extent of their crimes deserved.

The following were the names of the men condemned to death:

William Collins, alias Moseby, 88th Pennsylvania volunteers.

Patrick Delany, 83d Pennsylvania volunteers.

Andrew Meever, United States navy.

Terrence Sullivan, 72d New York volunteers.

John Sarsfield, 140th New York volunteers.

Charles Curtis, 5th Rhode Island artillery.

On Monday, July 11, 1864, a rude gallows was erected by our own men on a rising ground at the southwestern portion of the stockade. The gallows was a rude piece of workmanship, built out of material which the rebel officials, but too willingly in this case, provided. It was composed of two heavy, forked logs, which were fixed perpendicularly in the earth, with a strong crossbeam resting in the forks at the top. A platform, about six feet from the ground, was built and supported upon props, which, at the final moment, were to be cut away, and the unfortunate men launched between heaven and earth. Six men from the camp were designated to adjust the ropes about the necks of the condemned, and a seventh detailed to execute the dropping of the platform.

At five o'clock in the afternoon the southwestern gate was thrown open, and the prisoners were marched in, under guard of rebel soldiers, commanded by Captain Wurtz, accompanied by the colonel commanding the post. The solemn procession moved in front of the gallows, and halted.

By this time several thousand prisoners had assembled to witness the execution. Many sympathized with the unfortunate situation of their comrades. But the crime of stealing from a fellow-prisoner was always regarded not only as the most unprincipled of acts, but also a matter in which every one who suffered was reduced from a state of deplorable misery to absolute deprivation of probably the last hold he had upon life. The crime was much aggravated by the depredations committed upon the helpless sick. In view of these facts, however benevolent or yielding the wishes of the fellow-prisoners of the condemned, all wished the sentence carried to the melancholy end, as a warning, in the future, to others disposed to the same practices.

When the culprits were formed in line, the rebel captain stepped forward, and, as near as I could note them, after the affair was over, made the following remarks to those in charge of the execution:

"PRISONERS—I now hand over to you, in the same manner I received them, the men whom you have condemned to death on the gallows."

Then turning to the culprits, he said:

"You have been arrested and condemned by your own comrades; I now turn you over to them, and leave them to carry out the sentence, or do as they may see fit."

After this, the colonel, captain, and guards immediately left the inclosure.

The condemned now received the consolations of religion, administered by a Catholic priest, who was permitted by the rebel authorities to visit the stockade on different occasions. The priest accompanied the culprits to the foot of the gallows, and engaged in prayer. In the midst of these holy offices, Curtis took occasion to make an attempt at escape. He succeeded in breaking through the crowd, but was immediately pursued and returned.

The prayer being finished, the six criminals, each accompanied by the persons appointed to execute the sentence, stepped upon the platform. The criminals each said a few words, which were scarcely audible, proclaiming their innocence, and begging for mercy.

When they had concluded what they had to say, the ropes having been previously adjusted, a sack was drawn over their heads, and the six men who accompanied them descended.

At a given signal the platform was cut away, and five of the unfortunate men were struggling in mid-air. The rope, however, of the sixth broke, and the culprit fell to the earth. He begged piteously to be released, but his comrades were inexorable. Another rope was secured, and, when the five bodies were removed, he was hanged alone.

The bodies of the six men were removed from the stockade, and buried in a separate part of the graveyard, distinct from those who died in camp.

During the execution, I observed outside of the inclosure the whole of the rebel troops on duty at Camp Sumter were drawn up facing the gallows. This was, as I understood afterwards, a precautionary measure, supposing some treachery on the part of the prisoners.

At first thought, the above action on the part of the prisoners appears an act of useless severity on the part of the comrades of the men so dishonorably and summarily deprived of life. But our after experience in the evil which it was designed to correct, does not justify this opinion. The example of extreme punishment thus placed before the minds of others, of "raiding" proclivities, had a good result. It at once put a stop to this class of annoyance. During the remainder of the time I remained at Camp Sumter I did not hear of a single article being stolen, and the feelings among all classes of prisoners were stronger and more sympathizing, to an extent surprising, as the very natural selfishness created in times of extreme suffering, and which, in our case at Sumter, never relaxed, now changed to a bond of closer union; and it was not unusual to see men waiting upon each other, as kindly as though they had some important interest at stake.

CHAPTER XXII.

Removal to Macon—An agreeable Journey—Prison Life at Macon—An extraordinary Privilege—Description of Macon—More Prisoners Arriving—Preparations for another Transfer.

In the beginning of August, 1864, with seventy other officers, I was transferred to Macon, Georgia. It was, at least, with some regret that I left the unhappy scenes and associations of Camp Sumter. During my stay there I had formed intimate and agreeable acquaintances, which I was not sure would be my fortune elsewhere. I expected little improvement in camp living, and even with this inducement would have foregone much for the sake of companions, with whom the tardy hours of imprisonment were always made light and full of life.

On the day that I made my departure I met my friends to say a farewell. How solemn were these moments! How sadly against us were the chances of ever meeting again! Consumed by the devouring terrors of the place, some were already one foot in the grave. I cheered them all, though I felt myself on the verge of giving up. When we parted there was no farewell smile, but a tear of mutual commiseration and prayers for strength to outlive our sad lot.

It was known that the prisoners about leaving were to be confined at Macon; still, with a faint expectation that some of us might be exchanged, our parting was also given to messages of love to the dear ones at home, —a single word to cheer them and keep alive their hope.

We left Anderson by rail shortly after noon, and after a ride of four hours were landed at our destination.

This brief journey was one of the most agreeable I had yet experienced in the South. Though the day was oppressively hot, the open fields and fresh air had a cooling refreshing effect upon my feverish blood. I often wished, on the way, that a few hours of such a change could be, or rather would be, given the wretched inmates of Sumter. With all their deplorable wretchedness from hunger and disease, and the vitiated atmosphere of camp, in the pure air alone of the open country there was an invigoration which would have made their hearts leap with renewed strength, and a new lease of life given them, where before they watched and watched and felt every day the inevitable drawing near of its expiration.

When we arrived at Macon we were immediately confined in the officer's prison. In fact none but officers were permitted in the prisons at that place.

As might naturally be expected, the treatment which I received, in general with all others confined at Macon, was an improvement, though very little, on that endured by the wretched inmates of the stockade at Sumter. Our rations were a trifle better, and, what was rather novel to me, in quantity were sufficient to sustain life. This state of affairs evinced a partiality which at once convinced me of the depravity of sentiment which controlled the rebel leaders in their conduct towards prisoners. The almost powerless private was treated with a cruelty and rigor which will make all history blush to own such an unnecessary crime, while officers, who possessed more influence and weight with the Government, were somewhat respected. If all had been treated alike the case would have been different; but as it stands, there is plainly a fear standing out in the shameful policy of the South towards those whom the uncertainties of war had thrown into their power. The rank and file of our armies seemed to be persecuted, first from the impotent and inherent exasperation of the Southern leaders at the delay in the accomplishment of their aims of separate government; second, on account of the helplessness of their victims; and, third, to render as many as possible unfit, for a long time to come, for the duties of the soldier. In the case of officers, I found the persecutions less, as their cases would be much more easily and directly brought to the attention of their Government.

During my brief stay at Macon I enjoyed a privilege which was somewhat out of the *rôle* of my former experiences. By a remarkable act of kindness, on the part of one of the officers of the guard, I was permitted to spend a portion of an afternoon in perambulating the town, having, previous to my going, solemnly promised not to go beyond a certain limit, and to return at a certain time.

As I left the confinement of a prison, for the first time in a year, and unembarrassed by a guard, I never felt such a weight of sorrow removed as in the few hours of that pleasant afternoon. In fact so intense was the feeling of relief which I temporarily enjoyed, that, after my return, I could scarcely realize that I had been out at all; yet my mind and whole body were pervaded by an indescribable sensation and satisfaction almost too great to have any other foundation than in a pleasing dream.

My walk was confined entirely to the limits of the heart of the town. I met some persons on the streets, but very few, as the day was yet warm, and all who were not absolutely called out remained in doors. Of the town, however, I could form some opinion.

Macon, the county-seat of Bibb county, judging from the number of houses, had, before the war, a population of about four thousand souls. It is beautifully situated on the west bank of the Ocmulgee River, at the head of navigation, and at the intersection of the Macon and Western and Southwestern Railroads. From this fact the business of the place before the war was quite brisk, and since had greatly increased, particularly in the manufacturing interest, as much of the machinery of the insurgent party was set up here, as our armies advanced. The convenience of communication to all parts of the South made it an inviting centre for this purpose.

The residences of the town are generally plain but comfortable. There were several churches and a number of stores. The Wesleyan Female Institute, a place of some note in the South, was located here, and before the war was well attended from all parts of the Gulf States. Upon the general average, Macon, as far as my observation extended, was, and probably will be again, a town considerably above the standard of small Southern towns.

The batch of prisoners, in which I was transferred to Macon, was immediately followed by others. Every day there were fresh arrivals, until, at the expiration of five days, there were nearly six hundred congregated for some purpose, which we could not understand, though with the high expectations that we were to be immediately exchanged. With this thought were all correspondingly rejoiced. Nothing, however, was published on the subject until we were about to start.

CHAPTER XXIII.

Off for Charleston—Enthusiasm of the Prisoners—The Displeasure of the People—Under Fire—Nobody Hurt—Relieved—An Exchange—Presents from Home.

JUST one week after I reached Macon I resumed my melancholy perigrinations in the direction of Charleston. As we were about to depart we were gratuitously informed that "the Yankee government" had placed a large number of " Confederate" prisoners under fire on Morris Island, and that the " Confederate" government intended to do the same. This, I have since learned, was their side of the story, whereas ours shows the act, on our part, a retaliation for the same, first done by the rebel authorities in Charleston, and that we were sent to the city as a retaliation for a retaliation.

When we understood our destination, though it was not then known that the part of the national government was retaliatory, we all admitted it was for some wise purpose, and therefore submitted without saying a word. As we were obliged to be persecuted in some way, there was something extremely satisfying, indeed cheering, in the fact that it was for the Government. This feeling prevailing over all, I never saw a more ready, willing, I had almost said happy set of men, than those chosen to submit to the fire of their own countrymen.

As the train left Macon I witnessed and felt the first enthusiasm since I was taken prisoner. The officers cheered, as if they were going to battle for their flag, and sang the national songs as if their journey was nothing more than a mere holiday excursion. What a contrast, I thought, with our departure from the horrible scenes and recollections of Belle Island, and the deep sympathy felt as many of us left the pestilence and woe of Camp Sumter. We now seemed to have lost all thought of the circumstances by which we were surrounded, and looked only to the supreme satisfaction of being of service to our cause.

The enthusiasm of the prisoners as they left was evidently displeasing to the guard, as well as the people who had assembled about the train. A few women took occasion to exhibit their disapprobation, by twisting their mouths into all sorts of contortions, and at intervals displaying their tongues. A few old men also gave utterance to the requests, "Shut up your d——d noise." "What are you howling at, you're all going to get killed by your own men," and the like. One prisoner rather aptly replied,

"Well, it's better to be killed by a 'Yankee' than a 'rebel.'"

This was rather unpalatable to the person to whom it was addressed, as he was still of the ancient impression that one Southern man, particularly in the value of the earth of which he was made, was better than a dozen Yankees, and got out of hearing rather rapidly.

Our route to Charleston lay over the same road we travelled when we were sent to Anderson, namely, by the way of Millen, Augusta, Branchville, and thence to Charleston.

At once upon our arrival at Charleston we were transferred from the cars to the city jail-yard and workhouse. I had the honor of being one of the occupants of the former.

A few days after it was announced by the rebel commander that he would proceed immediately to place us under fire. This piece of information was loudly applauded, greatly to the disgust of the informant. We were now ordered to be in readiness to be moved. His orders were obeyed as promptly as they were magnificently given, and in a few hours we found ourselves confined in the Marine and Rosser Hospitals, under fire of our long-range guns.

There was something eminently pleasing in our situation at that time. We could look out upon the bay, and in the dim distance see the vessels of our Government, proudly investing and cutting off from the world the birthplace and cradle of treason. Occasionally the deep boom of a big gun from our batteries would be heard, almost speaking to us in familiar tones. We felt that the stars and stripes, which through the distance we could scarcely discern, were still there, moving over many stout hearts and willing hands in the service of the cause of right.

I must say, I never passed so many happy moments of reflection as during my imprisonment under fire. Everybody indeed seemed fired with a pride at being again the victims of this new phase of Southern chivalry. Though our rations were scant, our bodies were strong. All seemed to be lifted up, to live upon the thought of the sacrifices we were about to make for the government. But with all the efforts of the rebels to put us in exposed positions, not a single man was hurt by our shells. A fragment one day entered General Stoneman's room, but harmlessly lodged in the wall. There were numerous other instances of this kind, but not a single person killed or even wounded, though the buildings were well riddled.

For six weeks we were under fire, when, very unexpectedly, we were removed, and, much to our surprise, an exchange commenced almost immediately after. This was rather an incomprehensible piece of business, which was never explained; suffice it that I was not one of the fortunate ones exchanged.

Our prison-life at Charleston, in the way of comforts of food and clothing, was the same experienced everywhere by officers. There was less imposition, as might be expected, from the authorities, than that universally experienced by the privates. There were little of the robberies and schemes of extorting money, already mentioned as practised upon the soldier of the ranks. Indeed, in keeping with the general character of rebel officials in subordinate positions, they imposed only upon those whom they took to be their inferiors, though they were often much astonished to find even "Yankee" privates too wise for them.

During our stay at Charleston a number of boxes, containing various articles, arrived from the North. At first, to save the necessity and expense of a strong guard to watch us, the rebels took this means of endeavoring to extort a parole from the prisoners. We were up to the designs of this, and all peremptorily refused. For a short time the boxes were withheld from us, but the sense of shame was too deep for even a rebel official, and the most of the supplies were distributed.

When the boxes were received, and their contents well examined, there was a sense and universal expression of gratification, which it would be impossible to convey in words. These evidences of the thoughtfulness of the folks at home, were always deeply cherished, and were food for thought and conversation for weeks after. Even the rebels themselves could not withhold a look or a word of admiration of at least this one good side of a "Yankee" heart.

CHAPTER XXIV.

Transferred to Columbia, S. C.—The Expressions of the People on the Way—General Grant's Combinations Beginning to Pinch.

In September, 1864, the squad of which I was a member, resumed its travels. Before we left, I discovered our destination was Columbia, the capital of South Carolina. The rebel authorities were evidently of the opinion we were in favor of prison-life in Charleston, from the fact that we enjoyed accommodations vastly better than allowed to prisoners anywhere else in the South. It is true we were quite comfortably fixed in the way of sleeping conveniences, and it was with some disapprobation we heard the news of our contemplated removal.

Our journey to Columbia was performed by rail, again, in a series of dilapidated and antiquated box cars, considerably the worse for wear. The first stage of our travels was to Branchville. At this point we were delayed by trains passing North, until night, when we rode a few miles further to Orangeburg, and were obliged to wait for some wood to be chopped for the engine, and thence proceeded to Kingsville. It was morning when we reached the latter place; accordingly the train halted for several hours, to allow time for the distribution of rations. This very acceptable work accomplished, we pushed on about thirty miles further, when we entered Columbia.

During this trip we were subject to a more universal calling of hard names and epithets, than when I passed over the same road about seven months before. I accounted for this in the fact, that Lieutenant-General Grant, who we knew had been assigned to the general command of all the armies of the United States, and was more than a match for Lee, was very closely pressing down upon the rebel cause and territory, gradually reducing it to a very small compass. We were not sufficiently well advised to form any very correct ideas of the situation, yet from the rebel papers, which were willingly *sold* to "Yankees," we drew our inferences; and from what we gathered here and there from persons loitering about with the camp-guards, we concluded that General Grant's combinations were beginning to pinch.

In order to give an idea of prison life in Columbia, South Carolina, I submit some extracts which I have been permitted to use, from the diary of Lieutenant J. N. Whitney, 2d Rhode Island cavalry, not only an old friend, but for some time a messmate and intimate companion. His record presents, from day to day, a complete picture of all the scenes and incidents which came under our observation during our imprisonment. It is not, however, my intention to give his journal complete, but to select such portions as will convey a clear insight into his experience, without the natural repetition found in a diary covering an extended period. I find an interval running from October 20, 1864, soon after our arrival, up to November 22d following—a duration of one month —contains all this, and therefore make that my selection. It will be observed in his narrative, that, though our treatment was little less than that of brutes, still we were not reduced to the suffering and disgusting extremities which characterized the prisoners of war elsewhere. This is rather an unaccountable fact, confined as we were in the very capital of the first State to revolt, and among a people historically hostile and vindictive towards the people of the North.

I may add, that I accept Lieutenant Whitney's diary, not only on account of its merits as a daily record, but my inability to keep my own, while suffering from a severe illness which befell me soon after our arrival.

With this understanding, I will make the diary the subject of another chapter.

CHAPTER XXV.

Extract from the Diary of Lieutenant J. N. Whitney, 2d Rhode Island Cavalry.

OCTOBER 20, 1864.—To-day the weather is again fine. Nights frosty and cold. We commenced to live in a tent of our own. I will here give an account of our arrival from Charleston. We were turned into a new lot, in the suburbs of the town, lying on a hill bounded on the east by the main road from Columbia, running north. On the west by a deep valley, through which runs a small creek, tributary to the Saluda. This creek, I may add, runs through the lower portion of the camp. On the north we touch a heavy pine wood, which, with intervals of openings, and smaller growth, encircles the entire camp though at various distances from its boundaries. On the south ranges a low ridge, overgrown with brush and scattered pines. The site of the camp was originally covered with a stunted growth of small pines, which soon disappeared in the shape of huts for protection against the weather. The camp is completely invested by a guard-line and chain of sentinels. It has been a rule in camp to permit small parties to go into the woods, to carry fuel for cooking. Some have already collected sufficient spare wood to construct the walls of a cabin, which, covered with brush, are quite comfortable. Our quarters, which we hope to improve now, consist of two blankets sewed, or rather strung together, and fastened by the four corners to as many posts driven firmly into the ground, and rising from the surface about two feet. A wedge-pole, supporting the blanket in the centre, is fastened on two stakes, about six inches higher. Our bed (upon which six of us sleep) is made of pine logs, crossing each other at the ends, making a height of about one foot, on which a surface of logs has been laid. The greatest difficulty we find in sleeping on this bed is, to avoid the sharp corners, being almost entirely without any thing to lie upon, except a little brush and leaves, and these even are scarce. We are however satisfied with this, in the absence of an immediate prospect of any thing better.

To-day cutting down of our rations took place. The issue per man, for five days, is as follows:

Five quarts of corn-meal, very coarse.

One quart of sorghum.

Two tablespoonfuls of coarse salt.

Two tablespoonfuls of rice.

In addition to this, those who have money are permitted to purchase of the sutler. He being in league, no doubt, with some of the officers, has a monopoly, and is permitted to sell at his own price. His rates, in Confederate money, are:

Sweet potatoes, twenty dollars per bushel. Price in town, twelve dollars.

Butter, fifteen dollars per pound.

Fresh beef, two dollars and fifty cents per pound.

Mutton, the same.

Irish potatoes, thirty-two dollars per bushel.

Eggs, five dollars per dozen.

Salt, six dollars per quart.

Apples, two for a dollar.
Bacon, seven dollars per pound.
Tea, seventy-five dollars per pound.
Coffee, twelve dollars per pound.
Cigars (villanous), four for a dollar.
Shoes, sixty-five dollars per pair. Tapping-boots, twenty-five dollars.
Cotton cloth, formerly seven cents, three dollars per yard.
One sheet of paper, and one envelope, one dollar.
French flannel shirt, fifty dollars.
Tent-fly, one hundred dollars.
One tin pint measure, five dollars.
One three-quart pail, twenty dollars.

We have some difficulty in keeping the scant supplies which we receive. Our sorghum is kept in an old black bottle, which reminds us very forcibly of better cheer in former days. Its history is often a subject of amusement in our mess, talking over the many sprees it has witnessed. Our corn-meal is secured in a bag made out of an old coat-tail, picked up in the rubbish-heap of the camp. Never, during our prison experience, have we had any conveniences for safely securing rations from the weather, wastage, and dirt.

Our accommodations for cooking and eating are equally primitive and simple. In our mess, which is better supplied than the majority of others, we possess four earthen dishes of the rudest and roughest fabric, two tin plates, much battered and bent; two whole forks, and two with one prong; three knives without handles; one earthen cup of antique pattern, two earthen saucers; two tin pans; one huge tin pail, somewhat dilapidated and leaky, holding about twelve quarts. This answers also the purpose of a boiler. We have also one tin can, holding about one quart, used for making coffee. The repast which these conveniences and our limited rations permit us to make is spread upon the ground.

Our wardrobe, and that of the majority of officers in this prison, is confined to the clothes upon our backs. Under garments are rare, and many who once possessed them were obliged to throw them away on account of the vermin which had congregated in them.

October 21*st.*—One of the finest days in autumn. I often look out upon the fields around, and wish for one hour's liberty. To-day a new commander, a lieutenant-colonel, took charge of the camp. He has promised a reform and better times; but we have been promised this so often that we expect little.

October 23*d.*—Last evening occurred one of those painful scenes which we are called upon too frequently to witness. Lieutenant Young, of the 4th Pennsylvania cavalry, while sitting on a stool with a number of companions clustered about a fire near the northern boundary of the camp, was shot through the body, and died in about twenty minutes. His only words were, "I am hurt," and was immediately seized with a hemorrhage at the lungs. The guard, who was the cause of the lieutenant's death, said it was done accidentally, while adjusting the cap on his musket. But no one has ever been punished, or even reprimanded for their carelessness. I remember one instance, in Richmond, where a soldier, for a similar "accident," received a promotion and furlough. The same occurred during my imprisonment at Macon. A "Yankee" is never killed for any cause whatever, without evident signs of satisfaction on the part of the guard and their officers.

To-day the artillery, under the direction of our new commander, was removed to a hill at a greater distance, and giving better range to sweep the camp. This is probably a precautionary measure, suggested by the alarm of a few nights since. The affair was rather amusing. The particulars were these: About eight o'clock P. M., four shots were heard in quick succession from the west side of the camp. Immediately in the camp of the chivalry there was a great commotion. Men were flying hither and thither in evident consternation. One shouting,

"Where is company B?" Another, an officer, yelling at the top of his voice, "Fall in, company G." Another, "Rally on that yer artillery," and so on for five minutes, the whole reserve guard was in a wild clatter.

At last, they got into position, and became somewhat quiet. A small reconnoitering party ventured near the border of our camp, one exclaiming,

"Fetch out yer Yanks." Another, "We're ready for you now."

Finding no signs of disturbance, the party withdrew. Upon inquiry, I found that three prisoners ran by the guard, and were fired at. The guard, supposing a mutiny on the eve of breaking out, aroused their whole force, but only to find their alarms unfounded.

October 23d, Sunday.—Severe frost last night. We are having signs of the approach of winter, and few of us are prepared. The fires are nightly the centres of a shivering group.

There have been a number of instances in this camp of gross injustice in the distribution of supplies sent here for distribution by the sanitary commission. A few weeks ago, over one hundred quilts were received. If equitably distributed, they would have supplied nearly every destitute man in camp, or at least would have allowed one quilt to two. This, however, was not satisfactory to some. A colonel, for instance, whose name I forbear to mention, kept back about twelve for his own mess, which was well supplied before. Every morning the blankets can be seen hung about his tent airing, while there are upward of a hundred men who are obliged to pass the nights hugging the fires, and sleep by day.

Lieutenant Young, who was killed yesterday, was buried to-day. The funeral services were read by Lieutenant Ogden. Thus another victim of treason and treachery lies buried far away from home and friends. It is sad to think of this. How soon will the plowshare obliterate the ample mound which now marks his resting place!

October 25th.—A confederate soldier, caught stealing spoons, knives, forks, &c., during the evening roll call of prisoners, has been placed under arrest, his officers promising to punish him.

Lieutenant King arrived in camp from hospital in town. He reports Union feelings among the rebel soldiers, repeating a number of remarkable stories told by them of what they intend doing. Not being credulous, we listen to the lieutenant's story, because it is something new, and not because there is much confidence placed in it.

October 26th, Wednesday.—We commenced building a cabin for shelter against the approaching cold and storms of winter. For the past two weeks we have been "lugging" pine logs upon our shoulders from the woods, about a quarter of a mile distant. This was somewhat of a task in our weakened state, and the accumulation of material was necessarily very slow.

October 27*th, Thursday.*—Commenced splitting slabs for roofing.

October 28*th, Friday.*—To-day we succeeded in putting up the sides and one end of our hut. It is now raining, the first we have had for twenty days. In our present quarters it is impossible to keep dry. We are soaking wet, and will have to remain so until the weather clears, and we can again start the fires. These rains are uncharitable things. How many poor fellows I can now see sitting without shelter, and but half clothed, taking the rain in all its fury! All the huts and tents are crowded with wet and steaming clusters of men. Such misery! I often long, in the parlance of the prisoners, "for some northern hog pen." I hear a home sick prisoner exclaiming, "I wish I was in my father's barn." His father must be a farmer. Another sings out with a stoical indifference, "'Tis a place to be jolly in." Another, with a mixture of irony and sincerity, remarks, "I want to go home." There are some cheerful spirits amongst us who make sport over everything. Without them it would be hard to survive this miserable place.

October 29*th, Saturday.*—Still raining, no fires, nothing to eat, wet and weary. The day passed never so slowly. No sleep at night. The same sad spectacle of men seated on the leeward side of a hut hugging their knees, the rain pelting them mercilessly.

October 30*th, Sunday.*—The clouds broke during the night, and the sun rose beautifully this morning. Details of men have returned with wood, and the fires are again burning. Many are down sick with colds and pneumonia from the effects of the late exposure. A great many are laid up with hunger, the rain interfering with the supplies.

This afternoon was spent in bringing logs and brush for our hut.

October 31st, Monday.—Suffered unusually from hunger to-day. Our labor in building we find very exhausting.

November 1st, Tuesday.—Received a letter from mother, dated September 25th. It is the only one that has reached me since May 1st. These always welcome missives of home are rendered doubly valuable in the isolation of prison life. To read them over and over again is a pleasurable way of wiling away the dull hours.

November 2d, Wednesday.—Last night an officer attempting to make his escape was wounded in the leg; several, however, under cover of the fire which he drew, were more successful.

To-day we occupied our hut, which turns out more comfortable than an exterior view would suggest. Its dimensions are seven feet by ten, and about six feet in height. The sides are well secured with mud, and the roof, which is made of boughs and earth, is a tolerable protection from the weather. The internal conveniences are rather economical in variety, consisting principally of a platform of logs covering nearly the entire space within, and used for lounging on rainy days and a bed at night.

November 3d, Thursday.—The great event of to-day was a visit from a highly appreciated personage, an old porker. As he approached the camp his movements were closely watched by about a hundred hungry fellows. No sooner had his porkship crossed the "dead line" than he was enthusiastically greeted by a popular demonstration. At least a hundred fell upon him, some seizing him by the tail and ears, and every other portion of the animal furnishing a handle. Those who were unable to lay hold plunged their knives into him and clubbed him, the hog meanwhile squealing to the full extent. The hog, unable to endure this treatment, soon expired, then came the contest for a share in the spoils; finally, however, it fell in small quantities into the hands of about fifty, and the cooking soon spread through the camp an odor of fresh meat, which had been foreign to us for a long time.

November 4th, Friday.—To-day we have had considerable excitement on the subject of "counts." A short time since the number of officers confined in this prison was fifteen hundred, to-day but eleven hundred and sixty-four are all that can be accounted for. The cause of this deficit is the loose manner of paroling the men, who a short time since were permitted to go out alone for wood, provided they promised upon honor or oath that they would return. The applications were numerous, and the regulations not rigid. There were many who left the prison without giving their parole. These left the camp for our lines, some succeeding and others not.

November 5th, Saturday.—An officer who made his escape yesterday reached a distance of five miles on his journey, and returned for want of food and a blanket. Approaching a sentinel, the officer stated that he was an inmate of the hospital, and promised an order on another officer in camp for a new rubber blanket if the sentinel would give him his. The sentinel seized at the chance, and gave the officer his blanket. The officer again started on his journey, and the sentinel, after a delinquent search, found he was the victim of a "Yankee trick."

November 6th, Sunday.—Raining; cold and unpleasant. Our frail domicile proves rather leaky. Those who are unprovided with any shelter at all, are commencing to feel the effects of their unfortunate condition. Colds, rheumatism, and lung diseases, are commencing to spread. After the terrible experience of last winter, I dread the coming of the present one.

November 7th, Monday.—Left the camp on parole. Walked to the factory. Not permitted to enter. Saw a large number of the female operatives. They are, I find, the best of the lower class, but greatly inferior in intelligence, good-looks, and taste in dress, to the Northern factory girls. Towards prisoners they are generally kind, when an opportunity offers for them to show their feelings, though the rules are strict that they shall have nothing to do with a "Yankee."

Returned to camp in the afternoon, feeling much benefited by the exercise and fresh air enjoyed in my rambles. The only obstacle to our happiness, comparatively speaking, is a very limited supply of food to meet the cravings of excellent appetites.

November 8th, Tuesday.—Over sixty escaped prisoners have been reclaimed up to this time, many bitten by hounds used in their pursuit.

An officer named Murphy, a perfect specimen of an Irishman, was brought in this morning. Ever since, he has been narrating to an extensive and interested audience his perilous adventures and capture. He was out four days, and witnessed all sorts of sights, and passed through an infinite variety of hairbreadth escapes. He represents the people hospitable, but reports that they pick up every able-bodied man, friend or foe, who can not give a good account of himself. The country he represents uninviting, and difficult of travel.

November 10*th, Thursday.*—We are rapidly assuming the appearance of a winter encampment. More substantial " shebangs" than have answered the purpose of shelter during the summer are being erected.

The messes are each reduced five or six less in number, and work in common, carrying logs from the woods, a half mile distant. The sides of the winter " shebangs" are solid and secure, but the rooms, made of strips and brush, much expose the interior to the weather. Each " shebang" is provided with a chimney of wood, " cobbled," and lined with clay-mud. All the crannies are filled in the same way, making every thing very close. Each place has one door, but no windows. However, by the time everybody is accommodated, we will have, if not the most beautiful, at all events, under the circumstances, the most comfortable quarters now in a Southern prison-camp.

November 11*th, Friday.*—Last night a man was shot, attempting to pass the guard.

November 12*th, Saturday.*—More escaped prisoners brought in. All report poor prospects of discovering a passage out of the country, on account of its intricacies of roads and rivers.

November 13*th, Sunday.*—A beautiful Sabbath. The weather clear and sparkling. The air rather cool and damp. We enjoy few opportunities of religious instruction. Everybody's religion here is to reach God's country, as the North is termed, as soon as possible.

November 16*th, Wednesday.*—Nothing new. Monotony, bad weather, nothing to eat, and every thing else to make our confinement irksome.

November 17*th, Thursday.*—Thinking about trying my fortune in an effort to escape; been revolving in my mind a number of plans, none of which seem to answer the purpose.

November 18*th Friday.*—Had a conversation with Lieutenant G. M. Van Buren, 6th New York Cavalry, on the subject of escape. He agrees to be my companion. Passed the day in secret conversations on the subject.

November 20*th, Sunday.*—Our plans of escape, which were ready to be carried into effect to-night, were delayed by the arrival of a box from home, containing shirts and stockings. This comes at a very appropriate time, as I as well as my companion were in need of such supplies for our journey.

CHAPTER XXVI.

The Escape of Lieutenant Whitney and Captain Van Buren—Their Experiences on the Way—Attacked by Hounds—Arrival at a Mill—Obliged to Turn Back—A Sorghum Boiling.

By November 21st I had returned to my mess, and at once entered into the arrangements of escape suggested by Lieutenant Whitney. My strength was not sufficient for me to undertake any such journey; it was therefore understood that I should keep guard over the personal effects of the Lieutenant and his companion, and in event of not being recaptured, and returned to camp at the expiration of four weeks, the things in my possession were to be disposed of as I saw fit.

As Lieutenant Whitney and his companion were both brought back to Columbia, after being out a few weeks, I will let the diary of the former note their experience, and narrate their adventures.

The day before their departure two passes were written out, one for the Lieutenant, the other for Captain Van Buren. The Lieutenant assumed the name of Lieutenant Jackson, and his companion, Captain Mann. In addition to writing these passes themselves, they also took the privilege of signing the name of Captain Martin, officer of the guard.

We resume the diary where the Lieutenant and Captain left camp:

November 22d, Tuesday.—The sun rose clear this

morning, and every thing turned out to facilitate our escape. The understanding was to pass the guard singly. Bidding a quiet good-by to but two of our most intimate friends, we commenced our operations by a little manœuvring about the guard, to catch them without an officer. At the proper moment, with my pass in hand, my haversack under my coat, containing a few necessary articles of food, a blanket thrown over my shoulders, and with two loaves of corn-bread in my hand, I approached the guard, handed him my papers, at the same time adding, in the weakest voice at my command, that I wished to go to the "hospital where I belonged." The guard looked at the pass mechanically, looked at me, and then gave the document back, saying it was "all right." I crossed the line, and at once felt like another man, ready to undergo every privation and fatigue for liberty. I immediately hastened towards the hospital, where I was soon joined by the Captain. We remained about the hospital, but as much removed from attention as possible, until 7 o'clock P. M., when we set out on our uncertain journey, feeling strong and full of hope.

Our first duty was to elude the soldiers and inhabitants continually found in the vicinity of the camp, and having reached the country, we felt rather safe. Passing along the edge of the open field in the rear of the rebel headquarters, we could see the rebel soldiers seated around their camp fires, talking and laughing, singing and smoking, some stretched at full length on the ground, sleeping, and others standing. How unconscious they were that two "Yanks" were anxiously creeping by them on their way to "Yankeedom." We made our way through briers and mud-holes until we had effectually "flanked" the enemy, and came out on the road a short distance beyond. We halted a few moments to listen and reconnoitre. This was a wise precaution. We had scarcely set our ears to work than two rebel soldiers, talking enthusiastically upon various subjects that they knew nothing about, passed within a few rods of us. We dropped flat on the ground, and lay there in anxious suspense, every moment expecting them to challenge us. But they passed on, infinitely to our relief, without observing us. We lay in our cover about half an hour longer, until it was later, and consequently less probability of finding any one abroad. At length we arose, and struck out into the road, making our way directly for Columbia, whence we intended to take a road leading off to the right towards Augusta, Ga.,—the latter point being our destination, in hopes of falling in with some of Gen. Sherman's forces reported moving for that point and the coast.

After a great search, and considerable scratching through brambles, we ran into an inclosure, in which was a small cabin. The inmates were in a state of jollification, which was manifested by sundry exercises effected in unison with the labors of a negro fiddler, who was deeply engaged in extracting certain imitations of tunes from his instrument. We passed the house without attracting any attention, and struck the road leading in the desired direction. Down this road we pushed with all speed. The night was clear and cold, and the ground frozen,—a good night for walking. We made no delay on our way, more than to stop occasionally and listen.

About five miles from Columbia, we struck a wide creek, crossing the road. There was no bridge, and the only way to cross it was by wading. Accordingly we stripped our feet and legs, and walked in with a shiver. When less than half the distance across, the water reached our pantaloons. We gave a glance at the opposite shore, which was, at least, twice as far distant as the space we had crossed. There was but the alternative to strip or turn back. Adopting the latter, we turned about and walked out, to make an effort to find some more practicable and convenient means of getting over.

After reconnoitring in the darkness, on both sides of the road, we discovered something which, upon investigation, was found to be a foot-bridge. Upon this we cautiously crossed, and again took the road.

About midnight we passed a plantation on the roadside. This was the first and only one during our first night's travel. The negro huts were close to the road, and as we went by, we could see the bright fires shining through the chinks, and hear the negroes earnestly talking. We kept on our way without attracting their attention. Soon after, we came to a mill, in which there were a number of men at work. We searched diligently for a crossing, but could find none except by passing through the mill. Not deeming it prudent to hazard such an alternative, we turned back, and struck another road, which, though not following our general direction, we hoped would bring us out on another road leading south. Southern roads, we found, were not the most regularly surveyed, nor excellently constructed. They are nothing more than wagon-tracks winding in every direction through forests, over plantations, and across streams without bridges. Any obstacles, such as a fallen tree, are conveniently avoided by making a detour. The roads, consequently, are much obstructed, and difficult to travel. In the darkness, more than once we lost the track, and several times were thrown to the ground across logs and stumps in our way.

During the night, we made as much distance as possible. As day was breaking, we reached a plantation, yet we ventured past. The house stood off some distance, but the barn was immediately on the road. We heard several voices in the barn, and soon two men came out. We sprang into a thicket on the road-side, and ran about a hundred yards into a ravine.

November 23d, Wednesday.—Having remained quiet in the ravine for fully a half an hour, and feeling assured that we were not detected by the two men from the barn, we looked about us for a secluded spot where we might be secure from discovery. It was now broad daylight. After a little search, we found a dense cluster of briers, thickly surrounded by large trees. We felt it would be impossible for any one to find us, unless they accidentally walked right into the bushes. This was not a probable contingency, so we opened our haversacks, and ate sparingly of our food, a little bacon and a little bread. We here discovered one cause of distress, we were without water, and had been since early yesterday. As it would be dangerous to attempt to satisfy our thirst, we determined to wait until night.

We now lay down for rest, covering ourselves with the blanket I had brought. We both fell into a sound sleep, from which we awoke long after noon. An hour before dark, we took another meal, but could find no water.

When night had set in, we resumed our journey. After fairly "flanking" the plantation, we again entered the road. Having tramped but a half a mile on our way, we reached a cross-roads. Van Buren climbed the sign-post, and read the directions, which indicated that we had come out on the main Columbia and Augusta road. We followed the index finger pointing to Augusta. No incident occurred during the night. We passed a number of plantations, in the houses of which lights were burning, but the buildings standing away from the road, we experienced no danger in getting by.

November 24*th*, *Thursday.*—During last night my legs pained me severely, probably from the effects of the attempt to wade the stream across the road on our first night out. But I gave no attention to my suffering, hoping another night's exercise might restore them to good walking order.

At dawn this morning we reached a densely populated district, that is, for the South. While passing a house near the road four hounds sprang at us. We took to the bushes, they after us. Fortunately we were not discovered on the road, and the uproar occasioned by the hounds was not an unusual annoyance, so no attention was paid to them, else we should have been detected at once.

After holding us at bay for about an hour the dogs went off, evidently satisfied that they had annoyed us enough. We now kept under cover of the bushes in the bottom of a ravine, where we discovered a beautiful little stream. Our thirst, which by this time had become almost intolerable, was heartily quenched.

We both now, soon after, lay down, and fell into a sound sleep, from which we were called to our senses about ten o'clock, shaking with the cold. We now ate our breakfast; in fact, it was the remnant of our whole stock of food. After washing in the stream, we both felt refreshed, and hid ourselves in the bushes for the remainder of the day. The long hours were spent in laying out plans over our future movements, with intervals of sleep, and no dinner.

Late in the afternoon we gathered a number of acorns. There were a number of hogs near us engaged in the same search, and seemed to look upon our labors as an intrusion upon the already precarious supply of this article of diet.

About an hour after dark we again ventured on the road, and resumed our journey. For two hours, we moved onward without incident. We passed several plantations and a number of negro quarters, but attracted only the attention of an occasional hound, which saluted us as we passed with one or two mournful howls.

Shortly before ten o'clock in the evening, we approached a sorghum boiling. The glare of the fires lit up the road for some distance. There were a large number of whites and blacks superintending the operations. Our greatest concern was to get by without eliciting observation. We left the road as we drew near the light; in fact, we were expedited in this manœuvre by the sudden appearance in our rear of a planter galloping towards us on a mule. We lay in the bushes about twenty feet from the road until he passed, and then rose, and started to make a detour of the sorghum boilers. We experienced the greatest difficulty in forcing a passage through the briers, and suffered greatly from the lacerations thus occasioned both to our bodies as well as our clothes. We suffered much from a want of water, and were obliged to drink from hog wallows, in which frequently stood a small quantity of stagnant water from the last rain. By this time also the pains in my limbs became so great that I hobbled along with the assistance of two sticks, and with the greatest difficulty.

CHAPTER XXVII.

Off the road—Discover a Pea-stack—Rest—Morning—Where the travellers found themselves—Making themselves known to the Negroes—The Hospitality of the Negroes.

November 25*th, Friday.*—Shortly after 3 o'clock in the morning, during the darkness, we strayed from our road into a large field. For at least an hour we wandered about unsuccessfully, endeavoring to extricate ourselves. At last we came to a number of stacks of cow-peas. To satisfy our hunger, we set to and ate a large quantity of them, after which, lying close up to the stack, and covering ourselves with a goodly supply of the damp vines, sank into a sound slumber.

At dawn, we were aroused by a negro, who crossed the yard on which we were lying, and disappeared in a cornfield. Before creeping from our cover, we made a good preliminary optical reconnoissance of our locality. We found ourselves in an extensive field, and two hundred yards from the negro quarters, which stood between us and the plantation house, a short distance beyond.

At sunrise the negroes could be seen flocking from their comfortable cabins, ready to begin their day's work. Some went to the fields; several fat wenches took a conspicuous position near the stack in which we lay, and set up a tremendous "Coo-o-hoo," "Coo-o-hoo." In a few moments, this summons was answered by the appearance of a large number of hogs, apparently in great excitement in expectation of their morning meal. While watching these proceedings a patriarchial negro passed in a wagon, singing vociferously a psalm, in the favorite doleful minor key.

A few minutes after sunrise, about a dozen negroes, male and female, had congregated in front of their quarters, and were holding an earnest conversation, judging from their manner, on an important subject. Our object now was to attract the attention of one, without alarming the others. Directly an aged and a middle-aged negro, with axes on their shoulders, crossed the field, and approached the stack-yard. They entered the inclosure, and commenced to work within a few feet of our concealment. After laboring for a few minutes they held up, and again entered into conversation, probably a continuance of that in which they indulged at their quarters. We listened attentively. The old darkey was talking.

"I tink," said he, "dis here war had to be, and I tink God is on de side ob de Yankees. 'Tis just as in de days ob pfore, when dey sprinkled de sides ob de houses wid blood, and de nation was smote, 'cause of its wickedness."

The younger African fully coincided with this observation, and they resumed their work.

A few minutes after, they took another breathing spell. This time the subject of their talk was a matter which deeply interested both of us, relating to several officers who designed attempting their escape the same night of ours. The old negro alluded to one in unmistakable terms, and mentioned having given him food the night before.

The younger African passed a compliment on the stranger, to the effect that he was a "man who used the most correctest language dey heard in all der days—dat massa was no comparson."

Basing our conclusions of their feelings from this conversation we had listened to, we determined at once to discover ourselves to them.

In an undertone, but still covered with the pea-vines, my head alone exposed, I addressed the elder of the negroes, calling him "uncle." The two stopped work, when one of them, seeing me, came up. I said to him—

"Uncle, do you know who we are?"

"I kind o' 'spec youse Yankees," said the old negro.

His companion now joined him, and we assured the two that we were Yankees. At first they were in doubt whether to believe us, but a few minutes sufficed to convince them. Their countenances immediately lit up with satisfaction, and they seemed heartily glad to see us, dirty, ragged, haggard, and travel-worn as we were. The two negroes offered their kindness, which we accepted in the same spirit of gratitude with which it was tendered.

Their first thought was to get us out of the stack-yard, which they knew was not safe.

The old negro, speaking, remarked—

"Massa, dis place am very unsartain; when de boss comes out, he comes right here, so I speck dat de safest way am to git out ob dis stack, and lay away somewhar else."

We at once mentioned our confidence to the negroes, and that we would be guided by their directions.

After the ancient negro thoroughly reconnoitred about the premises, and found the coast clear, they hastened us to a thicket on the edge of the field, where we were told to remain, while they resumed their work, until "Boss," whom they were expecting at the stacks, should return to the house.

Two hours thus passed away. We had crept a short distance into the bushes, in order to be more secure, and were discussing our future movements, when the younger of the two negroes made his appearance, with a bottle of sorghum, some sweet potatoes, and an immense pone, made mostly of flour, which being a luxury among negroes, he had saved it, probably, since the beginning of the war. In our half-famished state we devoured it without much ceremony, and much to the astonishment and sympathy of our benefactor.

Having concluded our meal, the negro appeared decidedly anxious to know something about the progress of the war. After over a year's imprisonment, we were almost as ignorant on the subject as himself; though in prison we had all kinds of rumors and reports, and an occasional sight of a newspaper. We told him, however, that General Sherman, with ever so many more men than all the rebel army put together, was marching across Georgia, for Augusta. This was then the general impression among the prisoners. This information greatly excited the joy of the negro; he laughed and swung his hat, but when we told him that General Sherman would soon be in South Carolina, and set all his brethren free, his delight knew no bounds. He rolled on the ground, kicked and cut up a variety of antics, and was only restrained from shouting by a thoughtful consideration of our safety.

At each pause in our remarks, the negro would chime in, "To be shoo;" and when we finished said, "Ise gwine to 'Gusta to-day, after his nice gold watch ; he's afeerd de Yankees cotch it ; yah, yah." Judging from this remark the master evidently expected the Yankees there himself, and the negro had now discovered the meaning of sending him for the watch.

A half an hour after the negro who brought us food had joined us, another came up, and, in a few minutes, the old negro, whose name, I learned, was Uncle Ben. The old man was a venerable looking old African, and, I have no doubt, the embodiment of all rare virtues attributed by fiction writers to the higher order of slaves. I formed an affection for the old man at first sight, and was greatly strengthened in it by his many kindnesses to us in our forlorn and dependent condition. Uncle Ben, from all accounts, was an important negro among his race in the vicinity. He could read and write, and was the oracle of the neighborhood. He frequently smuggled a paper, from which he enlarged his ideas for the edification of his people.

This day I shall never forget. As we sat surrounded by our three generous protectors, I could scarcely suppress a tear of sympathy that so much goodness of heart should be wasted in the abject and forced servitude of bondage. As we sat on the thick leaves, and told them of the war, of the Emancipation Proclamation, and many other things, they displayed an eagerness seldom witnessed in the most intelligent. From their masters, in whom they had no confidence, they had overheard many marvellous stories, but with wonderful sagacity sifted the truth from fiction. Indeed they seemed to possess a very good idea of the war, and laughed to think that their masters took them to be such fools as to believe their stories. Here the old negro spoke of their sufferings, their privations, and particularly the universal imposition of the masters, and their encroachment upon prerogatives they and their ancestors had enjoyed, time out of memory. The old negro said he was willing to work, if he got paid for it. Their ideas are of necessity incoherent, and liberty in their mind is merely an indescribable sensation. At least, so I judged from Uncle Ben's views.

We were particularly cautious against "tory" negroes, as the old man termed them, adding, "Some niggers haint got no sense." The word tory was one applied by the inhabitants of South Carolina to all persons of Union sentiments, while the negroes used it to signify a negro who exposed the Yankees.

About noon all the negroes left us, promising to return with food towards evening.

It was five o'clock, and we had just aroused from a sound sleep, when the three negroes reappeared, with a bountiful supply of boiled bacon, wheat bread, boiled and roasted sweet potatoes, boiled chickens, and every delicacy within their reach. We ate our fill, and the remnants being sufficient for a number of meals, were nicely deposited in our haversacks. Though the kindness was the act of hospitality, we paid the negroes handsomely for their food, and felt, whatever might have been the drain upon their stock, they possessed the means of replacing it by purchase; otherwise it is probable they would have suffered for their kindness.

CHAPTER XXVIII.

The Travellers again on the Way—Their Guide—Peleg's Home—A final Parting—Dense Forests—Again off the Road—Strike the Savannah River—Efforts to find a Negro—Run into a Rebel Picket—Again in the Hands of the Enemy.

DESIGNING to resume our journey, we now commenced to discuss the best route of travel. Peleg, the youngest and best-looking of the darkies, spoke up, and informed us he was going a distance of six miles to see his wife, and offered to guide us by a shorter route than the one we proposed to take.

Very soon after dark we were ready, and, bidding adieu to our good friends, started, led by Peleg. As we separated from these simple, noble-hearted negroes, I felt a gratitude deeper than I ever felt before, and again thought what a worth of human feeling slavery withheld from the world.

With a thoughtfulness rather remarkable, the negro insisted upon carrying our haversacks, in order to relieve us as much as possible, saying we had "a long ways to travel." He strove to make himself agreeable. He told us that he had been married five years, and in all that time, rain or shine, had not missed a single night in seeing his wife.

After an hour's walk we reached a stream, about forty yards in width, which was considerably swollen, insomuch that the foot-bridge was submerged about twelve inches. The night was cold, and the water not at all agreeable to the feet. However, following the example of our guide, we took off our shoes, rolled up our pantaloons, and walked in, following the bridge by a horizontal pole, answering the purpose of a railing. Having reached the other side, we again put on our shoes and resumed our journey.

A short distance beyond this stream we came to the cabin of our guide. It was a rude structure, but as near as we could judge in the dark, comfortable, and prettily situated in the midst of a small plot of ground, adorned with shrubbery. We expected him to ask us in to rest, but not so. When we got close up to the rear of the cabin, he said:

"Massas, dis place am filled wid de tory niggars, who, if dey was to see you, would run right away an tell de boss; derfore, you must stay right here, till I come back."

We promised him to remain. Accordingly, he disappeared in his cabin.

During the absence of the negro, we talked over several plans for our future movements; but being unfamiliar with the country, and without a compass, we determined to leave our route to our negro companion.

The negro was gone nearly an hour, and we had almost given him up, when, much to our surprise, he joined us, heavily laden with all sorts of provisions for our journey. He brought his wife with him, as he said, to see "de Yankees." It was evident that the negro was pleased with us, and took an immense amount of delight in turning us around, and laughing with great satisfaction at the opportunity of showing his faithful spouse two live "Yankees."

From the goodly store of provisions brought by the negro we ate heartily, and deposited in our haversacks as much as we could conveniently carry, returning the rest.

When all was ready for us to again set out, we offered the negro money for his kindness; but he peremptorily refused to take any thing at all, exclaiming: "Dis am de charity dat de Lor says must be given to dose who suffer."

This speck of religion was all the more forcible by a very hearty "Amen," emanating from Peleg's wife.

It would have been a crime to destroy such pure and conscientious impulses; we accordingly accepted the donation with the deepest feelings and expressions of gratitude.

Our next subject was, which route we should take. The negro proposed, as the most direct, and with little care in keeping on the lookout, ahead and in the rear, just as safe, and certainly more sure for night travel, the main road to Augusta, by way of Leesville, striking the Charleston and Augusta railroad about Aiken, thence pursuing that line until near the city, when we would be able to hide in the swamps until General Sherman came up.

The suggestion was satisfactory, and entirely in accordance with our own views on the subject. Bidding good-by to the wife of our friend, Peleg accompanied us on the road a short distance, and got us fairly started, when he returned to his little cabin, and we moved on our way to liberty.

November 26th, Saturday.—After parting with our negro friend last night, we walked until the break of dawn this morning. We crossed several streams, and passed a number of plantations, but met no person on the road. Therefore the night passed without incident.

During nearly all of to-day we slept. The distance from Columbia to Augusta is about sixty miles. We are now more than two-thirds on our way.

November 27*th, Sunday.*—At eight o'clock last evening we were again on our feet, and making our way carefully. Passed a village during the night, making a detour to avoid discovery.

Towards morning, it became evident that we were approaching a large river. We pushed on rapidly, to get as near as possible, to make the other side during to-morrow night.

Passed the day in a swamp, a short distance off the road. Occasionally, from our retreat, we could spy persons on foot and in wagons.

November 28*th, Monday.*—At dusk, last evening, we came out on the road, and after carefully looking around, resumed our journey. Our route lay principally through dense forests and swamps. We passed no plantations during the night. Every thing had a wild appearance. We now feel sure we are in the vicinity of the Savannah, or some other large stream.

At daylight this morning there was no termination of the forest into which we had penetrated, and we had doubts whether we were on the Augusta road. In the darkness, we thought we might have strayed by the wrong path. At all events, we resolved to press on to the river, and then direct our course by the current.

After halting several hours for breakfast, and a little sleep, we resumed our journey. At noon, we came to a small village, which we avoided, and in less than two hours came out upon the river.

Our first act, after accomplishing this part of our journey, was to hunt up a negro, in which we failed. We also needed food, as our supply was well-nigh exhausted, and also wished to find some one to take us across the river.

It was agreed not to go into the village, but to follow down the stream, until we came to a negro quarters, where it was certain we would find both food and a boat.

We had walked probably about ten miles through one of the worst countries I ever witnessed, nevertheless making excellent time, when, to our despair, at a bend in the river, we ran into a road in full view of a rebel cavalry picket, guarding a crossing.

"Halt!" "halt!" exclaimed two rebel soldiers at the same time, one standing in the road about twenty yards distant, and another springing from a cluster of bushes not more than ten feet from us.

Almost simultaneously we could see a dozen men seize their muskets. At first I felt like darting back into the timber; but this was of no use, as I found, upon looking round, we were completely surrounded. There was, therefore, but the single alternative of surrender.

When summoned to halt, we obeyed instantly. One of the rebel guard approaching, looked at us closely, and remarked, after he got through—

"Yankees, eh! Well, we got you."

At first I thought of representing both of us as connected with some branch of the rebel service, on our way to Augusta; but this would not do, as our passes would at once identify us as Union soldiers, which, in case of a denial of the fact, would be sufficient to condemn us as spies. So neither of us said any thing.

"You are our prisoners," continued the guard. By this time nearly the whole picket off duty had gathered around us. "Where do you come from?"

"Well, that's more than we can tell," I replied, "as we know nothing about this country."

"Well, we'll soon teach you something about it," said the guard, "if you don't tell us where you belong, and where you're going."

I was puzzled at first which army to claim, whether Sherman or the troops at Hilton Head, because we were some distance out of the way of each. At length the thought struck me. I replied:

"We belong to Sherman's army, and got cut off in a skirmish in which our boys were badly whipped, and were trying to make our way to Augusta."

"Then," asked an officer, who had stepped up by this time, "you expect Sherman at Augusta?"

"Not exactly," I replied; "I do not know where he is aiming at. I thought if his main army did not go there, at least some troops might pass that way."

As my first remark announced a victory for the rebels, the guards were satisfied that we were punished enough, so we were taken to the guard quarters, and treated better than we expected.

A great many questions were asked about movements and so forth, which I evaded, claiming ignorance on the plea of being a "private." I learned from the guards, whom we impressed with the idea that we came from the other side of the river, that we struck the river twenty miles from Augusta, and at present we were ten miles from the town.

By a fortunate oversight we were not examined when first taken, and while seated alone we both took out our pipes and carelessly lit them with paper which we took from our pockets. These were our passes, and were the only evidence we had about us contradicting the account which we had given of ourselves.

CHAPTER XXIX.

Taken to Augusta—Back to Columbia—Meeting old Friends—Another Exchange—Prisoners transferred to the Yard of the Lunatic Asylum —Building Quarters—Suffering.

AFTER being detained in Augusta for several days, Lieutenant Whitney and his companion were returned to camp at Columbia. They were a pitiable spectacle, almost shoeless, their clothes ragged and dirty, and bore every other evidence of a distant and toilsome journey. It was on the evening of December 3, 1864, when they arrived, and just as I was about cooking some corn-cake for the mess. The new-comers were almost famished, and partook largely in our repast, after which we sat by our fire and listened to their narrative of the adventures which I have already given.

On the day after the return of the two prisoners, the subject of exchange was again agitated, and created great excitement. During the same day two men were shot, one while attempting to escape, and the other while walking within the limits of the camp. The discipline of the camp, all of a sudden, and without notification, became very rigid. Sherman's movements towards the coast had created a great deal of alarm, particularly at this time, when it was known that there was no doubt of the complete success of the movement. Rebel papers, which we were hitherto allowed, were of a sudden withdrawn, and it was accordingly only by smuggling that we now got them.

On December 8th, two hundred names were called for exchange. There was immediately the usual "pulling" and bribery among those especially ardent in their efforts to get off. I always found, and in this instance particularly, in the matter of exchange there was great injustice done. Those who were longest in prison always stood the poorest chance of being released, and day after day for long months we wore our lives away in almost hopeless waiting, while those who were in prison but one or two months were sure to be among the first exchanged.

On the 9th of December the exchanged men left camp. In calling the names a number were absent, but others stepped up and answered in their places. In this piece of pardonable fraud, under the circumstances, two men were detected, and sent back, but the others all got away. In this exchange we got rid of one nuisance in camp, a Colonel ———, who showed great partiality for his favorites, to the exclusion of justice and every thing else.

On Monday, December 12th, we received orders from the rebel officer in command to "pack up" for a move. They claimed it was for humanity's sake, but, as this was a rare virtue, we at once concluded that General Sherman was on his way to Columbia.

As soon as orders came, the men at once set to burning their quarters. The rubbish accumulated made quite a conflagration, which was still at its height as we left.

The march to the city was a perfect mob; everybody tried to be first, in hopes, at the end, of getting better quarters. As we went along, we were paraded through the main streets. The people, however, manifested very little feeling or excitement. "The Yanks are coming" had become too common to be much heeded. It occurred to me still more forcibly, after this transfer, that General Sherman was certainly expected, sooner or later. The people, I observed, paid much more deference to "Yankees."

On the way I noticed a lady waving a handkerchief at the men. A rebel officer stepped up to her and asked—

"Madam, do you mean that for those Yankees?"

The lady, expressing some surprise, replied—

"Sir, I thought they were our men."

The manner in which this was said was sufficient to interpret her real meaning.

As we passed the hotel, a rebel officer, of the old school, was standing in front. As we came up he opened a volley of epithets upon us, and made a complete ass of himself. Growing still more excited, he threw off his coat, and swore he could whip the best "Yankee" among us. The only recognitions we made of his enthusiasm were groans, and a few expressions from the prisoners, as, "Go it, old pudding-head;" "Why don't you go to the front," etc.

When we reached the Lunatic Asylum, which we now found was our destination, we were drawn up in line; when Major Griswold, commanding the post, made a speech. His words were as follows:

"You are prisoners; I intend to do all in my power for your comfort. As you enter that yard you will see a line of boards near the wall. That is the "dead-line." Any man crossing that will be shot. You will be supplied with lumber and tools, with which you must build your own houses, under the direction of our master-joiner. Any thing about the grounds destroyed by you, its value will be deducted from your money. Any tools that are missing, kept back by you, after building, their value will also be deducted from your money."

After the major concluded his remarks, we were turned into the yard. There was at once a big rush for quarters. In five minutes the only building in the inclosure, to be used for the purpose, and capable of holding about two hundred, was packed full, with almost double that number. Those outside sat on the ground, without wood, shivering with cold, and no prospect of speedily being better off.

The yard in which we were confined contained about five acres, and was surrounded on three sides by a brick wall ten feet in height, while on the fourth was a board fence, the same height. There were two buildings, in addition to the one mentioned, used as hospitals. Sinks and water were convenient. The "dead-line," alluded to in the major's speech, was a row of boards about ten feet from, and within the wall, running around the entire inclosure. On the west, in the extension of our yard, was the Insane Asylum, pretty well populated, judging from the numerous doleful sounds emanating thence.

The night of December 12, the first at the asylum, was very cold; we, consequently, without shelter, were obliged to keep awake, and run up and down the inclosure to keep warm.

The next day the work on the buildings was continued. One was completed, and immediately occupied. They were built to accommodate thirty-six men, were without floors, no windows, and a mud chimney.

By December 26th, four buildings were erected, and one of which was occupied in part by our mess. There were, however, yet a large number under blankets, and exposed to the inclemency of the season. The delay in the building was no fault of the prisoners, but the tardy labors of those who were supplying the lumber. The sickness and suffering, which resulted from this state of affairs, was rapidly developing to an alarming degree, and deaths increased at a rate alarming, considering the altogether better general treatment given us, than experienced at Belle Island and Sumter.

CHAPTER XXX.

Sherman again in motion—Speculations as to his Destination—Removal of Prisoners to Charlotte—Our concealment—We leave our Hiding-place at Night—Fired upon—Meet two Rebels—Succored by a true Union Lady.

Tediously the days passed by, while in anxious watching we awaited the future movements of Sherman's army. His almost unopposed occupation of Fort McAllister and the abandonment of Savannah by the enemy, convinced us that he was sufficiently strong, and the general bold enough, to undertake another tramp northward.

Our speculations, however, upon the details of his subsequent operations, were entirely different from what really took place. Every one supposed that, from Savannah, he would move directly against Charleston, and invest that strong city, after which tedious process he would, probably, making his base at the fallen city, march into the interior. But this general has proven that a large army, as well as a small one, can move without a base.

In the early part of January, 1865, rumors prevailed in camp that Sherman was concentrating at Beaufort, S. C., a large portion of his forces. This act greatly deceived the rebel officers, as was apparent in the conversations of the camp-guards. They argued conclusively that the "Yankee" general was destined for Charleston.

In the latter part of January, we had later news in camp, which, to the rebels, was apparently quite astounding, namely, to the effect that two columns of " Yankees" were moving into South Carolina. Not only the one from Beaufort, but another across the Savannah River, pursuing a northern but parallel route. It was even then a question as to what point Sherman had in view.

While the exciting news of these operations was coming in, the prisoners were full of expectation. It was hoped that one of our columns would strike Columbia in its line of march. Nerved by this hope, it was gratifying to see the immediate effect upon the prisoners; even the sick were seen about the camps catching up every little item of news. It was confidently thought that a few weeks more would find them again under the shadow of their glorious flag. These feelings were better than all the medicine in the world, especially that part of the world temporarily known as the Southern Confederacy.

By the middle of February, the rebels were convinced that the "Yanks" were unquestionably striking for Columbia; so they determined to remove the prisoners to Charlotte.

A party of us learning this fact, determined to make an effort to escape. Within the camp inclosure there were two buildings, one of which was used by the Lunatic Asylum. The one which we chose for our purpose was two stories high, the upper rooms finished to the eaves and extending a portion of the distance with the roof. Between the highest part of the room, and the point of meeting of the two sides of the roof, there was a space of several feet perfectly dark. All the rooms were finished with boards instead of plaster. One of these boards, sufficiently large to admit the passage of a body, was sawed out by means of a saw-knife, and the board again secured in its place, to avoid detection.

On the 13th of February, the rebels commenced to remove the prisoners. Six hundred in round numbers were marched off to Charlotte the first day. The next day the rest were to follow. During the same night, thirty of us crept into the place of concealment determined upon. The following morning, the last batch of prisoners, all packed up, were assembled near the gate, ready to march, but awaiting the termination of the searches by a detail of rebels, to hunt up any "Yanks" who might have hid themselves. Every now and then some unfortunate fellow would be discovered, and drawn out of his hiding-place, whereupon the prisoners would set up a cry of "Fresh fish," "Fresh fish."

After the rebels were convinced that they had found everybody, they started on their journey, and by afternoon no sound was heard in the camp. It was consequently concluded that all had gone. However, it was not deemed prudent to come from our hiding-place too soon. So for two long days, without food, and suffering dreadfully from thirst, we remained secreted. On the third night, at eleven o'clock, several of us made our way down, and, as we passed across the camp, were fired upon by two rebel sentries, posted in a conspicuous position overlooking the grounds. No one was hurt, and we made good our escape over the wall.

Travelling as rapidly as we could, we made our way around towards the eastern edge of the town, and came in near the depot.

As we were walking along, two privates from Hampton's cavalry hailed us.

"Halt, there," said one of them, "What command do you belong to?"

We promptly halted, and replied,

"To the Telegraph corps."

"Ah, you belong to the bombproof department," said the rebel, laughing.

The other, upon both coming up, was very desirous to sell us some sugar; but, as we had no use for it, we declined, and went on our way.

After entering the town, our first move was for the house of a lady whom we knew to be unquestionably of Union sentiments. We approached her door quietly. We knocked. The lady promptly responded. It was now several hours after midnight, and our sudden appearance at such a time somewhat agitated her.

The door opened cautiously.

"Who's there?" the lady whispered.

"Friends," one of us replied.

"Are you Union officers?" again she whispered, half in fear.

"Yes," we replied.

"Come in, then, quick," again she whispered.

We went in, and related our story. The lady immediately gave us something to eat, and hid us away until the arrival of Sherman's army.

CHAPTER XXXI.

The Occupation of Columbia—We are within the Union Lines—The Burning of the House of our Benefactress—Our Efforts on her Behalf—Home.

On the 17th of February, we had the pride of witnessing the advance of the right wing of Sherman's army enter the capital of South Carolina. As our men marched in, the rebel picket stationed in the city rapidly disappeared, pursued for a short distance; and when assured that our cavalry were in undisputed possession, my companions and myself came from our hiding-places, to greet the incoming of the long columns of infantry, bronzed by long exposure, and as stout and hardy as veterans of such magnificent campaigns as Sherman's must necessarily have been.

It would be in vain for me to attempt to describe the sensations I felt, when I found myself again surrounded by the brave soldiers of the Union. Nineteen months in rebel prisons were a perfect blank in my career, as regarded every thing connected with the events of the war or the Government. The presence of national troops, though long expected, I could now scarcely realize as a fact. The battles and marches which must have filled up the interval, I thought, must have been terrible. There was the Army of the Tennessee, at the time of my capture, just consummating its brilliant operations against Vicksburg, now in the heart of South Carolina. It seemed impossible that such could be the fact. Yet it was true, remote as was its theatre of operations in July, 1863.

As the soldiers passed, a number, witnessing our forlorn appearance, questioned us as to our command, and other matters generally asked by soldiers. When we told them that we were fellow-soldiers, prisoners of war just escaped from the wretchedness of Southern inhumanity, they displayed their sympathy in the true soldier way. They offered us rations, and every thing to make us comfortable. In the course of a few minutes after it was known we were escaped prisoners, we were the centre of a large group, anxious to get a glimpse at us.

As soon as headquarters were established in the town, we reported ourselves, and were provided with uniforms and rations.

Returning to the house of the lady who had secreted us, we remained with her till the columns again moved. During the burning of Columbia, after the evacuation by our troops, unfortunately this lady's house was destroyed in the conflagration. Myself and companions did all in our power to save her property, but without avail. The flames spread, and in the devouring element we saw the home of one who had been really a friend to us destroyed. It was now our turn to reciprocate the kindness extended to us. By permission of the provost-marshal the lady was allowed to accompany the army to Fayetteville, thence to Wilmington; and before leaving there, I had the satisfaction of seeing her comfortably situated with her relatives.

From Wilmington I embarked for Fortress Monroe, as bearer of dispatches; which having delivered, I hastened North to greet once more the friends at home, and narrate to them the scenes which I have endeavored to give in the foregoing pages.

As a conclusion to this imperfect narrative of my own, and the experiences of thousands of others, who have undergone the trials and misery of Southern prisons, I can only hope that the Government will not overlook the sufferings which the innocent victims of the traitors' hate were brought to endure. We feel some commiseration for the misguided spirit in which all these gross acts of barbarism were committed, and therefore only ask for justice. Thousands of lives sacrificed to the vindication of the holy principle of the Government and the American Constitution is regretted, but still willingly made for the great and good ends which have been reached; but lives sacrificed by the wilful act of disappointed and wicked men should not be passed by. Even those who have outlived their cruel treatment are decrepit, and with constitutions broken, they have been restored, it is true, to their homes, but useless both to themselves and to society.

As I stated in the beginning, my efforts would not be directed to an attempt at literary effect, but to give a simple insight into prison life among the rebels. I feel confident that I have kept my promise in regard to the former; if I have been equally successful in the latter, my labors are amply repaid.

LIST OF UNITED STATES OFFICERS, PRISONERS OF WAR,

CONFINED AT COLUMBIA, SOUTH CAROLINA.

The following is a list of the officers confined at Columbia, South Carolina, during the winter of 1864 and 1865, giving name, command, date, and where captured.

Aldrich, C. S., Capt., 86th New York Vols., April 20, 1864, Plymouth, N. C.
Austin, J. W., 1st Lt., 5th Iowa Vols., Nov. 25, 1863, Mission Ridge, Ga.
Alter, J. B., Capt., 75th Ohio Vols., Aug. 17, 1864, Jamesville, Fla.
Allebrough, Wm., Capt., 51st Pennsylvania Vols., May 12, 1864, Spottsylvania, Va.
Alger, A. B., Lt., 22d Ohio Battery, Jan. 3, 1864, Jonesville, Va.
Avery, W. P., Capt., 132d New York Vols., July 25, 1863, North Carolina.
Allinder, W. F., 1st Lt., 7th Tennessee Cavalry, March 24, 1864, Mine City, Tenn.
Albro, S. A., Lt., 80th Illinois Vols., May 3, 1863, Rome, Ga.
Adair, W., Lt., 51st Indiana Vols., " " "
Adams, John, Lt., 80th Illinois Vols., " " "
Allstadt, C. L., Adjt., 54th New York Vols., July, 1863, Gettysburg, Pa.
Ahirn, M., 2d Lt., 10th Virginia Vols., Jan. 3, 1864, Morsfield, Va.
Ahleit, J. W., 2d Lt., 45th New York Vols., July 1, 1863, Gettysburg, Pa.
Adams, C. A., Capt., 1st Vermont Cavalry, Oct. 11, 1863, Brandy Station, Va.
Alban, H. H., Capt., 21st Ohio Vols., Sept. 25, 1863, Chickamauga, Ga.
Andrews, H. B., Capt., 17th Michigan Vols., May 12, 1864, Spottsylvania, Va.
Apple, H., 1st Lt., 1st Indiana Cavalry, June 9, 1863, Brandy Station, Va.
Anderson.
Aller, Abraham, Lt., 16th Illinois Cavalry, Jan. 3, 1864, Jonesville, Va.
Abernethy, H. C., 1st Lt., " " "
Acker, G. D., Lt., 123d Ohio Vols., June 15, 1863, Winchester, Va.
Adkins, P., Lt., 2d Tennessee Vols., Nov. 6, 1863, Rogersville, Tenn.
Asham, A. B., Lt., 7th Michigan Cavalry, May 11, 1864, Yellow Gap, Va.
Aigan, John, Capt., 5th Rhode Island Vols., May 5, 1864, Croton, N. C.
Adams, J. G. B., 1st Lt, 19th Massachusetts Vols., June 22, 1864, Petersburg, Va.
Alexander, E. P., 1st Lt., 26th Michigan Vols., " "
Anderson, H M., 1st Lt., 3d Maine Vols., June 20, 1863, Gum Springs, Va.
Abby, A. L., 1st Lt., 8th Michigan Cavalry, Aug. 5, 1864, Rosswell, Ga.
Anderson, J. S., 1st Lt., 2d Pennsylvania Vols., June 2, 1864, Gaines Mills, Va.

Arther, J. A., Capt., Kentucky Cavalry, Aug. 3, 1863, Todd. C. Y., Ky.
Artherrs, S. C., Capt., 67th Pennsylvania Vols., June 15, 1863, Winchester, Va.
Allen, S., Capt, 85th New York Vols., April 20, 1864, Plymouth, N. C.
Adams, S. B., Capt.,   "   "   "
Andrews, S. T., Capt,   "   "   "
Andrews, W. R., 1st Lt., 16th Connecticut Vols., April 20, 1864, Plymouth, N. C.
Albright, J., Capt., 87th Pennsylvania Vols., June 15, 1863, Winchester, Va.
Abbott, A. A., 2d Lt., 1st New York Dragoons, May 7, 1864, Wilderness, Va.
Anderson, R. W., 2d Lt., 122d Ohio Vols., June 15, 1863, Winchester, Va.
Armstrong, T. S.,   "   "   "   "
Airy, W., Capt, 15th Pennsylvania Cavalry, Dec. 24, 1863, Dandridge, Tenn.
Anderson, C. L., 2d Lt., 3d Iowa Vols., July 12, 1863, Jackson, Miss.
Applegatt, A. S., 2d New York Cavalry, June 12, 1864, Macon, Tenn.
Allen, Robert, 2d New York Dragoons.
Adir, M., Capt., 15th New York Cavalry, May 20, 1863, Front Royal, Va.
Anshutz, H. S., Lt., 12th Virginia Vols., June 15, 1863, Winchester, Va.
Adams, H. W., Lt., 29th Indiana Vols., Sept. 19, 1863, Chickamauga, Ga.
Austin, G. A., A. Q. M., 14th and 15th Illinois, Oct. 4, 1864, Acworth, Ga.
Albin, H. S., Lt., 79th Illinois Vols.
Andrews, E. E., Lt., 22d Michigan Vols.
Allen, O. C., Lt., 112th Illinois Vols., May 20, 1864, Cap. Station, Ga.

Belger, James, Capt., 1st Rhode Island Vols., May 16, 1864, Drury's Bluff, Va.
Baker, S. S., 1st Lt., 6th Missouri Vols., October 29, 1863, Blue Creek, Mo.
Butler, C. P., 1st Lt., 29th Indiana Vols., Sept. 19, 1863, Chickamauga, Ga.
Baird, J. F., 2d Lt., 1st Virginia Vols., Sept. 11, 1863, Moorefield, Va.
Bricker, W. H., 2d Lt., 3d Pennsylvania Vols., August 22, 1863, Burbers, Va.
Bick, W. C., Capt., 62d Pennsylvania Vols., May 5, 1864, Wilderness, Va.
Brady, S., Lt., 2d New Jersey Cavalry, June 11, 1864, La Grange, Miss.
Bulver, A., Lt., 3d New Jersey Cavalry, July 6, 1864, Petersburg, Va.
Burdick, C. H., Capt., 1st Tennessee Cavalry, June 10, 1864, Stilesboro, Ga.
Bertram, D. S., 2d Lt., 2d Connecticut Vols., July 1, 1863, Gettysburg, Pa.
Brown, J. A., Capt. 85th New York Vols., April 20, 1864, Plymouth, N. C.
Bradley, A. B., R. Q. M.,   "   "   "
Butts, L. A., 1st Lt., R. Q. M.,   "   "   "
Brown, G. W., Capt., 101st Pennsylvania Vols.,   "   "   "
Benner, H. S., Capt., 101st Pennsylvania Vols.,   "   "   "
Bowers, G. A., 1st Lt., 16th Connecticut Vols.,   "   "   "
Blakesly, B. F., 2d Lt., 16th Connecticut Vols.,   "   "   "
Bruns, H., 2d Lt., 16th Connecticut Vols.,   "   "   "
Buison, R. R., 1st Lt., 103d Pennsylvania Vols.,   "   "   "
Burns, S. D., 2d Lt., 103d Pennsylvania Vols.,   "   "   "
Bierbower, W., 2d Lt., 87th Pennsylvania Vols., June 16, 1863, Winchester, Va.
Beagle, D. F., 1st Lieut., 101st Pennsylvania Vols., April 20, 1864, Plymouth, N. C.
Brion, J. H., 2d Lt., 184th Pennsylvania Vols., June 22, 1864, Petersburg, Va.
Berry, A., Capt., 3d Maryland Cavalry, February 11, 1864, La.
Bruiting, G., 2d Lt., 5th Maryland Vols., June 15, 1863, Winchester, Va.
Bascomb, R., 1st Lt., 50th N.Y. Vols., April 20, 1864, Plymouth, N. C.

A PRISONER OF WAR. 177

Baldwin, M. R., Capt., 2d Wisconsin Vols., July 1, 1863, Gettysburg, Pa.
Blake, ——, 2d Lt., 3d Maine Vols., June 20. 1863, Aldn, Va.
Brown, W. H., 1st Lt., 93d Ohio Vols., Jan. 17, 1864, Dandridge, East Tenn.
Baird, J. V., Lt., 89th Ohio Vols., Sept. 20, 1863, Chickamauga, Ga.
Byron, C., Capt., 3d Ohio Vols., May 3d, 1863, Rome, Ga.
Banks, B. V., Capt., 13th Kentucky Cavalry, Dec. 14, 1863, Clynile Mount, Tenn.
Burch, J., Capt., 42d Indiana Vols., September 20, 1863, Chickamauga, Ga.
Baily, G. W., Lt. 3d Ohio Vols., May 3d, 1863, Rome, Ga.
Brownnell, F. J., Lt., 51st Indiana Vols.,   "   "
Booker, A., Lt., 73d Indiana Vols.,   "   "
Brown, J. L., Lt., 73d Indiana Vols.,   "   "
Barlow. J. W., Lt., 51st Indiana Vols.,   "   "
Bath, W., 2d Lt., 132d New York Vols., February 2d, 1864, Newbern, N. C.
Binding, H. R., Capt., 61st Ohio Vols., July 2d, 1863, Gettysburg, Pa.
Bush, J. G. Capt., 16th Illinois Cavalry, January 3d, 1864, Jonesville, Va.
Blinn, L. B., Capt., 100th Ohio Vols, Sept. 3, 1863, Lime Stone. Tenn.
Baldwin, H. A., 1st Lt., 2d New York Vols., May 5, 1864, Wilderness, Va.
Bastley, R., 2d Lt., Signal Corps, U. S. A.
Bradley, G., Capt., 2d New York Vols., May 14, 1864, Spottsylvania, Va.
Brandt, C. W, 1st Lt., 1st New York Cavalry, March 10, 1864, Keys Ford, Va.
Bouten, C. W., Capt., 4th Vermont Vols., June, 23. 1864. Petersburg, Va.
Barrett. D. M., Capt., 89th Ohio Vols., September 20, 1863, Chickamauga, Ga.
Brandt, O. B., Lt., 17th Ohio Vols., September 20, 1863, Chickamauga, Ga.
Byers, S. H. M, Lt., 5th Iowa Vols., November 25, 1863, Mission Ridge. Ga.
Barker, H. P., Lt., 1st Rhode Island Cavalry, June 18, 1863, Middleburg, Va.
Boone, S. G., Lt., 88th Pennsylvania Vols., July 1, 1863, Gettysburg, Pa.
Besbee, L. C., Lt., 16th Maine Vols.,   "   "
Besbee, G. D., Capt., 16th Michigan Vols.,   "   "
Brittan, G. C., Lt., 22d Michigan Vols., September 20, 1863, Chickamauga, Ga.
Beeby, H E., Lt., 22d New York Cavalry, May 8, 1864, Wilderness, Va.
Butler, T. H., Col., 5th Indiana Cavalry, July 31, 1864. Limestone Church. Ga.
Boen, C. D., Capt., 18th Connecticut Vols., June 15, 1863, Winchester, Va.
Bennett, D., Capt., 22d New York Cavalry, June 29, 1864, Reams Station. Va.
Brush. Z. T., 1st Lt., 100th Ohio Vols., September 8, 1863, Limestone, Tenn.
Bigley, C. H., 2d Lt., 82d New York Vols., June 22, 1864, Petersburg, Va.
Burns, M., Lt, 13th New York Cavalry, July 6, 1864, Aldn, Va.
Bassett, M. M., Lt., 53d Illinois Vols., July 13, 1863, Jackson, Miss.
Bostwick, N., Capt., 20th Ohio Vols., June 11, 1864, Wavellum Station, Va.
Brown, C. A., Lt., 1st New York Artillery. May 18, 1864, White Church Va.
Benson, J. F., Capt., 120th Illinois Vols., June 12, 1864. North Mississippi, Miss.
Bospard, W. R., Lt., 1st New York Vols, May 17, 1864. Spottsylvania, Va.
Burns, J., Lt., 57th Pennsylvania Vols., July 2, 1863, Gettysburg, Pa.
Burton, J. L., Lt., 49th Pennsylvania Vols., May 10, 1864, Spottsylvania, Va.
Beebe, B. L., Capt., 13th Indiana Vols., May 10, 1864. Drury's Bluff, Va.
Buchanan, W., Lt., 76th New York Vols., May 5, 1864, Wilderness, Va.
Benson, A. N., Capt., 1st D. C. Cavalry, June 27, 1864, Reams Station, Va.
Barkley, C., Lt., 149th Pennsylvania Vols., July 1, 1863, Gettysburg, Pa.
Blasse, W., Lt., 43d New York Vols., May 6th, 1864, Wilderness, Va.

Bristol, J. H., Lt., 1st Connecticut Cavalry, May 5, 1864, Wilderness, Va.
Berpee, E. A., Capt., 18th Maine Vols., June, 1864, Petersburg, Va.
Bryant, J. W., Capt., 5th New York Cavalry.
Bubel, H., Capt., 6th Connecticut Vols., May 14, 1864, Drury's Bluff, Va.
Bixby, H. L., Lt., 9th Maine Vols., June 1, 1864, Cold Harbor, Va.
Byrns, J. M., Capt., 2d Pennsylvania Rifles, July, 1863, Gettysburg, Pa.
Barrett, J. A., Capt., 7th Pennsylvania Rifles, May 5, 1864, Wilderness, Va.
Burkholder, D. W., Lt., 7th Pennsylvania Rifles, May 5, 1864, "
Beale, E., Capt., 8th Tennessee Vols., April 21, 1864, Bulls Gap, Tenn.
Bayard, J. A., Capt., 148th Pennsylvania Vols.
Brunn, S., Lt., 80th Illinois Vols.
Brady, W. H., Lt., 2d Delaware Vols., June 22, 1864, Petersburg, Va.
Brion, J., Lt., 148th Pennsylvania Vols.
Bishoff, P., Lt. 6th United States Artillery, April 12, 1864, Fort Pillow.
Burnett, E. W., Lt, 4th Indiana Cavalry.
Blair, B. T., Adjutant, 123d Ohio Vols., June 15, 1863, Winchester, Va.
Boyce, T. W., Lt., 123d Ohio Vols.,   "   "
Breckenridge, F. A., Lt., 123d Ohio Vols.,   "   " .
Boyed, W. I., Lt, 5th Michigan Cavalry, June 29, 1864, Reams Station, Va.
Bick, W. C., Capt., 62d Pennsylvania Vols., May 5, 1864. Wilderness, Va.
Brown, W. L., Lt., 14th Tennessee Vols., October 20, 1863. Philadelphia, Tenn.
Burrows, S. W., Lt., 1st New York Cavalry, June 13, 1864, Monterey, Va.
Brown, T., United States Navy, October 23, 1863, Rappahannock River, Va.
Beeman, W. M., Capt., 13th Virginia Cavalry, October 11, 1863, Brandy Sta., Va.
Boas, E. P., Capt., 20th Illinois Vols., May 24, 1863. Raymond, Miss.
Bryan, G., Adjt., 18th Pennsylvania Cavalry, Nov. 18, 1863, Germania Ford, Va.
Bath. A., Lt., 45th New York Vols., July 1, 1863, Gettysburg, Pa.
Beadle, M., Lt., 123 New York Vols., July 2, 1863,   "
Bigelow, A. J., Capt., 79th Illinois Vols., September 19, 1863, Chickamauga, Ga.
Borehess, T. F., Lt., 67th Pennsylvania Vols., June 15, 1863, Winchester, Va.
Borehess, L. T., Capt., 67th Pennsylvania Vols., June 16, 1863,   "
Brown, G. L., Lt., 101st Pennsylvania Vols., April 20, 1864, Plymouth, N. C.
Blanchard, G. A., Capt., 85th Illinois Vols., July 19, 1864. Atlanta, Ga.
Bradford, John, A. C. S., 4th New Jersey Vols., Oct. 15, 1863, Chantilly, Va.
Barns, O. P., Lt., 3d Ohio Vols., May 3, 1863, Rome, Ga.
Beeman, S., Capt., 3d Michigan Vols., May 5, 1864, Wilderness, Va.
Brickenhoff, M., Lt., 42d New York Vols., June 22, 1864, Petersburg, Va.
Barse, George R., Lt., 5th Michigan Cavalry, Oct. 19, 1863, Buckland, Va.
Bliss, A. T., Capt., 10th New York Cavalry, June 29, 1864, Petersburg, Va.
Buckly, H., Lt., 4th New Hampshire Vols., May 16, 1864, Bermuda Hundred, Va.
Bader, H., Lt., 29th Missouri Vols., November 27, 1863, Ringgold, Ga.
Blue, J. G., Lt., 3d Ohio Vols., May 3, 1863, Rome, Ga.
Boughton, S. H., Lt., 71st Pennsylvania Vols., July 2, 1863, Gettysburg, Va.
Barnes, A. T., Lt., 14th Illinois Battery, October 4, 1864, Acworth. Ga.
Beasley, J., Lt., 81st Illinois Vols., September 2, 1864, East Point, Ga.
Baker, H. D., Capt., 120th Illinois, Vols., June 5, 1864.
Burke, T. F., Capt., 16th Illinois Vols., June 3, 1864.
Barnes, W. G.

Bennett, W. F., Capt., 39th Iowa Vols., Oct. 5, 1864, Allatoona, Ga.
Bassett, W. H., 1st Lt., 79th Illinois, Sept. 19th, 1863, Chickamauga, Ga.
Botts, W. S., Lt., 10th Wisconsin Vols., Sept 20, 1863, Chickamauga, Ga.
Briggs, J., Lt., 123d Illinois Vols., " "
Bennett, F. T., Lt., 18th U. S. I., " "
Brown, J. P., Lt., 15th U. S. I., " "
Bryant, M. C., Lt., 42d Illinois Vols., " "
Butler, W. O., Lt., 10th Wisconsin Vols.
Brooks, E. P., Adjt.
Berrington, A., Lt., 140th New York Vols., June 3, 1864, Cold Harbor, Va.
Ballard, S. H., Lt., 6th Mich. Cav., July 2, 1863, Gettysburg, Pa.
Brown, J. H , Capt., 17th Iowa Vols., Oct. 13th, 1864, Allatoona, Ga.
Byron, S., Lt., 2d U. S. I., April 11, 1864, Callett Station, Va.
Blaire, Geo. E., Lt., 17th Ohio Vols., Sept 20, 1863, Chickamauga, Ga.
Bishop, F. P., Lt., 4th Tenn. Cav., August 15, 1864, Westport, Ga.

Coleman, T. S., 1st Lt., 12th Kentucky Cav., Oct. 11, 1863. Sweetwater, Tenn.
Charlpret, J. F., Capt., 11th Pa. Vols., May 9, 1864, Wilderness, Va.
Call, C. H., Capt., 29th Illinois Vols., June 23, 1864, Leclere, Miss.
Caswell, H., 2d Lt., 91st Illinois Vols., April 19, 1864, Big Black, Miss.
Carpenter, E. D., 2d Lt., 18th Ct. Vols., June 15, 1863, Winchester, Va.
Caldwell, C., 2d Lt, 1st Wis. Cav., April 13, 1864, Cleveland, Tenn.
Cook, A. A., 2d Lt., 9th Ohio Cav., April 13, 1864, Florence, Ala.
Casdroph, C. H., 2d Lt., 8th Virginia Vols., Dec. 19, 1863, Jackson River, W. Va.
Castler, B. G., Capt., 154th New York Vols., July 1, 1863, Gettysburg, Pa.
Cook, J. L., Lt., 6th Iowa Vols., May 14, 1863, Holly Springs, Miss.
Cusac, I., Capt., 21st Ohio Vols., Sept. 20, 1863, Chickamauga, Ga.
Camfield, S. S., Capt. 21st Ohio Vols., " "
Cotton, M., " " " "
Coffin, V. L., Lt., 31st Maine Vols., May 7th, 1864, Cold Harbor, Va.
Chandler, G. A., Lt., 5th Maine Vols., July 24, 1863, White Plains, Va.
Conn, J. H., Lt., 1st Va. Cav., April 30, 1863, Bridgeport, Ga.
Culver, F. B., Lt., 123d Ohio Vols., June 16, 1863, Winchester, Va.
Caruthers, I. Q., Lt., 123d Ohio Vols., May 3, 1863, Raymond, Miss.
Cildghorn, A. C., Lt., 21st Ohio Vols., Sept. 20, 1863, Chickamauga, Ga.
Carey S. E., Lt., 13th Mass. Vols., July 3, 1863, Gettysburg, Pa.
Campbell, L. A., Lt., 152d New York Vols., June 22, 1864, Petersburg, Va.
Carnes, W. C., Capt., 2d Tenn. Vols., Nov. 6, 1863, Rogersville, Tenn.
Center, A. P., " " " " " "
Carrolle, E., Lt., 11th Tenn. Vols., Feb. 22, 1864, Lubec, Va.
Carr, C. W., Lt., 4th Virginia Vols., June 23, 1864, Petersburg, Va.
Cunningham, J., Lt., 7th Pa. R., May 5, 1864, Wilderness, Va.
Caslett, C., Lt., 115th Pa. Vols.
Cooper, R., Lt., 7th New York Vols.
Creurford, C. H., Lt., 183d Pa. Vols., May 12, 1864, Spottsylvania, Va.
Cromack, S. O., Lt., 77th New York Vols., May 6th, 1864, Wilderness, Va.
Cornell, H., Lt., 2d Vermont Vols., " "
Cornell, C. H., Lt., 95th New York Vols., May 5th, 1864, Wilderness, Va.

Cutter, C. H., Lt., 95th New York Vols., May 1864, Wilderness, Va.
Crasey, G. W., Lt., 35th Mass. Vols., May 24, 1864, North Anna River, Va.
Chute, R. A., Lt., 59th Mass. Vols.,   "   "   "
Cross, H. M.,   "   "   "   "   "   "
Chapin, H. A., Lt., 95th New York Vols., May 5, 1864, Wilderness, Va.
Clyder, J., Capt., 76th   "   "   "
Cahill, W., Lt.,   "   "   "   "
Casler, J. L., Lt.,   "   "   "
Chisman, H., Lt., 7th Ind. Vols., May 16, 1864, Wilderness, Va.
Cooper, A., Lt., 12th New York Cav., April 20, 1864, Plymouth, N. C.
Cribben, H., Lt., 140th New York Vols., June 2, 1864, Cold Harbor, Va.
Curtis, G. M., Lt.,   "   "   "
Caldwell, J. S., Lt., 16th Illinois Vols., June 3, 1864, Jonesville. Va.
Caslin, C. J., Lt., 151st New York Vols., Nov. 29, 1863, Mine River, Va.
Crossly, L., Lt., 118th Pa. Vols., June 2, 1864, Mechanicsville, Va.
Chenney, C. R., Capt., 34th Mass. Vols., July 22, 1864, Atlanta, Ga.
Carlisle, L. B., Lt., 145th Pa. Vols., June 16, 1864, Petersburg, Va.
Conner, S. D., Capt., 125th Illinois Vols., Sept. 21, 1863, Chickamauga, Ga.
Cole, O. L., Lt., 54th Illinois Vols., Sept. 20, 1863, Chickamauga, Ga.
Cane, J. H., Lt., 140th New York Vols., July 1, 1863, Gettysburg, Pa.
Cassell, E. F., Lt., 11th Iowa Vols., July 22, 1864, Atlanta, Ga.
Chambers, J. H., Lt., 103d Pa. Vols., April 20, 1864, Plymouth, N. C.
Cottingham, E., Lt., 35th Ohio Vols., Sept. 20th, 1863, Chickamauga, Ga.
Coddington, J. P., Lt., 8th Iowa Vols., July 30, 1864, M———, Ga.
Cole, A. F., Capt., 59th New York Vols., June 22, 1864, Petersburg, Va.
Curtis, W. M., Adjt., 19th Mass. Vols.,   "   "
Clark, J. W., Lt., 59th New York Vols., May 12, 1864, Spottsylvania, Va.
Case, D. S., Adjt., 102d New York Vols., July 22, 1864, Atlanta, Ga.
Clark, J. H., Lt., 1st Mass. Art., May 19, 1864, Spottsylvania, Va.
Cope, J. D., Lt., 116th Pa. Vols., June 22, 1864, Petersburg, Va.
Corse, J. W., Lt., 6th Va. Cav., June 26, 1864, Springfield, Va.
Coulter, W. J., Lt., 15th Mass. Vols., June 22, 1864, Petersburg, Va.
Culburtson, W. M., Lt., 30th Indiana Vols., Sept. 19, 1863, Chickamauga, Ga.
Casey, J., Lt., 42d New York Vols., June 22, 1864, Petersburg, Va.
Carter, W. H., Lt., 5th Pennsylvania Vols., May 10, 1864, Spottsylvania, Va.
Chittenden, J. S., Lt., 5th Indiana Cavalry, July 31, 1864, Sunshine Church, Ga.
Cowney, W. H., Lt., 69th New York Vols., June 22, 1864, Petersburg, Va.
Cameron, P., Lt., 16th New York Cavalry, Feb. 22, 1864, Leesburg, Va.
Campbell, W. S., Lt., 51st Pennsylvania Vols., May 12, 1864, Spottsylvania, Va.
Cameron, J. F., Lt., 5th Indiana Cavalry, June 29, 1884, Petersburg, Va.
Carr, J. P., Capt., 93d Indiana Vols., June 12, 1864, Selema, Miss.
Clegg, M., Lt., 5th Indiana Cavalry, July 31, 1864, Clinton, Ga.
Curtis, H. A., Lt., 157th New York Vols., July 1, 1863, Gettysburg, Pa.
Coffin, J. A.,   "   "   "   "
Collins, W. A., Capt., 10th Wisconsin Vols., Sept. 20, 1863, Chickamauga, Ga.
Crocker, G. A., Capt. and A. A. I. G., 1st Cav. Div., Oct. 11, 1863, Brandy Sta., Va.
Carlisle, J. B., Lt., 2d Virginia Cavalry, Sept. 11, 1863, Smith Co., Va.
Christopher, W., Lt., 2d Virginia Cavalry, July 4, 1863, Raleigh, Va.

Chandler, G. W., Lt., 1st Virginia Cavalry, July 2, 1863, Gettysburg, Pa.
Chatburn, J., Lt., 150th Pennsylvania Vols., July 1, 1863, Gettysburg, Pa.
Childs, J. H., Lt, 16th Maine Vols., July 1, 1863, Gettysburg, Pa.
Chase, H. R., 1st Lt., 1st Wisconsin Artillery, June 23, 1864, Petersburg, Va.
Conover, W. H., Lt., 22d New York Cavalry, June 9, 1864, Turner's Bridge, Va.
Clark, J. A., Capt., 7th Michigan Cavalry, March 2, 1864, Mechanicsville, Va.
Cook, W. B., Lt., 140th Pennsylvania Vols., July 2d, 1863, Gettysburg, Pa.
Calef, B. S., Lt., 2d U. S. S. S., May 5, 1864, Wilderness, Va.
Cook, E. F., Major, 2d New York Cavalry, March 3, 1864, Stevensville, Va.
Cook, H. P., Capt. and A. A. G., May 7, 1864, Wilderness, Va.
Crocker, H., Lt., 1st New Jersey Cavalry, June 9, 1863, Brandy Station, Va.
Camp, T. B., Capt., 52d Pennsylvania Vols., July 3, 1864, Fort Johnson, S. C.
Clark, S., Capt.
Chapin, H. C., Capt., 4th Vermont Vols., June 23, 1864, Petersburg, Va.
Cunningham, J. B., Lt. Col., 52d Penn. Vols., July 3, 1864, Fort Johnson, S. C.
Christopher, J., Capt., 16th United States Inf., Sept. 19, 1863, Chickamauga, Ga.
Corcoran, N A.,   "   "   "   "   "
Causten, M. C., Lt.,   "   " 20,   "   "
Chubbuch, D. B., Lt., 19th Massachusetts Vols., June 22, 1864, Petersburg, Va.
Carpenter, S. D., Lt., 3d Ohio Vols., May 3, 1863, Rome, Ga.
Curley, A. A., Capt., 73d Indiana Vols.,   "   "
Connelly, R. J., Lt.,   "   "   "
Cartwright, A. G., Capt., 85th New York Vols., April 20, 1864, Plymouth, N. C.
Clark, M. L., Capt., 101st Pennsylvania Vols.,   "   "
Comphor, A.,   "   "   "   "
Clapp, J. B., Adjt., 16th Connecticut Vols.,   "   "
Case, A. G., Lt.,   "   "   "   "
Cralty, E. G., Capt., 103d Pennsylvania Vols.,   "   "
Coates, H. A., Capt., 85th New York Vols.,   "   "
Crooks, S. J., Col., 22d New York Cavalry, June 30, 1864, Ream's Station, Va.
Case, F. S., Capt., 2d Ohio Vols., June 29, 1864, Ream's Station, Va.
Cutter, J., Capt., 34th Ohio Vols., July 18, 1863, Wytheville, Va.
Couchlin.
Cord, T. A., Lt., 19th United States Infantry, Sept. 20, 1863, Chickamauga, Ga.
Cohs, F., Lt., 18th Connecticut Vols., June 15, 1863, Winchester, Va.
Cloadt, Capt., 119th New York Vols., July 1, 1863, Gettysburg, Pa.
Calkins, W. W., Lt., 104th Illinois Vols., Sept. 20, 1863, Chickamauga, Ga.
Craig, J., Capt., 1st Virginia Vols., Sept. 20, 1863, Morefield, Va.
Calville, J., Capt., 5th Michigan Vols., June 22, 1864, Petersburg, Va.
Crossley, T. J., Lt., 57th Pennsylvania Vols., July 2, 1863, Gettysburg, Pa.
Cohen, M., Lt., 4th Kentucky Vols., Sept. 21, 1863, Stevens Gap, Ky.
Copeland, J., Capt., 7th Ohio Vols., Nov. 6, 1863, Rogersville, Tenn.
Curtis, R., Lt., 4th Kentucky Vols., Sept. 21, 1863, Stevens Gap, Ky.
Clements, J, Lt., 15th Kentucky Vols., June 29, 1863, Jackson, Miss.
Caldwell, D. B., Lt., 75th Ohio Vols., July 2, 1863, Gettysburg, Pa.
Cubison, J., Lt., 101st Pennsylvania Vols., April 20, 1864, Plymouth, N. C.
Crawford, H. P., Capt.
Chase, E. E., Capt., 1st Rhode Island Cavalry, June, 1863, Middleburg, Va.

Coffin, G. A., Adjt., 29th Indiana Vols., Sept. 19, 1863, Chickamauga, Ga.
Cochran, T. G., Lt., 77th Pennsylvania Vols., " "
Conrad, W F., Capt., 25th Iowa Vols., May 24, 1863, Raymond, Miss.
Cox, J. L., Capt., 21st Illinois Vols., Sept. 21, 1863, Chickamauga, Ga.
Carpenter, J. Q., Lt., 105th Pennsylvania Vols., July 1, 1863, Gettysburg, Pa.
Copeland, W. A., Lt., 10th Michigan Vols., Oct. 19, 1864, Ringgold, Ga.
Cuniffe, H., Lt., 13th Illinois Vols., Nov. 24, 1863, Lookout Mountain, Ga.
Carpenter, E., Capt., 6th Pennsylvania Cavalry, May 7, 1864, Todd's Tavern, Va.

Day, J. W., Lt., 14th Massachusetts Vols., Feb. 1, 1864, Newbern, N. C.
Damrell, W., Lt., 13th Massachusetts Vols., May 21, 1864, Spottsylvania, Va.
Deering, G. A., Lt., 16th Maine Vols., July 1, 1863, Gettysburg, Pa.
Dufer, T. J., Lt., 5th Michigan Cavalry, Oct. 10, 1863, Robinson River, Va.
Dickerson, A. A., Lt., 16th Connecticut Vols., April 20, 1864, Plymouth, Va.
Donaghy, J., Capt., 103d Pennsylvania Vols., " "
Davis, W. G., Lt., 27th Massachusetts Vols., May 16, 1864, Drury's Bluff, Va.
Day, A. P., Lt., 15th Connecticut Vols., April 20, 1864, Plymouth, Va.
Derous, J. H., Major, 13th Pennsylvania Cavalry, June 24, 1864, Malvern Hill, Va.
Daniels, E. S., Capt., 35th United States Infantry, May 23, 1864, Florida.
Dietz, Henry, Capt., 45th New York Vols., July 1, 1863, Gettysburg, Pa.
Dody, C. C., Capt., 30th Michigan Vols., June 2, 1864, Mechanicsville, Va.
Duffenboch, A., Lt., 73d Pennsylvania Vols., Nov. 23, 1863, Mission Ridge, Ga.
Dewees, T. B., Lt., 2d United States Cavalry, June 9, 1863, Brandy Station, Va.
Dooly, A. T., Lt., 51st Indiana Vols., May 3, 1863, Rome, Ga.
Doroning, O. J., Capt., 2d New York Cavalry, May 12, 1864, Richmond, Va.
Denny, W. N., Capt., 51st Indiana Vols., May 3, 1863, Rome, Ga.
Delano, J. A., Lt., " " "
Davis, V. P., Lt., 143d Ohio Vols., June 15, 1863, Winchester, Va.
Derrickson, J. G., Capt., 66th New York Vols., June 22, 1864, Petersburg, Va.
Dean, S. A., Lt., 145th Pennsylvania Vols., " 16, " "
Dailey, W. A., Capt., 8th Pennsylvania Cavalry, Oct. 12, 1863, Sulphur Springs, Va.
Davis, C. G., Lt., 1st Massachusetts Cavalry.
Domschkee, B., Capt, 26th Wisconsin Vols., July 1, 1863, Gettysburg, Pa.
Dennis, J. B., Capt., 7th Connecticut Vols., July 17, 1864, Petersburg, Va.
Davis, L. R., Capt., 7th Ohio Vols.
Drake, L., Lt., 22d Michigan Vols., Sept. 20, 1863, Chickamauga, Ga.
Dutton, W. G., Lt., 67th Pennsylvania Vols., June 16, 1863, Winchester, Va.
Dillam, C. D., Lt., 7th Iowa Vols., July 13, 1863, Corinth, Miss.
Drenan, J. S., Lt., 1st Vermont Artillery, June 20, 1864, Petersburg, Va.
Dean, T., Lt., 5th Michigan Cavalry, Oct. 10, 1863, James City, Va.
Dunn, J., Lt., 164th New York Vols., June 3, 1864, Coal Harbor, Va.
Dunning, E. J., Lt., 7th New York Artillery, June 22, 1864, Petersburg, Va.
Davinport, J. F., Capt., 75th Ohio Vols., Aug. 17, 1864, Gainsville, Ga.
Davis, H. C., Capt., 18th Connecticut Vols., June 15, 1863, Winchester, Va.
Davis, T. C., Lt., 38th Illinois Vols., Sept. 20, 1863, Chickamauga, Ga.
Dirlam, C. G., Capt., 72d Ohio Vols., June 12, 1864, Ripley, Miss.
Doughton, O. G., Lt., 111th Ohio Vols., Sept. 5, 1863, Jonesboro, Tenn.
Day, A. R., Capt., 3d Maine Vols., June 20, 1863, Gum Springs, Va.

Donavan, J., Lt., 2d New Jersey Vols., May 6, 1864, Wilderness, Va.
Dusbrow, W., Capt., 40th New York Vols., May 12, 1864. Spottsylvania, Va.
Dyer, E. B., Lt., 1st Connecticut Cavalry, June 29, 1864. Ream's Station, Va.
Dinsmore, R., Capt., 5th Pennsylvania Vols., Oct. 13, 1863, Auburn, Va.
Duzenberg, A., Capt., 35th New Jersey Vols., July 22, 1864. Decatur, Ga.
Dorris, W. C., Lt., 111th Illinois Vols., July 22, 1864, Atlanta, Ga.
Dodge, H. G., Lt., 2d Pennsylvania Vols., June 24, 1864, Virginia.
Dixon, L., Lt., 104th New York Vols., July 1, 1863, Gettysburg, Pa.
Dunn, M., Major, 19th Massachusetts Vols., June 22, 1864, Petersburg, Va.
Doane, E. B., Capt, 8th Iowa Vols., July 30, 1864. Marian, Ga.
Davidson, J. H., Lt, 6th New York Artillery, Oct. 11, 1863, Brandy Station, Va.
Drake, J. W, Lt., 136th New York Vols., July 3, 1863, Gettysburg, Va.
Downs, C., Lt., 33d New York Vols., July 20, 1864, Atlanta, Ga.
Davis, J. W., Lt., 115th New York Vols., Feb. 20, 1864, —— Point, Ga.
Duren. J., Lt., New Hampshire Vols., June 3, 1864, Cold Harbor, Va.
Dushane, J. M., Capt. 142d Pennsylvania Vols., July 1, 1863, Gettysburg, Pa.
Davis, W. H., Capt., 4th Maryland Vols., May 5, 1864, Wilderness, Va.
Dercks, C. S. F., 1st Middle Tennessee Vols., June 26, 1863, Davidson, Ga.
Devine, J. S., Lt., 71st Pennsylvania Vols, July 3, 1863. Gettysburg. Pa.
Diemer, M., Lt., 10th Missouri Volunteers, May 16, 1863, Jackson, Miss.
Dingley, F., Lt., 7th Rhode Island Vols., July 13, 1863, "
Durfee, W. H., Lt., 5th Rhode Island Vols., May 5, 1864, Croton, N. C.
Durbaym, G, Lt., 66th New York Vols., June 17, 1864. Petersburg. Va.
Donohey, G. B., Capt., 7th Pennsylvania Rifles, May 5, 1864, Wilderness, Va.
Diffenbuch, W. H., Lt. "   "   "
De Lay, R., Lt, 3d Iowa Cavalry.
Demmick, C. W., 11th New Hampshire Vols., June 17, 1864, Petersburg, Va.
Drake, C. H., Lt., 142d Pennsylvania Vols., July 1, 1863, Gettysburg, Pa.
Dygert, K. S., Capt., 16th Michigan Vols.,   " 3, "   "
Dick, L., Lt, 72d Ohio Vols., June 11, 1864, Ripley, Miss.
Davis, S. B., Capt., 93d Indiana Vols., June 11, 1864, Salem, Miss.
Dillen, F. W., Capt., 1st Kentucky Cavalry, May 25, 1863. Fishing, Ky.
Dahl, O. B., Lt., 15th Wisconsin Vols., Sept., 20, 1863, Chickamauga, Ga.
Dickey, M. V., Lt., 94th Ohio Vols.,   "   "
Davis, Byron, Lt., 71st Pennsylvania Vols., July 2, 1863, Gettysburg, Pa.
Day, E., Capt, 89th Ohio Vols., Sept. 20, 1863, Chickamauga, Ga.
Dutton, G. A., Lt., 22d Michigan Vols., "   "
Dickerson, E., Lt., 44th Wisconsin Vols., Oct. 5, 1864. Allatoona, Ga.
Dirmand, J., Lt., 16th United States Infantry, Sept. 19, 1863, Chickamauga, Ga.
Dunn, H. C., Lt., 10th Kentucky Vols.,   "   "
Drescott, D., Lt., 24th Missouri Vols., Oct. 12, 1864, Tilton, Ga.
Davis, E. G., Lt., 44th Illinois Vols., Sept. 20, 1863, Chickamauga, Ga.
Duggan, J., Lt., 35th Indiana Vols.
Dow, H. G., Lt., 4th Massachusetts Cavalry, Oct. 2, 1864, Magnolia.

Everett, Chas., Lt., 70th Ohio Vols., Aug. 26, 1864, Atlanta, Ga.
Eastman, F. R., Lt., 2d Pennsylvania Cavalry, June 22, 1864, St. M. Church, Va.

Elkins, J. L. F., Adjt., 1st New Jersey Vols., May 6, 1864, Wilderness, Va.
Eastmond, O., Capt., 1st North Carolina Vols., April 20, 1864, Plymouth, N. C.
Evans, T. E., Lt., 52d Pennsylvania Vols, July 3, 1864, James Island, S. C.
Egestone, J. W., Lt., 19th Iowa Vols., July 22, 1864, Atlanta, Ga.
Ellinwood, W. B., Lt., 10th Wisconsin Vols., Sept. 20, 1893, Chickamauga, Ga.
Edwards, D C., Lt., 2d Maryland Vols., January 4, 1864, Burlington, Va.
English, D., Major, 11th Kentucky Cavalry, July 31, 1864, Sunshine Church, Va.
Elder, S. S., Capt., 1st U. S. Artillery, June 24, 1864, Petersburg, Va.
Ekings, T. K., Lt., New Jersey Vols., May 8, 1864. Spottsylvania. Va.
Evans, B. W., Capt., 4th Ohio Vols., May 6, 1864, Wilderness, Va.
Erickson, J. H., Lt., 57th New York Vols., Oct. 14th, 1863, Bristow, Va.
Eaverheart, H. H., Capt., 120th Ohio Vols., May 24, 1863, Raymond, Miss.
Eagan, M., Capt., 15th Virginia Vols., May 19, 1864, Meadows Bluff, Va.
Evans, N. C., Capt., 184th Pennsylvania Vols, June 22, 1864, Petersburg, Va.
Eglin, A. R., Capt., 45th Ohio Vols., November 15, 1863, Knoxville, Tenn.
Ewing, M., Capt., 21st Wisconsin Vols., Sept. 20, 1863, Chickamauga, Ga.
Eagan, John, Capt., 1st U. S. Artillery, July 1, 1864, Ream's Station, Va.
Elder John, Capt., 8th Illinois Vols., July 22, 1864, Atlanta, Ga.
Edwards, T. D., Chief Engineer U. S. N., April 20, 1864, Plymouth, N. C.
Edmiston, S., Lt., 89th Ohio Vols., September 20, 1863, Chickamauga, Ga.

Flick, M., Lt., 67th Pennsylvania Vols., June 15, 1863, Winchester, Va.
Fritz, J., Lt., 11th Tennessee Vols., February 22, 1864, Ynlee, Tenn.
Fay, S. A., Lt., 55th New York Vols., April 20, 1864, Plymouth, N. C.
Frost, C. W., Lt.,   "   "   "
Freeman, D. W. D., Capt., 101st Penn. Vols., April 20, 1864, Plymouth, N. C.
Fish, J. E., Capt., 2d Mass. Heavy Art.,   "   "
Fish, O. M., Lt.,   "   "   "
Finke, A. L, Lt., 103d Pennsylvania Vols.,   "   "
Fuhs, J., Capt., 87th   "   "   "
Foot, M. C., Lt., 92d New York Vols.,   "   "
Fontaine, J, Lt., 73d Pennsylvania Vols., November 25, 1863, Mission Ridge, Ga.
Fairbanks, J., Lt., 72d Ohio Vols., June 12, 1864, Salem, Miss.
Follett, W. H., Lt., 2d Massachusetts Vols., Nov. 22, 1863, Chancellorsville, Va.
Fry, Alfred, Lt., 73d Indiana Vols, May 3, 1863.
Fish, G. W., Lt., 3d Ohio Vols., May 3, 1863, Rome, Georgia.
Frazier, J., Col, 140th Pennsylvania Vols., June 22, 1864, Petersburg, Va.
Flemming, C. R., Maj., 1st Vermont Heavy Art., June 23, 1864, Petersburg, Va.
Foster, J. W., Capt, 42d Illinois Vols., Sept. 20, 1863, Chickamauga, Ga
Fales, J. M., Lt., 1st Rhode Island Cavalry, June 18, 1863, Middleburg, Va.
Finney, G. E, Lt., 19th Indiana Vols., May 5, 1864, Wilderness, Va.
Fowler, J. H., Lt., 100th Ohio Vols., September 8, 1863, Limestone, Tenn.
Fox, G. B., Maj., 75th Ohio Vols., August 17, 1864. Gainesville, Ga.
Farr, W. V., Capt., 106th Pennsylvania Vols., June 22, 1864, Petersburg, Va.
Forbes, W. H., Maj., 2d Massachusetts Cavalry, July 6, 1864, Alldee, Va.
Fort, E. W., Capt., 9th Minnesota Vols., June 11, 1864, Salem, Miss.
Ferris, J. M, Lt., 3d Michigan Vols., June 1, 1864, Gaines Mills, Va.
Fairchild, H., Lt., 10th Wisconsin Vols., September 20, 1863, Chickamauga, Ga.

Funk, J. W., Capt., 39th New York Vols., May 10, 1864, Spottsylvania, Va.
Faye, E. M., Lt., 42d New York Vols., May 12, 1864, "
Fungerson, J., Lt., 1st New Jersey Vols., " "
Flannery, D. F., Lt., 4th New York Vols. " "
Fowler, H. M., Lt., 15th New Jersey Vols., " "
Fisk, W. M., Capt., 73d New York Vols., May 6, 1864, Wilderness, Va.
Fluger, G. M., Lt., 11th Pennsylvania Rifles, May 5, 1864, Wilderness, Va.
Fagan, C. A , " " "
French, II., Lt., 3d Vermont Vols., " "
Francis, J. L., Capt., 135th Ohio Vols., July 3, 1864, "
Field, A., Capt., 94th New York Vols., July 3, 1863, Gettysburg. Pa.
Fritchy, A. W., Lt., 20th Missouri Vols., Nov. 26, 1863, Mission Ridge, Ga.
Fortescue, L. R., Lt., 29th Pennsylvania Vols., July 4, 1863, Emmettsburg, Md.
Fellows, M., Lt., 149th Pennsylvania Vols., July 1, 1863, Gettysburg, Md.
Fisher, R., Lt., 17th Missouri Vols., November 27, 1863, Ringgold, Ga.
Fenner, W., Lt., 2d Rhode Island Cavalry, July 2d, 1863, Port Hudson, La.
Fox, J. D., Lt., 16th Illinois Vols., January 3, 1864, Jonesville, Va.
Fritz, C., Lt., 24th Illinois Vols., September 20, 1863, Chickamauga, Ga.
Fisher, L. W., Lt., 4th Vermont Vols., June 23, 1864, Petersburg, Va.
Fatzer, S., Lt., 108th New York Vols., June 17, 1864, "
Fontaine, E. W., Lt., 7th Pennsylvania Rifles, May 5, 1864, Wilderness, Va.
Flamsburg, D., Capt., 4th Indiana Battery.
Forney, D., Lt., 80th Ohio Vols., July 22, 1864, Atlanta, Ga.
Fisher, S., Lt., 93d Indiana Vols., August 11, 1864, Salem, Miss.
Fiedler, J., Assistant Topographical Engineers, Jonesboro, Ga.
Finney, D. S., 14th and 15th Illinois Vt. Battery, October 4, 1864, Acworth, Ga.
Fairfield, O. B., Lt., 89th Ohio Vols., September 20, 1863, Chickamauga, Ga.
Fitzpatrick, L., 146th New York Vols., May 5, 1864, Wilderness, Va.
Freeman, H. B., Lt. 18th United States Infantry, Sept. 19, 1863, Chickamauga, Ga.
Foster, II. II., Lt., 23d Indiana Vols., June 21, 1864, Atlanta, Ga.

George, G. J., Lt., 40th Illinois Vols., June 29, 1864, Kenesaw, Ga.
Gillespie, J. B., Capt., 120th Illinois Vols., June 12, 1864, Northern Mississippi.
Gunn, F. N., Lt., 21st Kentucky Volunteers.
Gilbert, E. C., Capt., 152d New York Vols., June 22, 1864, Petersburg, Va.
Gill, A. H., Capt., 4th New York Volunteers, May 6, 1864, Wilderness, Va.
Grebble, C. E., Lt., 6th Michigan Cavalry, November 18, 1863, Knoxville, Tenn.
Green, J. H., Lt., 100th Ohio Vols., September 8, 1863, Limestone, Tenn.
Golshall, J., Adjt., 55th Pennsylvania Vols., May 16, 1864, Drury's Bluff, Va.
Godown, J. M., Lt., 12th Maryland Vols., July 12, 1864, Atlanta, Ga.
Grover, J. E., Lt., 6th Indiana Cavalry, September 16, 1863, Beans Station, Tenn.
Gayer, II., Lt., 133d Virginia Vols., September 12, 1863, Centreville, Va.
Gatch, O. C., Capt., 89th Ohio Vols., September 20, 1863, Chickamauga, Ga.
Gross, J. M., Capt., 18th Kentucky Vols., " "
Gulbraith, II. E., Capt., 22d Michigan Vols., " "
Goatz, J., Capt., " " "
Gray, W. L., Capt., 151st Pennsylvania Vols., July 1, 1863, Gettysburg, Pa.
Gross, C. M., Lt., 110th Ohio Vols., June 15, 1863, Winchester, Va.

Grant, G. W., Lt., 88th Pennsylvania Vols., July 1, 1863, Gettysburg, Pa.
Grant, H. D., Lt., 117th New York Vols., May 16, 1864, Drury's Bluff, Va.
Grey, R. H., Lt., 15th United States Infantry, Sept. 20, 1863, Chickamauga, Ga.
Gariss, J. A., Adjt., 1st Maryland Cavalry, June 9, 1863, Brandy Station, Va.
Gates, A. L., Lt., 10th Wisconsin Vols., September 20, 1863, Chickamauga, Ga.
Goodwin, J. A., Lt., 1st Massachusetts Cavalry, May 10, 1864, Beaver Dam, Va.
Gamble, G. H., Adjutant, 8th Illinois.
Gates, R. C., Lt., 18th U. S. Infantry, September 20, 1863, Chickamauga, Ga.
Gilmore, J. A., Lt., 79th New York Vols., July 10, 1863, Jackson, Miss.
Gamble, H., Lt., 73d Indiana, May 3, 1863, Rome, Ga.
Grant, E., Capt., 1st Wisconsin Cavalry, June 29, 1864, Stony Creek, Va.
Granger, C. M., Lt., 88th New York Vols., June 22, 1864, Petersburg, Va.
Goodrich, J. A., Adjt., 85th New York Vols., April 20, 1864, Plymouth, N. C.
Glozier, W. W., Lt., 2d New York Cavalry, October 10, 1863, Bickland Mills, Va.
Goodin, A., Lt., 85th Ohio Vols., July 3, 1863, Gettysburg, Pa.
Gordon, C. O., Lt., 1st Michigan Cav., June 24, 1864, St. Mary's Church, Va.
Green, E. H., Capt., 107th Pennsylvania, May 21st, 1864, Spottsylvania, Va.
Gimber, H. W., Capt., 159th Pennsylvania, July 1, 1863, Gettysburg, Pa.
Gilman, Lt., 3d Maine Vols., June 20, 1863, Alldie, Va.
Gottland, C., Lt., 134th New York Vols, July 1, 1863, Gettysburg, Pa.
Gettman, D., Capt., 10th New York Cavalry, June 9, 1863. Brandy Station, Va.
Griffin, H. G., Lt., 112th Illinois, November 18, 1863, Knoxville, Tenn.
Gordon, E., Lt., 81st Indiana, September 20, 1863, Chickamauga, Ga.
Geasland, S. A., Lt., 11th Tenn. Cavalry, Feb. 22, 1864, Cumberland Gap, Tenn.
Gay, F. C., Lt., 11th Pennsylvania Vols, July 1, 1863, Gettysburg, Pa.
Green, C. W., Lt., 44th Indiana Vols., September 22, 1863, Chickamauga, Ga.
Goss, J. W., Lt., 1st Massachusetts Artillery, June 22, 1864, Petersburg, Va.
Grafton, P., Capt., 64th Ohio Vols., September 20, 1863, Chickamauga, Ga.
Gates, J., Capt., 33d Ohio Vols.,   "   "
Grant, A., Capt., 19th Wisconsin Vols., July 28, 1864, Petersburg, Va.
Green, G. W., Capt., 19th Indiana Vols., July 1, 1863, Gettysburg, Va.
Goodrick, A. L., Capt., 8th New York Vols., June 29, 1864, Stony Creek, Va.
Gamble, S. B., Lt., 63d Pennsylvania, July 19, 1863, Harper's Ferry, Va.
Garbelt, D., Lt., 77th Pennsylvania, Sept 19, 1863, Chickamauga, Ga.
Good, T. G., Lt., 1st Indiana Cav., June 9, 1863, Brandy Station, Va.
Gordon, H. M., Lt., 143d Pennsylvania, May 5, 1864, Wilderness, Va.
Gray, P., Lt., 77th Pennsylvania, Sept. 19, 1863, Chickamauga, Ga.
Gallagher, J., Lt., 4th Vermont Vols., June 23, 1864, Petersburg, Va.
Galloway, L. J., Capt., A. D. C.
Green, E. A., Lt., 81st Illinois Vols.
Green, J. L., Capt.
Goove, W. A., Lt., 3d Massachusetts Cavalry.
Grant, S., Lt., 6th Michigan Art., Nov. 8, 1863.
Griffin, T., Adjt., 55th U. S. I.
Goove, J. B., Lt., 115th Illinois Vols., Sept 24, 1863, Lookout Mountain, Tenn.
Gross, T. E., Lt., 21st Illinois Vols., Sept. 20, 1863, Chickamauga, Ga.
Gorelon, G. C., Capt., 24th Michigan Vols., July 1, 1863, Gettysburg, Pa.
Gisbardt, Lt., 24th Illinois Vols., Sept. 20, 1863, Chickamauga, Ga.

A PRISONER OF WAR. 187

Gageby, J. H., Lt., 19th U. S. I., Sept. 20, 1863, Chickamauga, Ga.
Gutjahr, Capt., 16th Illinois Cav., May 12, 1864, Dalton, Ga.
Galloway, Lt., 15th U. S. I., Sept, 20, 1863, Chickamauga, Ga.
Graham, P., Capt., 24th Pennsylvania Vols., May 15, 1864, New Market, Va.
Godley, M. L., Lt., 17th Iowa Vols., Oct. 13, 1864, Tilton, Ga.
Gould, D., Capt., 133d W. Va., Sept. 12, 1863, Centreville, Va.

Huey, Pennock, Col., 8th Penn. Cav., June 24, 1864, St. Mary's Church, Va.
Helster, J. W., Capt., 9th Ohio Cav., April 13, 1864, Florence, Ala.
Haker, D. W., Lt., Connecticut, April 20, 1864, Plymouth, N. C.
Halsey, T. J., Mjor, 11th New Jersey Vols., June 22, 1864, Petersburg, Va.
Hutchinson, J., Lt., 2d Virginia Vols., Sept. 24, 1863, Cheat River, Va.
Hoffman, M., Lt., 5th Iowa Vols., Nov. 25, 1863, Missionary Ridge, Ga.
Hinds, H. H., Lt., 51st Pennsylvania Vols., July 2, 1863, Gettysburg, Pa.
Haggles, J. S., Capt., 5th Tennessee Vols., May 21, 1863, East Tennessee.
Helms, M. B., Lt., 1st Virginia Vols., Sept. 11, 1863, Morefield, Va.
Hall, C. B.,   "   "   "   "
Hallenbug, G., Lt., 1st Ohio Vols., Sept. 20, 1863, Chickamauga, Ga.
Hall, A. M., Lt., 9th Minnesota Vols., June 12, 1864, Jackson, Miss.
Handy, T., Capt., 79th Illinois Vols., Sept. 19, 1863, Chickamauga, Ga.
Hubbard, H. R., Lt., 119th Illinois Vols., Feb. 22, 1864, Miss.
Hoffman, J. M., Lt., 5th Illinois Vols., Nov. 25, 1863, Missionary Ridge.
Heffley, A., Capt., 142d Pennsylvania Vols., July 1, 1863, Gettysburg, Pa.
Hays, A. N., Capt., 7th Tennessee Cav., March 2, 1864, Union City, Tenn.
Hare, T. W., Lt., 5th Ohio Cav., Nov. 4, 1863, Waterloo, Tenn.
Helm, J. B., Lt., 101st Pennsylvania Vols., April 20, 1864, Plymouth, N. C.
Heffley, C. P., Lt., 142d Pennsylvania Vols., July 1, 1863, Gettysburg. Pa.
Hubbell, F. A., Lt., 67th Pennsylvania Vols., June 15, 1863, Winchester, Va.
Heffner, W., Lt., 67th Pennsylvania Vols.,   "   "
Harrington, B. F., Lt, 18th Penn. Cav., June 18, 1863, Germania Ford, Va.
Hart, E. R., Lt., 1st Vermont Artillery, June 23, 1864, Petersburg, Va.
Hanson, J. B., Lt, 1st Massachusetts Artillery, June 23, 1864, Petersburg, Va.
Hedge, W. E, Lt., 5th Maryland Vols., June 15, 1863, Winchester, Va.
Hawkins, S. W., Lt., 7th Tennessee Cav., March 24, 1864, Union City, Tenn.
Henry, C. D., Lt., 4th Ohio Cav., Sept. 20, 1863, Chickamauga, Ga.
Hays, N. W., Lt., 34th Ohio Vols., July 18, 1863, Wytheville, Va.
Hodge, P. M., Lt.
Hall, R. F., Lt., 75th Ohio Vols., Aug. 17, 1864, Gainsville, Ga.
Hate, J. D., Lt., 8th Iowa Cav., July 31, 1864, Nunan, Ga.
Hastings, T. J., Lt., 15th Massachusetts Vols., June 24, 1864, Petersburg, Va.
Hawk, A., Capt., 68th New York Vols., July 1, 1863, Gettysburg, Pa.
Hill G., W., Lt., 7th Michigan Cav., May 16, 1864, Yellow Tav., Va.
Heslitt, Lt., 3d Pennsylvania Cav., Nov. 27, 1863, Parker's Station, Va.
Hazell, E. J., Lt., 6th Pennsylvania Cav., May 2, 1864, Todd's Tav., Va.
Hamon, J., Lt., 115th Illinois Vols., Sept. 20, 1863, Chickamauga, Ga.
Herrick, B. C., Lt., 1st New York Cav., March 10, 1864, Charlestown, Va.
Hyne, J. J., Lt., 100th Ohio Vols., Sept. 18, 1863, Tilton, Tenn.
Hubert, E., Lt., 80th Pennsylvania Vols., May 12, 1864, Spottsylvania, Va.

Harris, S., Lt., 5th Michigan Cav., March 2, 1864, Richmond, Va.
Heppard, T., Lt., 105th Pennsylvania Vols., April 20, 1864. Plymouth, N. C.
Hamilton, W., Lt., 2d Massachusetts H. Artillery, April 20, 1864, Plymouth, N. C.
Herstings, G. L., Lt., 24th New York Artillery, April 20, 1864, Plymouth, N. C.
Horton, S. H., Lt., 101st Pennsylvania Vols., April 20, 1864, Plymouth, N. C.
Huff, H. B., Capt., 184th Pennsylvania Vols., June 22, 1864, Petersburg, Va.
Hampton, C. G., Lt., 15'h New York Cav., Feb. 20, 1864, Upperville, Va.
Hurd, W. B., Lt., 17th Michigan Vols., May 12, 1864, Spottsylvania, Va.
Hill, J., Capt., 45th New York Vols., July 1, 1863, Gettysburg, Pa.
Hauf, A., Lt., 45th New York Vols., " "
Hitt, W. R., Capt., 113th New York Vols., June 10, 1864. Briers Cross Roads, Miss.
Harris, W., Capt., 24th Mobile Vols., March 24. 1864, Union City, Tenn.
Habbie, C. A., Capt., 17th Connecticut, May 19, 1864, Pilatka, Fla.
Holden, E., Lt., 1st Vermont Cav., Sept. 26, 1863, Richard's Ford, Va.
Hedges, S. P., Lt., 112th New York Vols., June, Richmond, Va.
Hinds, H. C., Lt., 102d New York Vols., July 20, 1864, Atlanta, Ga.
Hall, W. P., Maj., 6th New York Cav., June 8, 1864, King William's County, Va.
Hart, R. K., Capt., 19th U. S. I., Sept. 20, 1863, Chickamauga, Ga.
Hodge, A., Capt., 80th Illinois Vols., May 3, 1863, Rome, Ga.
Harvey, H., Lt., 51st Indiana Vols., May 3, 1863, Rome, Ga.
Hay, D., Capt., 80th Illinois Vols., May 3, 1863, Rome, Ga.
Harmer, R. J., Lt., 80th Illinois Vols., May 3, 1863, Rome, Ga.
Hart, C. M., Lt., 45th Pennsylvania Vols., Dec. 14, 1863, Clinch Mountain, Tenn.
Hopper, J. A., Lt., 2d New York Vols., June 22, 1864, Petersburg, Va.
Hand, G. T., Lt., 51st Pennsylvania Vols., May 3, 1863, Rome, Ga.
Hertzog, H. O., Capt., 1st New York Cav., April 23, 1863, Shenandoah Valley, Va.
Hagler, J. S, Capt., 5th Tennessee Vols., May 21, 1863, Morgan County, Tenn.
Hintz, H., Capt., 16th Connecticut Vols., April 20, 1864, Plymouth, N C.
Hunt, C. O., Capt., 5th Maine Battery, June 18, 1864, Petersburg, Va.
Halpin, G., Capt, 106th Pennsylvania Vols., July 2, 1863, Gettysburg, Pa.
Haginbach, J. C., Lt., 67th Pennsylvania, June 15, 1864, Winchester, Va.
Hogan, P. A., Lt., 7th Maryland Vols., Oct. 19, 1863, Haymarket, Va.
Hullen, W., Lt., 8th Indiana Cav., July 31, 64, Sunshine Church, Va.
Hawkins, H. E., Capt., 78th Illinois Vols., Sept., 22, 1863. Mission Ridge, Ga.
Hur, B. A., Capt., 28th Ohio, June 5, 1864, New Hope, Va.
Hart, G. D., Capt., 5th Pennsylvania Cav., June 10, 1864, Petersburg, Va.
Hull, G. W., Lt, 135th Ohio, July 3, 1864, N. Mountain, Ga.
Hoyt, H. B., Capt., 40th N. Y. I., May 5, 1864, Wilderness, Va.
Hamilton, H. G., Lt., 1st New York I., May 5, 1864, Wilderness, Va.
Hezelton, D. W., Lt., 22d New York Cav., June 28, 1864, Stony Creek, Va.
Hovey, W., Lt., 98th Illinois, Sept. 22, 1863, Mission Ridge, Ga.
Hume, L. J., Capt., 19th Massachusetts, June 22, 1864, Petersburg, Va.
Holahan, C. P., Lt., 19th Pennsylvania Cav., June 12, 1864, Ripley, Miss.
Hamilton, H. N., Lt. 59th New York, June 22, 1864, Petersburg, Va.
Happin, H. P., Lt., 2d Massachusetts Artillery, April 20, 1864, Plymouth, N. C.
Huntington, E. S., Lt., 11th U. S. I., June 2, 1864, Mechanicsville, Va.
Hutchinson, R. C., Capt, 8th Michigan, May 6, 1864, Wilderness, Va.
Hoyt, W. H., Lt, 16th Indiana, July 22, 1864, Atlanta, Ga.

Hart, P. H., Lt., 19th Indiana, July 1, 1863, Gettysburg, Pa.
Hughes, R. M., Lt., 14th Illinois Cav., July 31, 1864, Sunshine Church, Va.
Henekay, D., Lt., 10th Wisconsin, Sept. 20, 1863, Chickamauga, Ga.
Harkness, R., Capt., 10th Wisconsin, Sept. 20, 1863, Chickamauga, Ga.
Herbett, W., Lt., 105th Pennsylvania, May 12, 1864, Spottsylvania, Va.
Hastings, C. W., Capt., 12th Massachusetts, May 12, 1864, North Anna River, Va.
Heston, J., Lt., 4th New Jersey, May 12, 1864, Spottsylvania, Va.
Hays, E., Capt., 95th New York, May 6, 1864, Wilderness, Va.
Heffelfinger, J., Lt., 7th Pennsylvania R. V. C., May 6, 1864, Wilderness, Va.
Harvey, J. T., Lt., 2d Pennsylvania Artillery, June 2, 1864, Mechanicsville, Va.
Hurst, T. B., Lt., 7th Pennsylvania R. V. C., May 5, 1864, Wilderness, Va.
Hobart, J. V., Capt., 7th Wisconsin V., May 5, 1864, Wilderness, Va.
Heek, R. B., Capt., 12th New York Cav., April 20, 1864, Plymouth, N. C.
Holman, W. H., Capt., 9th Vermont, Newport, N. C.
Hadley, J. V., Lt., 7th Indiana, May 6, 1864, Wilderness, Va.
Hall, C., Lt., 13th Wisconsin Cav., Sept. 20, 1863, Chickamauga, Ga.
Hagden, J. A., Capt., 11th P. R., May 6, 1864, Wilderness, Va.
Hill, J. B., Lt., 14th Massachusetts, Feb. 1, 1864, Newbern, N. C.
Hallett, M. V., Lt., 2d Pennsylvania Cav., July 12, 1864, Ream's Station, Va.
Hodge, W. S., Capt., 120th Illinois, June 10, 1864, Northern Miss.
Henry, A. J., 120th Illinois, June 12, 1864, Northern Miss.
Hamlen, S. G., Capt., 134th New York, July 1, 1863, Gettysburg, Pa.
Hulladay, A. J., Lt., 18th Indiana Cav., August 2, 1864, Carrolton, Ga.
Havens, D., Lt., 85th Illinois, July 19, 1864, Peach Creek, Ga.
Hays, C. A., Lt., 111th Pennsylvania, July 20, 1864, Atlanta, Ga.
Hastings, J. L., Adjt., 7th Pennsylvania R., May 5, 1864, Wilderness, Va.
Hunter, A. N., Lt., 2d U. S. Artillery, April 12, 1864, Fort Pilllow, Tenn.
Harris, J. W., Lt., 62d Indiana Cav.
Hellemus, J. B., Capt., 18th Kentucky, June 23, 1864, Ringgold, Ga.
Herzberg, F., Lt., 66th New York, June 17, 1864, Petersburg, Va.
Henry, J. M., Lt., 154th New York Vols., July 1, 1863, Gettysburg, Pa.
Harris, G., Lt., 79th Indiana Cav., Sept. 20, 1863, Chickamauga, Ga.
Holt, W. C., Capt., 6th Tennessee Vols., March 24, 1864, Baldin, Tenn.
Harrison, C. E., Lt., 89th Pennsylvania Vols., Sept. 20, 1863, Chickamauga, Ga.
Huey, R., Lt., 2d Tennessee Vols., Nov. 6, 1863, Rogersville, Tenn.
Henderson, J. H., 14th and 15th Vet. Bat. 3d Ill. Vols., Oct. 4, 1864, Acworth, Ga.
Height, T.
Higley, E. H., Lt., 1st Vermont Cav., June 24, 1864, Stony Creek, Va.
Hall, G. W., Lt., 135th Ohio Vols., Sept. 12, 1863, Chickamauga, Ga.
Hamilton, W. B., Lt., 22d Michigan Vols., Sept. 20, 1863, Chickamauga, Ga.
Hendricks, F., Capt., 1st New York Cav., June 15, 1864, Winchester, Va.
Henderson, R., Lt., 1st Massachusetts H. A., June 26, 1864, Petersburg, Va.
Howe, Charles, Lt., 21st Illinois, Sept. 20, 1863, Chickamauga, Ga.
Hefflefinger, J., Lt., 88th Indiana, Sept. 20, 1863, Chickamauga, Ga.
Himroa, P., Capt., 105th Ohio, Oct. 27, 1864, Dairsville, Ga.

Irwin, C. L., Lt., 78th Illinois Vols., September 22, 1863, Mission Ridge, Ga.
Imbrie, J. M., Capt., 3d Ohio Vols., May 3, 1863, Rome, Ga.

Isett, J. H., Major, 8th Illinois Vols., July 30, 1864, Newman, Ga.
Irwin, W. H., Adjutant, 163d Pennsylvania Vols., April 20, 1864, Plymouth, N. C.
Irsch, F., Capt., 15th New York Vols., July 1, 1863, Gettysburg, Pa.

Jackson, R. W., Lt., 21st Wisconsin Vols., September 20, 1863, Chickamauga, Ga.
Jenkins, R. M., Adjt., 21st Wisconsin Vols.,   "   "
Johnson, H. A., Lt., 3d Maine Vols., May 5, 1864, Wilderness, Va.
James, H. H., Lt., 6th Indiana Cavalry, January 19, 1864, Big Springs, Tenn.
Jones, S. T., Capt., 80th Illinois Vols.,   "   "
Johnson, G., Lt., 16th Connecticut Vols., April 20, 1864, Plymouth, N. C.
Judd, J. H., Lt., 27th Massachusetts Vols., May 16, 1864, Drury's Bluff, Va.
Jacobs, J. H., Capt., 4th Kentucky Vols., July 31, 1864, Fayetteville, Ga.
John, E., Lt, 135th Ohio Vols., July 3, 1864, Virginia.
Johnson, J. C., Capt., 149th Pennsylvania Vols., July 1, 1863, Gettysburg, Pa.
Job, B. A., Capt., 11th Pennsylvania Reserve Vols., May 30, 1864, Cold Harbor, Va.
Johnson, T. W., Lt., 10th New York Cavalry, October 14, 1863, Auburn, Va.
Jones, J. A., Lt., 21st Illinois Vols., September 20, 1863, Chickamauga, Ga.
Johnson, C. K., Lt., 1st Maine Cavalry, June 24, 1864, St. Mary's Church, Va.
Jennings. J. T., Capt., 45th Ohio Vols., November 15, 1863, Knoxville, Tenn.
Judson, S. C., Capt., 106th New York Vols., May 6th, 1864, Wilderness, Va.
Jenkins, H., Capt., 40th Massachusetts Vols., May 16, 1864, Drury's Bluff, Va.
Jackson, C. G., Capt., 84th Pennsylvania Vols., May 6, 1864, Wilderness, Va.
Jones, J. P., Lt., 55th Ohio Vols., July 2, 1863, Gettysburg, Pa.
Jenkins, G. W., Lt., 9th Virginia Vols.
Jones, C. W., Lt., 16th Pennsylvania Cavalry.
Justus, J. C., Lt., 2d Pennsylvania R., May 24, 1864, North Anna River, Va.
Jackson, J., Lt., 4th Indiana Cav., May 7, 1864, Wilderness, Va.
Johnson, J. D., Capt., 10th New York Vols., May 7, 1864, Wilderness, Va.
Jones, S. E., Capt., 7th New York Artillery, June 16, 1864, Petersburg, Va.
Jones, H., Lt, 5th U. S. Cav., Oct. 29, 1863, Elk Run, Va.
Jackson, J. S., Capt., 22d Illinois, Sept. 23, 1863, Chickamauga, Ga.
Johnson, R., Capt., 6th New York Cav., June 25, 1863.
Johnson, J. W., Lt., 1st Massachusetts Artillery, June 22, 1864, Petersburg, Va.
Johnson, W. N., Army correspondent, June 13, 1864, Staunton, Va.
Jones, Webster, Lt, 3-th Ohio Vols., Oct. 19, 1864, Rough Station, Ga.
Jones, M. P., Lt., 115th Illinois Vols., Oct. 3, 1864, Mill Creek, Ga.

Kelly, D. O., Lt., 100th Ohio Vols., Sept. 8, 1863, Tenn.
Krohn, P., Lt., 5th New York Cavalry, June 1, 1864.
Keeler, O. M., Capt., 22d Michigan, September 20, 1863, Chickamauga, Ga.
Kelly, D. A., Capt., 1st Kentucky Vols., Nov. 14, 1863, East Tennessee.
Kendricks, E., Adjt., 10th New York Vols., May 14, 1864, Wilderness, Va.
Kuehn, A., Lt., 5th Maryland Vols., June 15, 1863, Winchester, Va.
Kendall, S., Lt, 15th U. S. Infantry, September 20, 1863, Chickamauga, Ga.
Knapp, F. H., Lt, 9th Ohio Cavalry, April 12, 1864, Florence, Ala.
Karr, S. C., Lt., 126th Ohio Volunteers, May 6, 1864, Wilderness. Va.
Keis, G. W., Lt., 18th Connecticut Vols., June 15, 1863, Winchester, Va.
Kennedy, J. B., Lt., 8th Ohio Cavalry, June 19, 1864, Liberty, Ga.
Kempton, F., Lt., 75th Ohio Vols., August 17, 1864, Gainsville, Va.

Kline, D. J., Lt., 75th Ohio Vols., August 17, 1864. Gainesville, Va.
Kennedy, J. W., Lt., 134th New York Vols., July 1, 1863, Gettysburg, Pa.
Kidd, J. H., Lt., 1st Maryland Artillery, June 21, 1864, Salem, Va.
Kendrick, R. H., Lt., 25th Wisconsin Vols., July 21, 1864, Decatur, Ga.
Kenyan, G. C., Lt., 113th Illinois Vols., June 12, 1864, Ripley, Miss.
Kidder, G. C., Lt., 113th Illinois, " "
Kelly, H. K., Capt., 118th Pennsylvania Vols., June 2, 1864, Mechanicsville, Va.
Knox, G. W., Lt., New York Vols., July 20, 1864, Atlanta, Ga.
Kelly, S. M., Lt., 4th Tennessee Vols., July 30, 1864, Noonan, Ga.
Kirbey, W. M., Lt., 3d New York Artillery, Feb. 2, 1864, Newbern, N. C.
King, T., Quartermaster, 1st Pennsylvania Vols., April 20, 1864, Plymouth, N. C.
Keniston, J., Lt., 100th Illinois, Sept. 20, 1863, Chickamauga, Ga.
Krisgee, A., Lt., 67th Pennsylvania Vols., June 15, 1863, Winchester, Va.
Kendall, Capt., 40th Massachusetts Vols.
King, H., Capt., 16th Connecticut Vols., April 20, 1864, Plymouth, N. C.
Kendall, H. S., Adjt., 5th Pennsylvania Vols., May 7, 1864, Wilderness, Va.
Knowles, R. A., Lt., 116th Ohio Vols., June 15, 1864, Winchester, Va
Keister, W. H. H., Lt., 103d Pennsylvania Vols., April 20, 1864, Plymouth, N. C.
Kirk, J. B., Lt., 101st Pennsylvania Vols., " "
Kautz, J. D., Lt., 1st Kentucky Vols., September 10, 1863, Graysville, Ga.
Keith, C. E., Lt., 19th Illinois Vols., September 20, 1863, Chickamauga, Ga.
Kellog, J. H., Lt., 5th Michigan Cavalry, July 14, 1863, Falling Waters, Va.
Krounmyre, C., Capt., 52d New York Vols., May 10, 1864, Spottsylvania, Va.
Kelly, A., Capt., 126th Ohio Volunteers, May 6, 1864, Wilderness, Va.
Knowles, E. M., 42d Indiana Vols., Sept. 19, 1863, Chickamauga, Ga.
King, M. D., Lt., 3d Ohio Volunteers, May 3, 1863, Rome, Ga.
Kendall, J., Capt., 13th Indiana, " "
Kenkell, E., Lt., 45th New York Vols., July 1, 1863, Gettysburg, Pa.
King, G. E., Capt., 103d Illinois, June 10, 1864. Brier's Cross Roads, Miss.
Kandler, H., Lt., 45th New York Vols., July 1, 1863, Gettysburg, Pa.
Knight, H. R., Lt., 20th Michigan Vols., May 9, 1863, Monticello, Ky.
Kelly, J. R., Lt., 1st Pennsylvania Cavalry.
Keen, J., Lt., 7th Pennsylvania R., May 5, 1864, Wilderness, Va.
Kirkpatrick, G. W., Lt., 15th Iowa Vols., Feb. 29, 1864, Canton, Miss.
Knox, J. C., Lt., 4th Indiana Cavalry.
Kephart, J. S., Lt., 5th Indiana Vols., May 18, 1863, East Tennessee.
Kreuger, W., Lt., 2d Missouri Vols., Sept. 20, 1863, Chickamauga, Ga.
Kerin, J., Lt., 6th United States Cavalry, June 9, 1863, Bealton Station, Va.
Kenyon, P. D., Capt., 14th and 15th N. Y. Vet. Bat., Oct. 14, 1864, Acworth, Ga.
Kreps, F. A. M., Lt., 77th Pennsylvania, Sept. 19, 1863, Chickamauga, Ga.
King, Lt., 15th Illinois Cavalry, May 3, 1863, Rome, Ga.
Kane, T., Lt., 38th Indiana, September 20, 1863, Chickamauga, Ga.
Kessler, J. G., Capt., 2d Indiana Cavalry, July 30, 1864, Newman, Ga.

Lindemyer, L., Capt., 45th New York Vols., July 1, 1863, Gettysburg, Pa.
Lamson, A. T., Capt., 104th New York, July 1, 1863, Gettysburg.
Logan, W. S., Capt., 17th Michigan, May 12, 1864, Spottsylvania, Va.
Love, J. E., Capt., 8th Kansas Vols., Sept. 17, 1863, Chickamauga, Ga.

Lodge, G. R., Lt., 53d Illinois, July 12, 1863, Jackson, Miss.
Lucas, W. D., Capt., 5th New York Cavalry, July 6, 1863, Hagerstown, Md.
Little, J., Capt., 142d Pennsylvania, May 5, 1864, Wilderness, Va.
Lee, A., Lt., 152d New York Vols., June 22, 1864, Petersburg, Va.
Longnecker, J. H., Adjutant, 101st Pennsylvania, April 20, 1864, Plymouth, N. C.
Landon, H., Lt., 16th Connecticut, " "
Laughlin, J. K., Lt., 103d Pennsylvania, " "
Lyman, J., Lt., 27th Massachusetts, May 16, 1864, Drury's Bluff, Va.
Ladd, J. O., Lt., 35th United States Infantry, May 23d, 1864. Florida.
Litchfield, A. C., Lt.-Col., 7th Michigan Cavalry, March 1, 1864, Atleys, Va.
Langworthy, D. A., Capt., 85th New York, April 20, 1864, Plymouth, N. C.
Lyon, W. C., Lt., 23d Ohio, February 3, 1864, Kanawha, Va.
Lewis, C. E., Lt., 1st New York Dragoons. May 7, 1864, Wilderness, Va.
Laycock, J. B., Lt., 7th P. R. C., May 5, 1864, Wilderness, Va.
Lynch, C. M., Major, 145th Pennsylvania, June 22, 1864, Petersburg, Va.
Lintz, C. J., Lt., 8th Tennessee, October 6, 1863, Morristown, Tenn.
Lesley, J. D., Lt., 18th Penn. Cav., Oct. 11, 1863, Stafford Court-House, Va.
Leonard, A., Lt., 71st New York, October 11, 1863, Brandy Station, Va.
Ladd, M., Lt., 16th Iowa, July 22. 1864. Atlanta, Ga.
Lyman, H. H., Lt., New York, May 5, 1864, Wilderness, Va.
Luther, J. C., Lt., 1st Pennsylvania R., May 30, 1864, Cold Harbor, Va.
Larrabee, W. H., Lt., 7th Maine, May 6, 1864, Wilderness, Va.
Lane, L. N., Lt., 9th Minnesota, June 12, 1864, Ripley, Miss.
Lynn, J. L., Lt., 145th Pennsylvania, June 16, 1864. Petersburg, Va.
Lauison, F. D., Lt., 3d Maryland Vols., June 29. 1864, Stony Creek, Va.
Lytte, E. A., Capt., 145th Pennsylvania, June 10, 1864, Petersburg, Va.
Loomis, A. W., Lt., 18th Connecticut, June 15, 1863, Winchester, Va.
Lock, W. H., Lt., " "
Laning, A., Lt., 24th Michigan, May 5, 1864, Wilderness, Va.
Leith, S., Lt., 103d New York, February 20, 1864, North Carolina.
Lindsley, A. H., Lt., 18th Connecticut, June 15, 1863, Winchester, Va.
Long, C. H., Lt., 1st Maryland Vols., June 29, 1864, Duffield's Depot, Va.
Lewis, D. B., Lt., 12th Pennsylvania Cavalry, June 29, 1864, Duffield's Depot, Va.
Livingston, Lt., 1st Virginia Cavalry, July 18, 1863, Weytheville, Va.
Law, G., Capt., 6th Virginia Cavalry, June 26, 1864, Springfield, Va.
Lucas, John, Capt., 5th Kentucky Vols., September 19, 1863, Chickamauga, Ga.
Lovett, L. T., Capt., " " "
Lloyd, J. K., Capt., 17th Massachusetts, February 17, 1864, Newbern, N. C.
Leigh, T. J., Lt., A.D.C., May 5, 1864, Wilderness, Va.
Lemon, M. W., Lt., 14th New York Vols., June 2, 1864, Cold Harbor, Va.
Leeds, M. A., Lt.-Col., 153d Ohio, July 3, 1864, West Virginia.
Litchfield, J. B., Capt., 4th Maine, July 2, 1863, Gettysburg, Pa.
Lock, D. B., Lt., 8th Kentucky Cavalry, August 3, 1863, Kentucky.
Limbard, H., August 4, 1864, Ga.
Loyd, T. C., Lt., 6th Indiana Cavalry, Jan. 19, 1864, Big ——, Tenn.
Lavrince, G. H., Lt., 2d N. Y. M. Rifles.
Loud, E. D. C., Lt., 2d Pennsylvania Artillery, June 27, 1864, Petersburg, Va.
Ludwig, M. S., Lt., 53d Pennsylvania Vols., June 22, 1864, "

Loud, J. R., Capt., 66th Indiana Vols., Oct. 11, 1863, Colenville, Tenn.
Lombard, H. G., Adjt., 4th Michigan Vols., July 1, 1863. Gettysburg, Pa.
Lee, E. N., Capt., 5th Michigan Cavalry, Oct. 19, 1863, Buckland Mills, Va.
Lafler, J. A., Lt., 85th New York Vols., April 20, 1864. Plymouth, N. C.
Lowry, D. W., Lt., 2d Pennsylvania Artillery, July 24, 1864, Petersburg, Va.
Larkin, F. A., Lt., 18th Indiana Vols., June 4, 1863, Edwards ——, Tenn.

Myers, T., Lt., 107th Pennsylvania Vols., July 1, 1863, Gettysburg, Pa.
Moony, J., " " " "
Morris, W. J., Lt., 5th Maryland Vols., June 15, 1863, Winchester, Va.
Mettea, J. S., " " " "
Matson, C. C., Lt., 6th Indiana Cavalry, August 7, 1864, Atlanta, Ga.
Morgan, C. H., Lt., 21st Wisconsin Vols., Sept. 20, 1863, Chickamauga, Ga.
McGruder, W. H., Lt., " " "
Merrim, S. T. C., Lt., 18th Connecticut Vols., June 15, 1863, Winchester, Va.
Moore, G. W., Capt., 7th Tennessee Vols., March 24, 1864, Union City, Tenn.
McConnilee, W. J., Lt., 4th Iowa Vols., June 20, 1863, Vicksburg, Miss.
Martin, J. W., Capt., 4th Massachusetts Cavalry, August 17, 1864, Gainsville, Fla.
Martamhea, J. M., Lt., 75th Ohio Vols., " "
Morse, E., Lt., 78th Illinois Vols., Sept. 22, 1863, Mission Ridge, Ga.
McGiverin, J., Lt., 75th Pennsylvania Vols., Nov. 25, 1863, Mission Ridge, Ga.
Merssel, O., Capt., 65th New York Vols., July 1, 1863, Gettysburg, Pa.
Milios, V., Lt., " " "
Mooney, A. H., Capt., 10th New York Cavalry, April 16, 1864, Fairfax, Va.
McDowell, J. S., Capt., 77th Pennsylvania Vols., Sept. 19, 1863, Chickamauga, Ga.
McHugh, J., Capt., 69th Pennsylvania Vols., June 22, 1864, Petersburg, Va.
Marshall, W. S., Adjt., 55th Indiana Vols., May 3, 1863, Rome, Ga.
Moses, L., Lt., 4th Kentucky Vols., Sept. 20, 1863, Chickamauga, Ga.
Morrisson, M. V. B., Lt., 33d Ohio Vols., " "
Morly, H., Lt., 10th New York Vols., Oct. 12, 1863, Sulphur Springs, Va.
McColgin, J., Lt., 7th Ohio Vols., Nov. 6, 1863, Rogersville, Tenn.
Morris, J. H., Lt., 4th Kentucky Vols., July 30, 1864, Georgia.
McKruson, A. A., Lt., 10th Wisconsin Vols., Sept. 20, 1863, Chickamauga, Ga.
Meade, L. C., Lt., 22d Michigan Vols., " "
Madura, M. B., Lt., 6th Virginia Vols., April 8, 1864, Winchester, Va.
Marshall, W. S., Major, 5th Iowa Vols., Nov. 25, 1863, Mission Ridge Ga.
McKercher, D., Major, 10th Wisconsin Vols., Sept. 20, 1863, Chickamauga, Ga.
McLennom, P., Major, 22d New York Cavalry, June 29, 1864, Reams Station, Va.
Mattocks, C. P., Major, 17th Maine Vols., May 5, 1864, Wilderness, Va.
McQuiddy, H. C., Capt., 5th Tennessee Cavalry, May 3, 1863, Rome, Ga.
Meaney, D. B., Capt., 13th Pennsylvania Cav., June 15, 1863, Winchester, Va.
Mosely, H. H., Lt., 25th Ohio Vols., July 1, 1863, Gettysburg, Pa.
Morrissy, G. H., Quartermaster, 12th Iowa Vols., July 11, 1863, Jackson, Miss.
McKay, D. T., Lt., 18th Pennsylvania Cavalry, Sept. 13, 1863, Culpepper, Va.
Mayer, L., Lt., 12th " June 19, 1863, Front Royal, Va.
Merritt, H. A. P., Lt., 5th New York Cavalry, March 3, 1864, Stevensville, Va.
Matthews, A. S., Adjt., 22d Michigan Vols., Sept. 20, 1863, Chickamauga, Ga.
McFadden, W. M., Capt., 55th New York Vols., June 22, 1864, Petersburg, Va.

Metgger, J., Capt., 35th Pennsylvania Vols., May 16, 1864, Drury's Bluff, Va.
Moore, L. K., Capt., 77th Ohio Vols., June 11, 1864, Ripley, Miss.
McCain, J. C., Lt., 9th Minnesota Vols., " "
Morris, W. M., Lt., 93d Illinois Vols., Nov. 25, 1863, Mission Ridge, Ga.
Monaghan, J., Lt., 62d New York Vols., June 22, 1864, Petersburg, Va.
McCarty, W. W., Capt., 78th Ohio Vols., " Atlanta, Ga.
McKee. T. H., Capt.. 1st Virginia Vols., Sept. 11, 1863, Morefield, Va.
McGuire, T., Capt, 7th Illinois Vols., May 7, 1864, Florence, Ala.
McGowan, J., Lt., 29th Indiana Vols., Sept. 19, 1863, Chickamauga, Ga.
Makepeace. A. J., Capt., 19th " . July 1, 1863, Gettysburg, Pa.
Miller, J. W., Lt., 14th Illinois Cavalry, July 31, 1864, Sunshine Church, Va.
Murphy, J., Lt., 61st New York Vols., June 3, 1864, Cold Harbor, Va.
McIntosh, J. C., Lt, 145th Pennsylvania Vols., June 16, 1864, Petersburg, Va.
Matherson, E. J., Capt., 18th Connecticut Vols., June 15, 1863, Winchester, Va.
McKage, F., Lt.,   "   "   "
Mather, F. W., Lt., 7th New York Artillery. June 16, 1864, Petersburg, Va.
Murphy, J., Lt., United States Infantry, Sept. 19, 1863, Chickamauga, Ga.
Morgan, B., Lt., 75th Ohio Vols., August 17, 1864, Nunansville, Ga.
Mulligan, J. A., Lt., 4th Massachusetts Cavalry, August 17, 1864, Gainsville, Fla.
Meade, S., Capt.. 111th New York Vols., Dec. 7, 1863, Mine Run, Va.
McCall, O. M., Lt., 103d Pennsylvania Vols., April 19, 1864, Plymouth, N. C.
McKinley, J.. Lt., 98th Ohio Vols., Sept. 22, 1863, Mission Ridge, Ga.
Mathews, W. F.. Lt., 6th Maryland Vols., June 19, 1864, Duffield, Va.
McCreary, H., Capt., 145th Pennsylvania Vols., June 16, 1864, Petersburg, Va.
McDade, A., Lt., 154th New York Vols., July 1, 1863, Gettysburg, Pa.
Machrie, P. B., Lt., 73d " June 16, 1864, Petersburg, Va.
Merril, H. P., Capt., 4th Kentucky Vols., July 24, 1864, Jonesboro, Ga.
May, J., Capt., 15 Massachusetts Vols., June 16, 1864, Petersburg, Va.
Murphy, F., Capt., 97th New York Vols., July 1, 1863, Gettysburg, Pa.
Moore, N. H., Capt, 7th " June 16, 1864, Petersburg, Va.
Marion, N. J., Lt., 93d Indiana Vols., August 13, 1864. Salem, Miss.
McDonald, H. J., Capt., 11th Connecticut Vols., May 16, 1864, Drury's Bluff, Va.
Moody, J. E., Lt., 59th Massachusetts, June 15, 1864, Chickahominy, Va.
Myers, W. H., Lt., 76th New York Vols., May 5, 1864, Wilderness, Va.
McGeehan, J., Lt., 146th " " "
Miller, F. P., Col., 147th " " "
Mitchell, H. W., Lt., 14th " S. M., " "
Mallison, J., Lt., 94th " Vols., June 6, 1864, Cold Harbor, Va.
Morem, F., Lt., 73d " " July 3, 1863, Gettysburg, Pa.
Martin, J. C., Capt., 1st Tennessee Cavalry, Nov. 6, 1863, Rogersville, Tenn.
Mullin, D. W., Capt., 101st Pennsylvania Vols., April 20, 1864, Plymouth, N. C.
Melhorn, M., Capt., 135th Ohio Vols., July 7, 1864, Maryland Heights, Md.
Morrow. J. N.. Lt., 101st Pennsylvania Vols., April 20, 1864, Plymouth, N. C.
Moon, R. A., Lt., 6th Michigan Cavalry, Oct. 6, 1863, Chasledown, Va.
Mitchell, J., Lt., 79th Illinois Vols., Sept 19th, 1863, Chickamauga, Ga.
Mendenhall, J. A.. Lt., 75th Ohio Vols., July 2, 1863, Gettysburg, Pa.
McNice, A., Lt., 73d Pennsylvania Vols., Nov. 25, 1863, Mission Ridge, Ga.
Moore, M. M., 6th Michigan Cavalry, Oct. 18, 1863, Charlestown, Va.

A PRISONER OF WAR. 195

Manly, J. A., Capt., 64th New York Vols., May 12, 1864, Spottsylvania, Va.
McCutcheon, E. T., Lt., " " "
McWaim, E. J., Lt., 1st Vermont Artillery, " 23, " "
McCrary, D. B., Lt. Col., 145th Penn. Vols., " 16, " "
Murry, S. F., Capt., 2d U. S. S S, " 21, " "
McCune, A. W., Lt., 2d Ohio Vols., Sept. 20, 1863, Chickamauga, Ga.
McDowalled, H. N., Maj., 106th New York Vols., June 1, 1864, Cold Harbor, Va.
Moulton, O., Lt. Col., 25th, Massachusetts Vols., " 3, " "
McKennly, C., Lt., 85th New York Vols., April 20, 1864, Plymouth, N. C.
Miller, W. G., Lt., 16th Connecticut Vols., " " "
Mackey, J. F., Capt., 113th Pennsylvania Vols., " " "
Morrow, J. J., " " " "
McManus, P. W., Adjt., 27th Massachusetts Vols., May 16, 1864, Drury's Bluff, Va.
Moses, C. C., Capt., 58th Pennsylvania Vols., July 6, 1863, Washington, N. C.
Morringston, H., Lt., 87th " June 15, 1863, Winchester, Va.
McKeage, J., Capt., 184 " " 22, 1864, Petersburg, Va.
Manning, J. S., Lt., 111th Ohio Vols., " 15, 1863, Winchester, Va.
Mudgett, J. S., Capt., 11th Maine Vols., " 2, 1864, Drury's Bluff, Va.
McMahon, E., Lt., 72d Ohio Vols., " 15, " Salem, Miss.
Mash, P., Capt., 67th Pennsylvania Vols., " " 1863, Winchester, Va.
Muhleman, J. K., Major and A. A. G., Sept. 20, 1863, Chickamauga, Ga.
McNeil, J., Lt., 51st Ohio Vols., " "
Man, G., Lt., 80th " Nov. 25, 1863, Mission Ridge, Ga.
McKinstray, J., Lt., 16th Illinois Cavalry, Jan. 3. 1864, Jonesville, Va.
McEvoy, W., Adjt., 3d Illinois Vols., Aug. 15, 1863, Oxford, Miss.
McBeth, W., Lt., 45th Ohio Vols., Nov. 15, 1863, Knoxville, Tenn.
Merry, W. A., Lt., 106th New York Vols., June 16, 1863, Hagerstown, Md.
Marney, A., Capt., 2d Tennessee Vols., Nov. 6, 1863, Rogersville, Tenn.
Moore, D. T., Lt., " " "
Morton, G. C., Lt., 4th Pennsylvania Cavalry, June 11, 1864, Trevellyn Sta., Va.
Moffley, S. T., Adjt., 184th Pennsylvania Vols., June 22, 1864, Petersburg, Va.
McKay, A. G., Lt., 5th Michigan Vols., Sept. 23, 1863, Robson River, Va.
Molton, H., Lt., 1st United States Cavalry, June 21, 1863, Upperville, Va.
Montgomery, R. H., Lt., 5th " Oct. 29, 1863, Elk Run, Va.
Metcalf, C. W., Capt., 42d Indiana Vols , " "
Missick, J. W., Lt, " " "
Mackey, J. S., Lt., 66th United States Inf., Oct. 19, 1863, "
McDill, H., Lt., 50th Illinois Vols., May 3, 1863, Rome, Ga.
Maxwell, C., Lt., 3d Ohio Vols., " "
Mattison, O O., Capt., 12th New York Vols., May 5, 1864, Wilderness, Va.
Mull, D. H., Capt., 73d Indiana Vols., May 3, 1863, Rome, Ga.
Munday, J. W., Lt., " " "
Murdock, H. S., " " " "
McHolland, D. A., Capt., " " "
Marrow, H. C. A., Engineer U. S. N., May 7, 1864, James River, Va.
Mahoney, J. S., Lt, 21st Ohio Vols., Sept. 20, 1863, Chickamauga, Ga.
Mell, J. R., Lt., 61st Ohio Vols., July 1, 1863, Gettysburg, Pa.
McNeal, D., Lt., 13th Pennsylvania Cavalry, June 15, 1863, Winchester, Va.

Morgan, J. T., Capt., 17th Michigan Vols., Nov. 16, 1863, Campbell's Station, Va.
Manning, G. A., Capt., 2d Massachusetts Cav., Feb. 22, 1864, Drainesville, Va.
Mather, E., Lt., 1st Vermont Cavalry, June 3, 1863, Hanover Court-house, Va.
McDonald, C., Lt., 2d Illinois Artillery.
Mangus, H. F., Lt., 53d Pennsylvania Vols., June 16, 1864, Spottsylvania, Va.
Millie, H., Lt., 17th Michigan Vols., May 12, 1864, Petersburg, Va.
Moore, W. Q., Lt., 3d Indiana Cavalry, Feb. 11, 1864, Tangpahea, Fla.
McLaughlin, J., Lt., 53d Pennsylvania Vols., June 16, 1864, Petersburg, Va.
McCaferty, M. J., Lt., 4th U. S. Artillery, Feb. 22, 1864, West Point, Miss.
Millis, J., Lt., 66th Indiana Vols., Oct. 11, 1863, Colinville, Tenn.
McClure, T. W., Lt., 6th U. S. Artillery, April 12, 1864, Fort Pillow, Tenn.
McGinnis, W. A., Lt., 19th Massachusetts Vols., June 22, 1864, Petersburg, Va.
McNitt, R. J., Capt., 1st Penn. Cav., June 24, 1864, Sunshine Church, Va.
Mathews, A., Lt., 1st Vermont Artillery, June 23, 1864, Petersburg, Va.
Moree, A.,   "   "   June 11, 1864,   "
Maish, L., Capt., 87th Penn. Vols.,   "   "
Mason, J., Lt., 13th Penn. Cavalry, Oct. 12, 1863, Brandy Station, Va.
Morgan, S. M., Capt. and A. A. G., May 30, 1864, Cold Harbor, Va.
Mann, C. A., Capt., 5th Illinois Cavalry, June 27, 1863, Jones Co., Miss.
McDonald, J., Lt., 22d Tennessee, Nov. 6, 1863, Rogersville, Tenn.
Moore, F., Lt., 73d Pennsylvania I., Nov. 25, 1863, Mission Ridge, Ga.
Mead, W. H., Lt., 6th Kentucky Cavalry, Sept. 21, 1863, Chickamauga, Ga.
Morse, C. W., Capt., 16th Connecticut Vols., April 20, 1864, Plymouth, N. C.
Moore, M., Capt., 29th Indiana Vols., Sept. 20, 1863, Chickamauga, Ga.
McIntire, M., Capt., 18th Wisconsin Vols., Oct. 5, 1864, Atlanta, Ga.
Miller, C., Adjt., 14th Illinois Cavalry, Sept. 13, 1863, Bean's Station, Tenn.
McAdams, S. J., Lt., 10th Wisconsin Vols. Sept. 19, 1863, Jackson R., Va.

Norris, A. W., Lt., 107th Pennsylvania Vols., July 1, 1863, Gettysburg, Pa.
Norcrop, J. C., Lt., 2d Massachusetts Cavalry, July 12, 1863, Ashby's Gap, Va.
Neidenhoffer, C., Lt., 9th Indiana Vols., July 11, 1864, Briers' Cross Roads, Va.
Nice, W., Lt., 2d New York Cavalry, August 8, 1863, Thoroughfare Gap, Va.
Nelson, W. H., Lt., 13th U. S. Infantry, July 11, 1863, Jackson, Miss.
Nutting, J. H., Capt., 27th Massachusetts Vols., May 16, 1864, Drury's Bluff, Va.
Norris, O. P., Lt., 111th Ohio Vols., Nov. 15, 1864, Tennessee.
Nelson, P., Major, 66th New York Vols., June 17, 1864, Petersburg, Va.
Nelson, A., Lt.,   "   "
Noggle, O. L., Lt., 2d U. S. Infantry, June 2, 1864, Mechanicsville, Va.
Nichols, C. H., Capt., 6th Connecticut Vols., Jan. 2, 1864, Bermuda Hundred, Va.
Newbrandt, J. F., Lt., 4th Missouri Cavalry, July 10, 1863, Union City, Tenn.
Norwood, J., Lt., 76th New York Vols., May 5, 1864, Wilderness, Va.
Neal, A. S., Lt., 5th Indiana Cavalry, June 3, 1864, Sunshine Church, Va.
Napffer, A., Capt., 72d Ohio Vols., June 11, 1864, Ripley, Miss.
Norton, E. E., Capt., 24th Michigan Vols., May 5, 1864, Wilderness, Va.
Nolan, H. J., Capt., 14th New York Cavalry, June 15, 1863, Port Hudson, Miss.
Nealy, O. H., Lt., 11th U. S. Infantry, May 5, 1864, Wilderness, Va.
Netterville, W. Mc, Lt., 12th   "   "   "
Nash, W. H., Capt., 1st U. S. S. S.,   "   "

Neher, W., Lt., 7th Penn. R. V. C., May 5, 1864, Wilderness, Va.
Newscome, E., Capt., 81st Illinois Vols., June 13, 1864, Salem, Miss.
Nolan, L., Capt., 2d Delaware Vols., June 22, 1864, Petersburg, Va.
Nudham, J. B., Lt., 4th Vermont Vols., June 23, 1864, "
Niswander, D. N., Lt., 2d Pennsylvania Artillery, June 2, 1864, Cold Harbor, Va.
Newlin, C., Capt., 7th Pennsylvania Cavalry, June 20, 1864, Marietta, Ga.
Nyman, A. J., Lt., 19th Maine Vols., Oct. 27, 1864, Adairsville, Ga.

Outcast, R. V., Lt., 135th Ohio Vols., July 3, 1864, N. Mount, Va.
O'Harri, J., Lt., 7th New York Artillery, June 16, 1864, Petersburg, Va.
Ony, O. C., Lt., 2d Virginia Cav., May 12, 1863, Summerville, Va.
Ottingen, W., Capt., 8th Tennessee Vols., March 2, 1864, Greene Co., Va.
Osborne, F., Lt., 19th Massachusetts Vols., June 22, 1864, Petersburg, Va.
Oliphant, D., Lt., 35th New York Vols., July 22, 1864, Decatur, Ga.
O'Brien, E., Capt., 29th Missouri Vols., Nov. 27, 1863, Ringgold, Ga.
O'Shea, E., Lt., 13th Pennsylvania Cav., June 21, 1864, St. Mary's Church, Va.
Olcott, D. W., Capt., 134th New York Vols., July 1, 1863, Gettysburg, Pa.
O'Kane, Jr., Lt., 7th Illinois Cav., Nov. 8, 1863, Quinn's Mills, Miss.
Oats, J. G., Lt., 3d Ohio Vols., Jan. 12, 1864, Benton, Tenn.
O'Conner, C., Lt., 55th Pennsylvania Vols., May 16, 1864, Drury's Bluff, Va.
Owens, W. N., Major, 1st Kentucky Cav., Oct. 20, 1863, Philadelphia, Tenn.
Ogden, J., Lt., 1st Wisconsin Cavalry.
Ogan, H. W., Capt., 14th Ohio Vols., Oct. 19, 1864, Rough and Ready Station, Ga.

Pickinpaugh, A. C., Lt., 6th W. Virginia Vols., June 26, 1864, West Virginia.
Picquet, H., Lt., 32d Illinois Vols., July 22, 1864, Atlanta, Ga.
Parker, J. S., Lt., 13th Indiana Vols., July 22, 1864, Atlanta, Ga.
Purviance, J. J., Lt., 130th Indiana Vols., July 1, 1864, Marietta, Ga.
Pratt, J. E., Major, 4th Vermont Vols., July 23, 1864, Petersburg, Va.
Pumphry, J. B., Lt., 123d Ohio Vols., June 15, 1863, Winchester, Va.
Paxton, W. N., Lt., 140th Pennsylvania Vols., July 2, 1863, Gettysburg, Pa.
Parsons, W. L., Major, 2d Wisconsin Vols., May 5, 1864, Wilderness, Va.
Pierce, H. H., Lt., 7th Connecticut Vols., June 2, 1864, Bermuda Hundreds, Va.
Pasco, H. L., Major, 16th Connecticut Vols., April 20, 1864, Plymouth, N. C.
Pitt, G. W., Lt., 55th New York Vols., April 20, 1864, Plymouth, N. C.
Piggot, J. T., Capt., 5th Pennsylvania Cav., June 24, 1864, St. Mary's Church, Va.
Phelpos, L. D., Lt., 5th Pennsylvania Cav., Oct. 12, 1863, Warrenton Springs, Va.
Pease, W. B., Capt., 17th U. S. I., June 2, 1864, Mechanicsville, Va.
Pentzet, D., Lt., 4th New York Cavalry, Sept 16, 1863, Raccoon Ford, Miss.
Peetrey, J. G., Lt., 95th Ohio Vols., June 10, 1864, Tishimingo Creek, Miss.
Powers, D. C., Capt., 6th Michigan Cav., June 15, 1864, Trevellyn, Va.
Parmala, J. R. Capt., 7th Maryland Vols., Feb. 22, 1864, Okolona, Miss.
Penfield, J. A., 5th New York Cav., July 6, 1863, Hagerstown, Md.
Potter, E. A., Lt., 6th Michigan, July 4, 1863, Falling Waters, Va.
Peake, S. S., Lt., 55th New York Vols., April 19, 1864, Plymouth, N. C.
Pierson, E. C., Lt., 55th New York Vols., April 20, 1864, Plymouth, N. C.
Purlier, H., Lt., 20th Ohio Vols., Sept. 19, 1863, Chickamauga, Ga.
Powell, O., Lt., 42d Illinois Vols., Sept. 20, 1863, Chickamauga, Ga.

Pulliam, M. D., Lt., A.C.S., 11th Kentucky Cav., Oct. 20, 1863, Philadelphia, Tenn.
Patterson, J. B., Lt., 21st Ohio Vols., Sept. 20, 1863, Chickamauga, Ga.
Pruther, G. R., Lt., 116th Illinois Vols., July 22, 1863, ————, Miss.
Parson, M. P., Lt., 100th New York Vols., May 16, 1864, Drury's Bluff, Va.
Pemberton, H. V., Lt., 14th New York H. A., June 11, 1864, Petersburg, Va.
Pillsbury, S. H., Capt., 5th Maine Vols., July 24, 1863, White Plains, Va.
Parker, J., Capt., 1st New Jersey Vols., May 11, 1864, Wilderness, Va.
Powell, J. P., Capt., 146th New York Vols., May 6, 1864, Wilderness, Va.
Phares, W., Lt., 46th Pennsylvania Vols., Jan. 15, 1864, West Virginia.
Paul, A. C., Capt., A. A. G., May 9, 1864, Spottsylvania, Va.
Purley, J. P., Lt., 13th Michigan Vols., Sept. 20, 1863, Chickamauga, Ga.
Paine, L. B., Capt., 121st New York Vols., May 6, 1864, Wilderness, Va.
Partridge, W. H., Lt., 67th New York Vols., May 6, 1864, Wilderness, Va.
Petit, G., Capt., 20th New York Vols., June 1, 1864, Wilderness, Va.
Porter, E., Capt., 154th New York Vols., July 1, 1863, Gettysburg, Pa.
Poole, S. B., Capt., 154th New York Vols., July 1, 1863, Gettysburg, Pa.
Preston, A. S., Lt., 8th Michigan Vols., August 5, 1864, Gainesville, Ga.
Phinney, A., Lt., 9th Illinois Vols., July 22, 1864, Atlanta, Ga.
Provine, W. M., Lt., 84th Illinois Vols., July 20, 1864, Atlanta, Ga.
Pendleton, D. B., Capt., 5th Michigan Vols., June 11, 1864, Trevellyn, Va.
Porter, D. M., Capt., 120th Ill. Vols., June 11, 1864, Northern Miss., Va.
Purdell, T., Lt., 10th Iowa Vols., July 16, 1864, Atlanta, Ga.
Pennypacker, E. J., Capt., 18th Penn Cav., Oct. 4, 1863, Buckland Mills, Va.
Patterson, F. A., Capt., 3d Pennsylvania Cav., June 15, 1863, Winchester, Va.
Potter, H. C., Lt., 18th Pennsylvania Cav., July 6, 1863, Hagerstown, Md.
Potts, C. P., Lt., 151st Pennsylvania Vols., July 1, 1863, Gettysburg, Pa.
Paul, J. S., Lt., 122d Ohio Vols., June 15, 1863, Winchester, Va.
Powell, W. H., Lt., 2d Illinois Artillery, July 22, 1864.
Philipp, F., Lt., 5th Pennsylvania Cav., March 1, 1864, S. Mills, N. C.
Pierce, S. C., Capt., 3d New York Cav., June 29, 1864, Ream's Station, Va.
Price, C. A., Lt., 3d Michigan Vols., June 22, 1864, Petersburg, Va.
Pretzman, C. N., Lt., 7th Wisconsin Vols., Oct. 19, 1863, Haymarket, Va.
Potter, G. A., Lt., 2d Kentucky Vols., May 26, 1863, Murfreesboro, Tenn.
Peters, G., Lt., 9th New York Vols., May 16, 1864, Drury's Bluff, Va.
Pitt, J. H., Lt., 108th New York Vols., May 16, 1864, Drury's Bluff, Va.
Potts, J. H., Lt., 75th Ohio Vols., July 2, 1863, Gettysburg, Pa.
Post, James, Lt., 149th Pennsylvania Vols., May 23, 1864, Hanover Junction, Va.
Page, J. C., Capt., 5th Iowa Vols., Nov. 25, 1863, Mission Ridge, Ga.
Pierce, G. S., Capt., 19th U. S. Infantry, Sept. 20, 1863, Chickamauga, Ga.
Pace, N. C., Capt., 80th Illinois Vols., May 3, 1863, Rome, Ga.
Piper, S. B., Lt., 3d Ohio Vols., May 3, 1863, Rome, Ga.
Palmer, E. L., Lt., 57th New York Vols., Aug. 1, 1863, Morrisville, Va.
Phelps, J. D., Capt., 73d Indiana Vols, May 3, 1863, Rome, Ga.
Parker, J. M., Lt., 45th Illinois Vols., July 18, 1864, Atlanta, Ga.
Penny, F. W., Capt., 10th Wisconsin Vols., Sept. 20, 1863, Chickamauga, Ga.
Poston, J. L., Capt., 13th Tennessee Vols., April 12, 1864, Fort Pillow, Tenn.
Pitson, S. V., Lt., 126th Ohio Vols., Nov. 27, 1863, Mine Run, Va.
Poole, J. F., Lt., 1st Virginia Cavalry, July 18, 1863, Hagerstown, Md.

Peterson, C. G., Lt., 1st Rhode Island Cav., June 18, 1863, Middleburg, Va.
Parker, E. B., Lt., 1st Vermont H. Artillery, June 23, 1864, Petersburg, Va.
Peck, H. D., Lt., 2d New York Cav., June 22, 1864, Ream's Station, Va.
Pelton, E. W., Lt., 2d Md. Vols., June 3, 1864, Morefield, Va.
Patterson, G. W., Lt., 135th Ohio Vols., July 3, 1864, N. Mount, Va.
Powers, J. L, Lt., 157th New York Vols., July 1, 1863, Gettysburg, Pa.
Price, J. C., Lt., 75th Ohio Vols., Aug. 17, 1864, Nunanville, Ga.
Paine, H. C., Lt., 20th Illinois Vols., Sept. 22, 1863, Mission Ridge, Ga.
Porter, P. B., Capt., 10th New York Art., June 22, 1864, St. Mary's Church, Va.
Perrin, L., Lt., 77th Ohio Vols., June 12, 1864, Ripley, Miss.
Platt, S. H., Lt., 54 Massachusetts Volunteers.
Porter, L. G., Lt., 80th Illinois Volunteers.
Paine, J. A., Capt., 2d Indiana Cavalry.
Phelps, L. D., Major, 5th Virginia.
Palmer, J. H., Lt., 12th Ohio.
Pettijohn, D. B., Lt., 2d U. S. S. S., July 2, 1863, Gettysburg, Pa.
Pickerell, W. F., Capt., 5th Iowa Vols., Nov. 25, 1863, Mission Ridge, Ga.
Pope, W. A., Lt., 18th Wisconsin, Oct. 5, 1864, Allatoona, Ga.
Ping, T., Capt., 17th Iowa Vols., Oct. 13, 1864, Tilton, Ga.
Park, A., Lt., 17th Iowa Vols.,   "   "

Quigg, D., Major, 14th Illinois Cavalry, Aug. 11, 1864, Athens, Ga.

Rus, M., Lt., 72d Ohio Vols., June 11, 1864, Ripley, Miss.
Robinson, J. L., Lt., 7th Tennessee Cav., March 2, 1864, Union City, Tenn.
Robins, M., Capt., 2d Missouri Vols., July 1, 1863, Gettysburg, Pa.
Rockwell, W. E, Lt., 134th New York Vols., July 1, 1863, Gettysburg, Pa.
Robinson, G. A., Lt., 80th Ohio Vols., Nov. 25, 1863, Chickamauga, Ga.
Rose, W. B., Lt., 106th Pennsylvania Vols., June 22, 1864, Petersburg, Va.
Reynolds, W. J., Capt., 75th Ohio Vols., Aug. 17, 1864, Newman, Ga.
Rough, J., Capt., 1st Illinois Artillery, June 31, 1864, Petersburg, Va.
Robbins, N. A., Lt., 4th Maine Vols., July 2, 1863, Gettysburg, Pa.
Reynolds, E. P., Lt., 5th Tennessee Cav., May 22, 1863, Huntsville, Ga.
Robison, J. F., Lt., 67th Pennsylvania Vols., June 15, 1863, Winchester, Va.
Ruff, J., Lt., 67th Pennsylvania Vols.,   "   "   "
Robertson, G. W., Lt, 2d Michigan Vols., Sept. 20, 1863, Chickamauga, Ga.
Rossman, W. C., Capt. 3d Ohio Vols., May 3, 1863, Rome, Ga.
Russel, M., Capt., 51st Indiana Vols.,   "   •   "
Randall, W., Lt, 80th Illinois Vols.,   "   "
Rosencranzs, A. C., Capt., 4th Indiana Vols., May 9, 1864, Dalton, Ga.
Rowley, G. A., Lt., 2d U. S. I., June 2, 1864, Mechanicsville, Va.
Richley, J. A., Capt., 73d Indiana Vols., May 3, 1863, Rome, Ga.
Roach, A. C., Lt., 57th Indiana Vols.,   "   "
Reid, J. A., Lt, 2d New York Vols., April 20, 1864, Plymouth, N. C.
Robins, B. E., Lt., 95th Ohio Vols., June 10, 1864, Tishimingo, Miss.
Ryder, S. B., Capt., 5th New York Cav., Oct. 11, 1863, James City, Va.
Russell, J. H., Lt., 12th Massachusetts Vols., July 1, 1863, Gettysburg, Pa.
Reynolds, W. H., Major, 14th New York Artillery, June 17, 1864, Petersburg, Va.

Robinson, W. A., Capt., 77th Pennsylvania Volunteers.
Russell, J. A.. Capt., 93d Illinois Vols., Nov. 25, 1863, Mission Ridge, Ga.
Roach, W. E., Lt., 49th New York Vols., June 30, 1864, Ream's Station, Va.
Rogers, O., Capt., 4th Kentucky Vols., Sept 21, 1863, Stephen's Gap, Va.
Rockwell, J. A., Lt., 99th New York Vols., July 1, 1863, Gettysburg, Pa.
Ruger, J. M., Lt., 57th Pennsylvania Vols., June 22, 1864, Petersburg, Va.
Raymond, H. W., Lt., 8th New York Artillery, June 3, 1864, Cold Harbor, Va.
Roach, S., Lt., 100th Illinois Vols., Sept. 20, 1863, Chickamauga, Ga.
Ross, C. W., Lt., 1st Kentucky M. D., Sept. 15, 1863, Lagrange, Ky.
Richards, L. S., Lt., 1st Vermont Artillery, June 20, 1864, Petersburg, Va.
Riggs, B. T., Capt., 11th Kentucky Vols., Sept. 20, 1863, Chickamauga, Ga.
Rose, J. E., Lt., 120th Illinois Vols., June 12, 1864, Northern Miss.
Rounds, J. R., Lt., 145th Pennsylvania Vols., June 12, 1864, Petersburg, Va.
Roberts, E. R., Lt., 7th Illinois Vols., May 7, 1864, Florence, Ala.
Read, J. H., Lt., 120th Illinois Vols., June 14, 1864, Northern Miss.
Richards. J. N., Lt., 1st Virginia Vols., June 21, 1864, Virginia.
Randolph, J. F., Capt., 123d Ohio Vols., June 15, 1863, Winchester, Va.
Ringe, G., Adjt., 100th Ohio Vols., Sept. 6, 1863, Jonesboro, Tenn.
Rice, J. S., Lt., 13th Indiana Vols., July 22, 1864, Atlanta, Ga.
Rienecker, G., Lt., 5th Pennsylvania Cav., June 29, 1864, Petersburg, Va.
Rothe, H., Lt., 15th New York Artillery, May 15, 1864, Spottsylvania, Va.
Richardson, H., Lt., 19th Indiana Vols., July 1, 1863, Gettysburg, Pa.
Rubb, W. J., Capt., 1st Virginia Vols., Jan. 31, 1864, Hardee County, Va.
Ramsey, E. R., Lt., 1st New Jersey Vols., May 6, 1864, Wilderness, Va.
Ross, C. H., Adjt., 13th Indiana Vols., June 2, 1864, Mechanicsville, Va.
Riley, L. H., Lt., 7th Pennsylvania R. V. Cav., May 5, 1864, Wilderness, Va.
Rice, J. A., Capt., 73d Illinois Vols., Sept. 20, 1863, Chickamauga, Ga.
Ratily, W. L., Lt., 51st Pennsylvania Vols., Sept. 20, 1863, Chickamauga, Ga.
Robbins, A., Capt., 123d Ohio Vols., June 15, 1863, Winchester, Va.
Rosembaum, O. H., Capt., 123d Ohio Vols., June 16, 1863, Winchester, Va.
Ray, T. J., Lt., 49th Ohio Vols., Sept. 19, 1863, Chickamauga, Ga.
Risden, J, Lt., 11th Tennessee Cav., Feb. 22, 1864, Lee County, Va.
Robs. E. W., Lt., 1st Tennessee Vols., Oct. 19, 1863. Rayler, Tenn.
Rahn, O., Lt., 184th Pennsylvania Vols., June 22, 1864, Petersburg, Va.
Ring, A., Lt., 12th Ohio Vols., May 12, 1864, Virginia.
Ruter, H., Capt., 52d New York Vols.. June 22, 1864, Petersburg, Va.
Richardson, J. A., Lt., 2d New York Cav., July 5, 1863, Emmettsburg, Pa.
Ruby, S. V., Lt., 7th Pennsylvania R., May 5, 1864, Wilderness, Va.
Romain, L., Lt., 2d New York Volunteers.
Roberts, G., Lt., 7th New Hampshire Vols., Feb. 20, 1864, Olustee, Fla.
Ross, G., Lt., 7th Vermont I., Feb. 9, 1864, Florida.
Reynolds, H., Lt., 42d Illinois Vols., Sept. 20, 1863, Chickamauga, Ga.
Rooney, J. C., Lt.
Robinson, G. B., Lt.
Richards, J. S., Lt.
Rugg, C. L., Lt., 6th Indiana Cav., Aug. 3, 1864, Athens, Ga.
Roger, J. R., Lt., 157th Pennsylvania Vols., April 16, 1864, Fairfax Court House, Virginia.

Sturgeon, W. R., Lt., 107th Pennsylvania Vols., July 14, 1864, Petersburg, Va.
Socks, J., Lt., 5th Maryland Vols., June 15, 1863, Winchester, Va.
Sweadner, J., Lt., " " "
Stewart, T. H., Lt., " " "
Smith, O. J., Major, 6th Indiana Cavalry, August 3, 1864, Atlanta, Ga.
Swift, E., Lt., 74th Illinois Vols., September 24, 1864, Jonesboro, Ga.
Sutherland, L. W., Capt., 85th New York Vols., April 20, 1864, Plymouth, N. C.
Shaefer, James, Capt., 101st Pennsylvania Vols., " "
String, E. E., Lt., 16th Connecticut Vols., " "
Sampson, J. B., Capt., 2d Massachusetts H. Artillery, " "
Sinclair, R. B., Lt., " " "
Starr, G. H., Capt., 104th New York Vols., July 3, 1863, Gettysburg, Pa.
Swift, R. R., Capt., 27th Massachusetts Vols., May 16, 1864, Drury's Bluff, Va.
Stroman, C. P., Lt., 87th Pennsylvania Vols., June 15, 1863, Winchester, Va.
Sibley, H. L., Lt., 116th Ohio Vols., " "
Spineller, J., Lt., 73d Illinois Vols., September 20, 1863, Chickamauga, Ga.
Spencer, S. A., Capt., 28th Indiana Vols., " "
Spafford, A. C., Lt., 41st Ohio Volunteers, " "
Smith, M. H., Lt., 123d " June 15, 1863, Winchester, Va.
Schuyler, J. F., Lt., " " "
Stover, J. C., Capt., 3d Tennessee Vols., July 24, 1864, Knoxville, Tenn.
Stover, M. H., Lt., 184th Pennsylvania Vols., June 22, 1864, Petersburg, Va.
Stevens, J. H., Lt., 6th Maine Vols., Dec. 14, 1863, Wilford Ford, Va.
Swan, E. L., Capt., 76th New York Vols., May 6, 1864, Wilderness, Va.
Sweet, W. H. S., Lt., 146th " " "
Stevens, F., Lt., 190th Pennsylvania Vols., June 13, 1864, Malvern Hill, Va.
Stewart, C., Lt., 124th New York Vols., June 1, 1864, Mechanicsville, Va.
Shanan, M., Lt., 140th " May 5, 1864, Wilderness, Va.
Stevens, J. R., 40th " May 6, 1864, "
Schell, G. L., Capt., 88th Pennsylvania Vols., July 1, 1863, Gettysburg, Pa.
Schofield, E. D., Capt., 88th Pennsylvania R., May 6, 1864, Wilderness, Va.
Shutter, H., Lt., 43d New York Vols., " "
Sealy, H. B., Lt., 86th " July 2, 1863, Gettysburg, Pa.
Sanders, A. H., Col., 16th Iowa Vols., July 22, 1864, Atlanta, Ga.
Shedd, W., Col., 30th Illinois Vols., " "
Strange, H. W., Capt., " " "
Smith, J. S. A., Capt., 16th Indiana Vols., " "
Steel, J. M., Lt., 1st Virginia Vols., Sept. 11, 1863, Morefield, Va.
Schroeders, E., Lt., 74th Pennsylvania Vols., July 1, 1863, Gettysburg, Pa.
Sittir, J. R., Lt., 2d Pennsylvania Cavalry, May 7, 1864, Todd's Tavern, Va.
Sweatland, A. A., Lt., " July 12, 1864, Petersburg, Va.
Schroad, J. C., Capt., 77th Penn. Vols., Sept. 19, 1863, Chickamauga, Ga.
Singer, G. P., Capt., 33d Ohio Volunteers, " 20, " "
Shaw, J. C., Lt., 7th " Nov. 6, 1863, Rogersville, Tenn.
Shepard, D. J., Lt., 7th Kentucky Vols., May 5, 1863, Nashville, Tenn.
Sherman, A. L., Lt., 3d Indiana Vols., June 29, 1864, Ream's Station, Va.
Spaulding, E. G., Lt., 22d Michigan Vols., Sept. 20, 1863, Chickamauga, Ga.
Snyder, J., Capt., 14th New York Vols., June 17, 1864, Petersburg, Va.

Smith, C. B., Lt., 4th New York Cavalry, Sept. 16, 1863, Raccoon Ford, Va.
Smith, A. M., Lt., 1st Tennessee Cavalry, July 31, 1864, Chattahoochee, Ga.
Sutter, C., Lt., 39th New York Vols., Dec. 2, 1863, Mine Run, Va.
Spaulding, E. J., Lt., 2d United States Cavalry, June 9, 1863, Brandy Station, Va.
Smythe, W. H., Lt., 16th " Infantry, Sept. 19, 1863, Chickamauga, Ga.
Schammerhorn, J., Capt., 42d Indiana Vols., Sept. 20, 1863, Chickamauga, Ga.
Shaffer, H. C., Lt., 2d New York Cav., Oct. 10, 1863, Culpepper, Va.
Swayzie, W. A., Capt., 3d Ohio Vols., May 3, 1863, Rome, Ga.
Sharp, E. E., Lt., 57th Indiana, " "
Smith, J. C., Lt., 24th Indiana Battery, July 31, 1864, Macon, Ga.
Simpson, G. W., Lt., 67th Pennsylvania Vols., June 15, 1863, Winchester, Va.
Schromforth, F., Lt., 24th Illinois Vols., Sept. 20, 1863, Chickamauga, Ga.
Saber, G. E., Lt., 2d Rhode Island Cavalry, August 3, 1863, Jackson, La.
Schroeder, E. L., Lt., 5th Maryland Vols., June 15, 1863, Winchester, Va.
Sullivan, J., Adjt., 7th Rhode Island Vols., July 13, 1863, Jackson, Miss.
Smith, J., Lt., 67th Pennsylvania Vols., June 15, 1863, Winchester, Va.
Smith, J. B., Lt., 5th Western Va. Cav., May 13, 1864, Middletown, Va.
Sandon, W., Lt., 1st Wisconsin Cav., May 9, 1864, Dalton, Ga.
Schortz, L., Capt., 12th Pennsylvania Cav., June 15, 1863, Winchester, Va.
Smith, E. B, Lt., 1st Vermont Artillery, June 23, 1864. Petersburg, Va.
Sharp, G. A., Lt., 19th Pennsylvania Cav., Feb. 13, 1864, Holly Springs, Va.
Stoughton, H. R., Lt. Col., 2d U. S. S. S., June 21, 1864, Petersburg, Va.
Stone, L. L. R., Quartermaster, 2d Vermont Vols., Oct. 26, 1863, Warrenton, Va.
Smith, L. S., Lt., 14th New York Cav., June 15, 1863, Port Hudson, La.
Stoke, G. W., Lt., 103d Pennsylvania Vols., April 20, 1864, Plymouth, N. C.
Spence, D. M., Lt., " " "
Smullin, F., Capt., " " "
Sanford, O. L., Major, 7th Connecticut Vols., June 2, 1864, Drury's Bluff, Va.
Stelle, J., Major, 3d Pennsylvania Cav., July 12, 1864, Petersburg, Va.
Smith, J. P., Lt., June 2, 1864, Cold Harbor, Va.
Skinner, J. L., Lt., 27th Massachusetts Vols., May 16, 1864, Drury's Bluff, Va.
Stevens, J. C., Lt., 52d Pennsylvania Vols., July 3, 1863, Fort Johnson, S. C.
Smith, T. W., Major, 7th Tenn. Cav., March 24, 1864, Union City, Tenn.
Spuce, L. B., Major, 7th Pennsylvania R., May 5, 1864, Wilderness, Va.
Skelton, A. S., Capt., 57th Ohio Vols., July 22, 1864, Atlanta, Ga.
Smart, G. F. C., Capt., 145th Pennsylvania Vols., June 16, 1864, Petersburg, Va.
Schurr, C., Lt., 7th New York Vols., " "
Swope, C. T., Lt., 4th Kentucky Vols., July 31, 1864, Jonesboro, Ga
Stewart, A. S., Lt., " " "
Singer, A. W., Lt., 21st Illinois Vols., Sept. 20, 1863, Chickamauga, Ga.
Schuttz, W., Capt., 37th Ohio Vols., July 22, 1864, Atlanta, Ga.
Strickland, E. P., Lt, 114th Illinois Vols., May 11, 1864, Tishimingo Creek, Miss.
Smith, P., Lt., 4th Tennessee Vols., August 1, 1864, Franklin, Ga.
Stanton, J. W., Lt., 5th Indiana Cavalry, July 31, 1864, Sunshine Church, Va.
Soper, M. H., Major, " " "
Shaffer, W. H., Lt., 5th Pennsylvania Cav., June 29, 1864. Petersburg, Va.
Stratford, S. A., Lt., 42d New York Vols., June 22, 1864, "
Sears, D. C., Lt., 94th " July 1, 1863, Gettysburg, Pa.

Sheppard, E., Lt., 6th Ohio Cavalry, Sept. 1, 1863, Bowlins Cross Roads, Va.
Scripture, F. E., Quartermaster, 7th N. Y. Art., May 27, 1864, Bowling Green, Va.
Smythe, S. S., Lt., 1st Illinois Vols., July 22, 1864, Atlanta, Ga.
Smith, A. B., Capt., 48th   "   July 21, 1864,   "
Simmons, A. B., Lt., 5th Indiana Cav., July 31, 1864,   "
Star, H. P., Lt., 22d New York Cav., May 8, 1864, Chancellorsville, Va.
Smith, J. E., Lt., 154th New York Vols., July 1, 1863, Gettysburg, Pa.
Sprung, B., Lt. 75th Ohio Vols., August 17, 1864, Nunan, Ga.
St. John, W. H., Lt., 5th Indiana Cavalry, June 3, 1864, Sunshine Church, Ga.
Schule, G., Lt., 45th New York Vols., July 1, 1863, Gettysburg, Pa.
Sampson, J. B., Lt., 12th Massachusetts Vols., July 1, 1863, Gettysburg, Pa.
Stover, A. E., Lt., 95th Ohio Vols., June 10, 1864, Tishimingo Creek, Miss.
Smith, D. D., Capt., 1st Tennessee Vols., May 3, 1863, Rome, Ga.
Stansbury, M. L., Capt., 95th Ohio Vols., June 10, 1864, Barbours Cross Roads, Va.
Schofield. R., Capt., 1st Vermont Cav., July 12, 1863, Hagerstown, Md.
Syring, Wm., Capt., 45th New York Vols., July 1, 1863, Gettysburg, Pa.
Stone, C. P., Lt., 1st Vermont Cav., June 1, 1864, Ashland, Va.
Spencer, F., Lt., 17th Ohio Vols., Sept. 20, 1863, Chickamauga, Ga.
Sheppard, E. A., Capt., 110th Ohio Vols., June 15, 1863, Winchester, Va.
Shroeder, C. H., Lt., 82d Illinois Vols., July 1, 1863, Gettysburg, Pa.
Shelton, N. H., Lt., 1st New York Artillery, May 5, 1864, Wilderness, Va.
Smith, M. S., Lt., 16th Maine Vols.,   "   6,   "   "
Scudder, A. A., Quartermaster, 35th Penn. Vols., Feb. 14, 1864, Brentsville, Va.
Scooville, H. C., Lt., 92d Illinois Vols., April 23, 1864, Ringgold, Ga.
Stebbins, J., Lt., 77th New York Vols., May 12, 1864, Spottsylvania C. H., Va.
Swartz, C. S., Lt., 2d New Jersey Cavalry.
Smith, H. J., Capt., 53d Pennsylvania Vols., June 16, 1864, Petersburg, Va.
Sailor, J., Lt., 13th Pennsylvania Cavalry, June 24, 1864, St. Mary's Church, Va.
Sergeant, W. G., Lt., 1st Vermont Artillery, June 23, 1864, Petersburg, Va.
Singer, H. C., Lt., 2d Maryland Vols., June 12, 1864.
Scott, R. F., Lt., 11th Kentucky Cavalry, November 14, 1863, Maysville, Tenn.
Schooley, D., Capt., 2d Pennsylvania Artillery, July, 1864, Petersburg, Va.
Stewart, R. K., Lt., 2d New York Vols., May 19, 1864, Spottsylvania, Va.
String, F. B., Capt., 11th Kentucky Cavalry, November 14, 1863, Maysville, Tenn.
Stone, D., Capt., 118th New York Vols., May 16, 1864, Drury's Bluff, Va.
Snowwhite, E. H. A., Lt., 1st Pennsylvania R., May 5, 1864, Wilderness, Va.
Stollman, C. H., Lt., 87th Pennsylvania Vols.
Stribling, M. W., Lt., 61st Ohio Vols., May 25, 1864, Dallas, Ga.
Stewart, A. J., Capt. and A. A. G., April 20, 1864, Plymouth, N. C.
Shoemaker, F. M., Lt.
Sill, E. E., Lt., 136th New York Vols., May 25, 1864, Dallas, Ga.
Scott, George, Lt., 10th Indiana Vols., July 6, 1864, Atlanta, Ga.
Sutcher, C. B., Capt., 16th Illinois Vols., May 12, 1864, Dalton, Ga.
Smith, J., Lt., 5th Pennsylvania Cavalry, June 29, 1864, Ream's Station, Va.
Stevens, C. G., Lt., 154th New York Vols., July 1, 1863, Gettysburg, Pa.
Simpson, J. D., Lt., 10th Indiana Vols., Sept. 20, 1863, Chickamauga, Ga.
Segar, F. W., Lt., 80th Illinois Vols., May 3, 1863, Rome, Ga.
Stout, J. O., Lt., Ohio Cavalry (McGloffen Squad), Oct. 5, 1864, Decatur, Ga.

Shepotmy, M. W., Lt., Ohio Cavalry (McGloffen Squad), May 21, 1864, Dallas, Ga.
Shurtz, E., Capt., 8th Iowa Cavalry, July 30, 1864, Macon, Ga.

Tuthill, P. A., Lt., 104th New York Vols., July 1, 1863, Gettysburg, Pa.
Thompson, B. E., Capt., 9th Ohio Vols., Sept. 20, 1863, Chickamauga, Ga.
Tainter, H. S., Lt., 82d New York Vols., May 25, 1864, Hanover Junction, Va.
Tamer, D., Lt., 118th Illinois Vols., May 24, 1863, Raymond, Miss.
Tomkins, A., Lt., 59th New York Vols., June 22, 1864, Petersburg, Va.
Thomas, D., Major, 135th Ohio Vols., July 3, 1864, North Anna River, Va.
Trout. B. W., Lt., 106th Pennsylvania, June 22, 1864, Petersburg, Va.
Thornburg, J. M., Lt., 39th Kentucky Vols., June 9, 1863, Boyd County, Ky.
Thompson, C. H., Major, 5th Indiana Cavalry, July 31, 1864, Sunshine Church, Va.
Tilloston, H. H., Lt., 73d Indiana Vols., May 3, 1863, Rome, Ga.
Teeter, A. J., Lt., 2d Ohio Vols., Sept. 20, 1863, Chickamauga, Ga.
Thompson, J. S., Lt., 10th Vermont Vols., June 1, 1864, Cold Harbor, Va.
Thorp, T. J., Lt. Col., 1st New York Drag.,   "   Trevellyn, Va.
Tenvilliger, J. E., Capt., 85th New York Vols., April 20, 1864, Plymouth, N. C.
Turner, M. C., Capt., 16th Connecticut,   "   "
Tilbrand, H., Capt., 4th N. H. Vols., May 16, 1864, Bermuda Hundred, Va.
Taylor, A. A., Lt., 122d Ohio Vols., June 15, 1863, Winchester, Va.
Thompson, R., Lt., 67th Penn. Vols.,   "   "
Taylor, E., Lt., 1st Connecticut Cavalry, May 4, 1864, Wilderness, Va.
Thayer, H. O., Lt., 67th Pennsylvania Vols., June 15, 1863, Winchester, Va.
Thorn, R. F., Lt., 5th Kentucky Vols., Sept. 21, 1863, S. Gap, Ga.
Tinninn, A., Lt., 16th Iowa Vols., July 22, 1864, Atlanta, Ga.
Tyler, L. D. C., Capt., 106th Pennsylvania Vols., June 22, 1864, Petersburg, Va.
Tiffany, A. W., Lt., 9th Minnesota Vols., June 11, 1864, Salem, Miss.
Tumer, J. H., Capt., 16th Indiana Vols., July 22, 1864, Atlanta, Ga.
Thompson, J., Capt.
Teneyck, S., Capt., 18th U. S. I., Sept. 21, 1863, Chickamauga, Ga.
Tayor, H., Lt., 55th Indiana Vols., Dec. 14, 1863, Bean's Station, Va.
Temple, H., Lt., 2d New York Cavalry, Sept. 19, 1863, Jackson, Va.
Thomas, A. V., Lt., 73d Indiana Vols., May 3, 1863, Rome, Ga.
Thompson, S. C., Capt., 95th New York Vols., May 6, 1864, Wilderness, Va.
True, Wm. M., Lt., 16th Iowa Cavalry, June 3, 1863, Jonesville, Va.
Thompson, J. J., Ass't Surgeon, 12th Ohio Vols., May 12, 1864, Cloyd House, Va.
Tybballs, H. G., Capt., 12th Ohio Vols., May 19, 1864, Meddon Bluff, Va.
Taylor, J., Lt., 2d Pennsylvania R., May 5, 1864, Wilderness, Va.
Templeton, O. F., Capt., 107th Pennsylvania Vols., July 1, 1863, Gettysburg, Pa.
Todd, H. H., Capt., 8th New York Vols., May 19, 1864, Spottsylvania, Va.
Todd, O., Lt., 18th Wisconsin Vols., Oct. 5, 1864, Allatoona, Ga.
Twiss. D. W., Lt., 17th Iowa Vols.
Thompson, T., Lt.,   "
Tipton, A. F., Lt., 8th Iowa Cavalry.

Unthank, C. L., Capt., 11th Kentucky Cavalry, May 24, 1864, Cap Station, Ga.
Ullenbaugh, G., Lt., 1st Ohio Vols., Sept. 20, 1863, Chickamauga, Ga.
Urwiller, S. C., Capt., 67th Pennsylvania Vols., June 15, 1863, Winchester, Va.

Ulem, J., Lt., 3d Ohio Vols., May 3, 1863, Rome, Ga.
Uptigrove, J. R., Lt., 73d Ind.Vols., May 3, 1863. Rome, Ga.
Underdown. J. D., Capt., 2d Tenn. Vols., Nov. 6, 1863, Rogersville, Tenn.
Ulffers, H. A., Capt. and A. A. G., June 6, 1864, Bethsalda Church, Va.
Underwood, J. W., Capt., 7th Ohio Vols., July 22, 1864, Atlanta, Ga.

Van Keiser, A., Capt., 20th New York Vols., June 20, 1864. A. R. Gap, Va.
Van Nutter, R. N., Lt., 1st Michigan Cavalry, July 6. 1863, Hagerstown, Md.
Van Valocha, D. D., Lt., 12th U. S. I., May 5, 1864, Wilderness, Va.
Vanderhoef, J., Capt., 45th New York Vols., July 1, 1863, Gettysburg, Pa.
Vettford, G., Lt., 54th   "   "   "
Vickers, D., Major, 4th New Jersey Vols., May 5, 1864, Wilderness. Va.
Von Helmrick, G., Lt. Col., 4th Missouri Cavalry, June 10, 1864, North Mississippi.
Von Ketterohnung, H., Lt., 103d New York Vols., June 2, 1864, Morris Is., S. C.
Vriary, F., Lt, 85th New York Vols., April 20, 1864, Plymouth, N. C.
Van Dorn, D., Lt., 72d Ohio Vols., June 11, 1864, Salem, Miss.
Van Ness, G. A., Lt., 73d Indiana Vols., May 3, 1863. Rome, Ga.
Van Ransslair, C., Lt., 148 N. Y. V., June 15, 1864, Petersburg. Va.
Vaughn, Z., Capt., 1st Maine Cav., May 11, 1864, North Anna River, Va.
Van Buren, G. M., Capt., 5th N. Y. Cav., July 6, 1863, Wilderness, Va.

Weakley, T. J., Lt., 110th Ohio Vols., June 15, 1863, Worcester. Va.
Whitney, J. N., Lt., 2d Rhode Island Cav., July 2, 1863. Port Hudson, La.
Willetts, W., Lt., 22d Michigan Vols., Sept. 20, 1863, Chickamauga, Ga.
Washeow, F., Lt., 54th New York Vols., July 1, 1863, Gettysburg. Pa.
Wiltshire, J. N., Lt., 45th Ohio Vols., Nov. 15, 1863, Knoxville. Tenn.
Weaver, J. R., Lt., 18th Pennsylvania Cav., Oct. 11, 1863, Brandy Station, Va.
Wilson, J., Capt., 57th Ohio Vols., July 12, 1864, Atlanta, Ga.
West, J. H., Capt., 4th Kentucky, July 29, 1864, Jonesboro, Ga.
Warner, J. B., Lt., 8th Michigan Vols., Aug. 5. 1864, Athens, Ga.
Warner, James, Lt., 33d N. Y. Vo's., July 30, 1864, Atlanta, Ga.
White, A. B., Adjt., 4th Pennsylvania Vols., Oct. 12, 1863, Lead Springs, Ga.
Wilson, R., Lt., 113th Illinois Vols., June 11, 1864, Ripley, Miss.
Williams, W. H., Capt., 4th New York Vols., Sept. 16, 1863, Virginia.
Whiteside, J. C., Capt., 94th New York Vols., July 1, 1863, Gettysburg, Pa.
Wicher. W. B., Capt., 21st Ohio Vols., Sept. 20, 1863, Chickamauga, Ga.
Wistbrook, U. S., Capt., 135th Ohio Vols., July 3, 1864, N. Mount, Va.
Woodward, J. E., Lt., 18th Connecticut Vols., June 15, 1863, Winchester, Va.
Wanzer, G. G., Major, 24th New York Cav., May 6, 1864, Wilderness, Va.
Warren, J. S., Lt., 1st Wisconsin Cav., Aug. 3, 1864, Atkins, Ga.
Wasson, J. M., Lt., 40th Ohio Vols., Sept. 20, 1863, Mission R., Ga.
Walker, J., Lt., 8th Tennessee Vols., Aug. 6, 1864, Atlanta, Ga.
Webb, G. W., Capt., 2d Pennsylvania Artillery, June 2, 1864, Cold Harbor, Va.
West, O. W., Lt., 1st New York Dragoons, May 9, 1864, Wilderness, Va.
Williams, R., Capt., 12th Ohio Vols., May 9. 1864, Newbern Department, W. Va.
Welch, J. C., Lt., 85th New York Vols., April 20, 1864, Plymouth, N. C.
Warwick, J., Lt., 101st Pennsylvania Vols., April 20, 1864, Plymouth, N. C.
Wheeler, J. D., Capt., 15th Connecticut Vols.,   "   "

Wilson, W. M., Capt., 122d Ohio Vols., May 6, 1864, Wilderness, Va.
Williams, Wm., Lt., 8th Michigan Cav., August 6, 1864, Macon, Ga.
Weaks, E. J., Lt., 67th Pennsylvania Vols., June 15, 1863, Winchester, Va.
Welch, W. H. H., Lt., 87th   "   "   "
Wilcox, C. W., Lt., 9th New Hampshire Vols., May 12, 1864, Spottsylvania, Va.
Winrick, J. E., Capt., 19th Pennsylvania Cav., April 8, 1864, Memphis, Tenn.
White, C. W., Capt., 3d Pennsylvania Cav., June 15, 1863, Wilderness, Va.
Williams, G., Lt., 8th Michigan Vols., August 7, 1864, Covington, Ga.
Wright, D. C., Lt., 51st Indiana Vols., May 3, 1863, Rome, Ga.
Williams, M. S., Lt., 15th Kentucky Vols., June 29, 1863, Jackson, Miss.
Wiley, M., Capt., 1st Tennessee Vols., August 1, 1864. Sweet Water, Ga.
Whittaker, E. B., Capt., 72d Pennsylvania Vols., June 22, 1864, Petersburg, Va.
Winters, J., Lt., 72d Ohio Vols., June 22, 1864, Ripley, Miss.
Wedimain, F., Lt., 16th Indiana Vols., July 22, 1864, Atlanta, Ga.
Wallace, J., Lt. Col., 47th Ohio Vols., July 22, 1864, Atlanta, Ga.
Wheeler, J. F., Lt., 149th New York Vols., July 20, 1864, Atlanta, Ga.
Williamson, J. B., Lt., 4th Virginia Vols., Jan. 3, 1864, Morefield, Va.
Wilder, G. O., Lt., 15th Missouri Vols., June 22, 1864, Petersburg, Va.
Wiston, C. F., Lt., Wisconsin Vols., Sept. 20, 1863, Chickamauga, Ga.
Wando, Capt., 22d Michigan Vols.,   "   "
Watson, J. C., Lt., 121st Ohio Vols., May 6, 1864, Wilderness, Va.
Windship, Lt., 88th Illinois Vols., August 30, 1864, East Point, Ga.
Wilson, W. C., Capt., 104th New York Vols., July 11, 1863, Gettysburg, Pa.
Widdis, C. C., Capt., 150th Pennsylvania Vols.,   "
Word, T. H., Lt., 59th U. S. I., June 19, 1864, Briss's Cross Roads.
Wheaton, J.,   "   "   "   "
Wright, R. J., Capt., 6th Ohio Vols., May 17, 1863, Richmond, Va.
Wright, W. R., Capt., 80th Illinois Vols., May 31, 1863, Rome, Ga.
Wilson, A.,   "   "   "   "
Whiting, J. D., Capt., 3d Ohio Vols.,   "   "
Wolbach, A. K., Lt.,   "   "   "   "
Willis, W., Lt., 52d Indiana Vols.,   "   "   "
Woodrow, I. A., Lt., 73d Indiana,   "   "   "
Wilcox, W. H. H., Lt., 10th N. Y. Infantry, Oct. 12, 1864, Bealton Station, Va.
Wallace, R. P., Lt., 120th Ohio Infantry, May 24, 1863, Raymond, Miss.
Wright, L. L., Lt., 51st Indiana, May 3, 1863, Rome, Ga.
Walpole, H. H., Capt., 122d New York, May 3, 1864, Spottsylvania, Va.
Wright, B. F., Capt., 141st New York, May 5, 1864, Wilderness, Va.
Woodruff, T. M., Lt., 76th New York,   "   "
Winner, C. N., Lt., 1st Ohio Vols., Sept. 19, 1863, Chickamauga, Ga.
Willis, H. H., Lt., 4th New York Vols., June 1, 1864, Hanover Junction, Va.
Wright, J. W., Lt., 10th Iowa Vols., Nov. 25, 1863, Mission Ridge, Ga.
Weatherbee, J., Lt., 51st Ohio Vols., Sept. 20, 1863, Chickamauga, Ga.
Welsheimer, F., Capt., 21st Illinois Vols., Sept. 20, 1863, Chickamauga, Ga.
Whitten, B. F., Lt., 9th Maine Vol. Infantry, June 1, 1864, Cold Harbor, Va.
Whiston, D., Lt., 13th Massachusetts Vols., July 1, 1863, Gettysburg, Pa.
Whitimore, B. W., Lt., 5th New York Cav., June 29, 1864, Ream's Station, Va.
Willis, A. R., Capt., 8th Michigan Vols., May 16, 1864, Drury's Bluff, Va.

Wadsworth, M. C., Lt., 16th Maine Vols., July 1, 1863, Gettysburg, Pa.
Wallace, J. J., Lt., 7th Tennessee Cav., March 24, 1864, Union City, Tenn.
Whitman, W. S., Lt., 66th Indiana Vols.,   "   "
Wentworth, M. E., Lt., 14th New York Vols., June 2, 1864, Cold Harbor, Va.
Walcott, W. S.
Worthen, T. A., Lt., 188th Illinois Vols., May 24, 1863, Raymond, Miss.
Wakefield, H. B., Capt., 53d Indiana Vols., June 29, 1864, Kenesaw Mt., Ga.
Wilson, H., Lt., 18th Pennsylvania Cav., Oct. 11, 1863, Brandy Station, Va.
White, H. G., Lt., 94th New York Vols., July 1, 1863, Gettysburg, Pa.
Wall, M H., Capt., 69th New York Vols., June 22d, 1864, Petersburg, Va.
Whitey, M. G., Capt., 29th Mo. Vols., Nov. 27, 1863, Ringgold, Ga.
Weisner, T. A., Capt., 14th and 15th Illinois Vet. Bat., Oct. 4, 1864, Acworth, Ga.
Walker, W. H., Lt., 21st Ohio Vols., July 9, 1864, Chattahoochee, Ga.
Woodson, C. W., Lt., 17th Iowa, Oct. 13, 1864, Tilton, Ga.
Wilson, E S., Lt., 1st Massachusetts Cav., May 10, 1864, Beaver Dam, Va.
Warren, D. H., Lt., Assist. Surgeon 8th Iowa Cav., July 30, 1864, Nunan, Ga.

Yearo, E. C., Lt., 67th New York Vols., May 6, 1864, Wilderness, Va.
Yentz, H. C., Capt., 126th Ohio Vols., June 14, 1863, Winchester, Va.
York, E. D., Lt., 2d North Carolina Vols., April 20, 1864, Plymouth, N. C.
Young, J. W., Major, 76th New York Vols., May 5, 1864, Wilderness, Va.
Yound, A., Lt., 4th Penn. Cav., June 24, 1864, Yellow Tavern, Va. (Since killed.)
Yates, C. H., Lt., 96th Illinois Vols., Sept. 22, 1863, Mission Ridge, Ga.
Young, J. W., Lt., 111th Illinois Vols., July 22, 1864, Atlanta, Ga.
Young, T. P., Lt., 4th Kentucky Vols., July 31, 1864, Nunan, Ga.
York, J. H., Lt., 63d Indiana Vols., June 27, 1864, Kenesaw Mountain, Ga.
Young, D. G., Capt., 81st Illinois Vols., June 11, 1864, Ripley, Miss.

Zobel, C., Lt., 15th New York H. A., May 6, 1864, Wilderness, Va.
Zeis, H., Capt., 80th Illinois Vols., June 3, 1863, North Alabama.
Zarracher, F., Capt., 18th Pennsylvania Cav., May 5, 1864, Wilderness, Va.
Zeigler, Aaron, Lt., 7th Pennsylvania R.   "   "
Zeigler, J. D., Lt., 104th Illinois, April 10, 1864, Brison's Cross Roads, Va.

www.ingramcontent.com/pod-product-compliance
Lightning Source LLC
Chambersburg PA
CBHW020825230426
43666CB00007B/1102